Bill Novelli

50+

50+

Igniting a Revolution to Reinvent America

Bill Novelli, *CEO of AARP*
with
Boe Workman

Foreword by Steve Case

ST. MARTIN'S PRESS ⚐ NEW YORK

www.stmartins.com

The quotation by Ogden Nash on page 96 is reprinted by permission of Curtis Brown, Ltd. Copyright © 1954 by Ogden Nash.

Library of Congress Cataloging-in-Publication Data

Novelli, William D.
    50+ : igniting a revolution to reinvent America / Bill Novelli.—1st ed.
        p.   cm.
    ISBN-13: 978-0-312-35524-1
    ISBN-10: 0-312-35524-6
    1. Baby boom generation—United States. Middle-aged persons—United States—Political activity. 3. Retirees—United States—Political activity. 4. Social reformers—United States. 5. Social change—United States. 6. Political participation—United States. 7. United States—Social conditions—1980– 8. United States—Social Policy. 9. United States—Politics and government—2001– I. Title. II. Title: Fifty plus. III. Title: 50 plus.

HN59.2.N68 2006
305.2440973—dc22   2006046265

First Edition: October 2006

10 9 8 7 6 5 4 3 2 1

This book is dedicated to
Celeste Novelli and Laura Bickell,
two women who raised families, helped
others, lived long, and left legacies.

contents

foreword

Americans deserve a revolution. With people living longer, and the first of the 78 million baby boomer generation turning 60 this year, America is on the brink of another wave of disruptive change. Both as individuals and as a nation, we need to be ready to take advantage of the emerging opportunities that will arise from this change. In *50+: Igniting a Revolution to Reinvent America,* Bill Novelli offers his vision of how to do that. He clearly identifies the opportunities for change that confront us today and tomorrow, and he shows us what he believes we should do to bring about these changes. But most important, he inspires us to become sparks to ignite a revolution to reinvent America for the twenty-first century . . . to make it better for all generations.

Revolutions, by their very nature, are driven by people coming together around a common desire to create change. My colleagues and I started AOL twenty years ago with a single, clear vision: to make the power of the online medium available to everyone. The conventional wisdom of that time was that consumers were couch potatoes. But I could see a world where interactivity was ubiquitous, with consumers in control. By challenging the conventional wisdom, we sparked a revolution that brought transformational change and helped usher in an era where interactivity is now a part of our daily lives. We ignited the revolution, but consumers changed the world.

Just as I saw a world twenty years ago where, given the proper tools, consumers would make interactivity a way of life, today I see a world where consumers are put at the center of the health system; where we focus more time and investment on keeping people healthy and fulfilled, as opposed to dealing with the resulting problems (poor health, unfulfilled lives) after the fact, to help people realize the kind of "life in the balance" they seek; and where we create experiences that truly reflect the uniqueness of their surroundings and the innate desire of people to connect—and disconnect. This is the focus of my new company, Revolution, which I launched in 2005. Revolution seeks to drive transformative change just as we did at AOL, by shifting power to consumers. Our mission is to give people more choice, more control, and more convenience in the important aspects of their lives. We don't just aim for a financial return—we seek to build companies that can bring about revolutionary change in their industries.

Bill Novelli is no stranger to revolutionary change. From his early days of attacking big health and social issues at Porter Novelli (the giant public relations firm he cofounded) to his years at CARE International helping impoverished people across the globe, to battling big tobacco at The Campaign for Tobacco-Free Kids, he has devoted most of his career to leading positive social change. Now, as chief executive officer of AARP, he is tackling perhaps his toughest and most wide-sweeping challenge, yet—the myriad changes America faces as it prepares for the aging of the vast baby boom generation.

Just as I did twenty years ago with AOL, and am doing now with Revolution, Bill is challenging the conventional wisdom. Many people view the aging of the boomers (combined with longer life expectancies) as a huge social *problem*, but Novelli sees it as a series of *oppor-*

tunities—the opportunity to transform health care, to reinvent retirement, to revolutionize the workplace, to build more livable communities, to change the marketplace, to advocate for a cause, and to leave a lasting legacy. While seizing upon these opportunities will not be easy, Novelli firmly believes we can do it. As he writes in the epilogue, "We can improve the quality of our own lives, and those of our families, by seizing the opportunities that spring from our increased longevity and our privileged place in the world. But we can also do much more. We can change society and make America a better place for all of our citizens, now and in the future."

I happen to believe he is right, just as I'm confident that Revolution will help bring about the kinds of transformational change Novelli talks about in this book. Passionate entrepreneurs are the architects of revolutionary change. Even though Novelli heads one of the largest membership organizations in the world (AARP has over 36 million members), he is an entrepreneur at heart. And he knows, as do I, that igniting this revolution will take entrepreneurs from all walks of life to come forward with innovative new products and services, with new breakthrough ways of doing things, with renewed passion for success and a strong desire to make the world a better place. It will also take much more. It will take all of us doing whatever we can, wherever we are to ignite this revolution. We must all be involved.

Regardless of your age, or where you are in life's journey, I believe you will find 50+: *Igniting a Revolution to Reinvent America* bold, enlightening, thought-provoking, and inspirational. This book is filled with the stories of people who are making a difference. All of them, each in their own way, are igniting the revolution. Americans deserve a revolution. And I hope that within the pages of 50+ you will find the spark that will rekindle your passion to do something to help ignite a revolution to reinvent America, not just for yourself, but for future generations.

STEVE CASE
Chairman and CEO, Revolution

acknowledgments

Just as it takes more than one person to reinvent America, it took more than one person to make this book possible. Many people contributed their talent, expertise, experience, and enthusiasm. While I can't mention them all, I would like to recognize a few.

First, I would like to thank Boe Workman, my colleague and collaborator at AARP, who was instrumental in this project from the beginning. Boe did much of the hard work. We are in this great adventure together. I also thank the talented folks at Wordworks, who helped us frame the book and shape it. Helen Rees was the person who suggested this project in the first place. I thank her for that and for her constant encouragement throughout the process. Also, I am indebted to Michael Flamini, my editor at St. Martin's Press. Michael is not just a skilled editor who knows how to make a book better, he also really wanted to do this project and ignited the fire of his colleagues at St. Martin's as well—many thanks to Lisa Senz, Ronni Stolzenberg, Vicki Lame, and all of the design and production people involved in the project.

This book could not have been done without the help of my many colleagues at AARP. John Rother, our policy guru, read drafts, made suggestions, and added accuracy, as did Mike Naylor and David Certner. Marie Smith, Joan Wise, and Hugh Delehanty read and commented on the drafts. Hugh, who is editor-in-chief of AARP publications, knows books and how to write them. He also helped guide the development of the chapters. My thanks also go out to Tom Nelson and Dawn Sweeney, two AARP teammates who encouraged me when so many other things were piling up on the agenda; to Kevin Donnellan, for leading our communications efforts around the book; to Sherla Allen, my valuable assistant, who continually juggled the many demands of my schedule to keep me on track; and to the AARP Board of Directors for their support and encouragement throughout the project.

I would also like to thank Steve Case for doing the foreword to the book; Lyle Minter and Budd Whitebook, who read drafts and provided valuable comments; our fact checkers, Andrea Andrews and Karen McMillan; my former colleagues at Porter Novelli, CARE International, and the Campaign for Tobacco-Free Kids; and the staff and volunteers at AARP who work hard every day on behalf of 50+ America. Finally, my gratitude goes out to all 50+ Americans, especially those whose stories are included in this book—who are doing their part to ignite a revolution to reinvent America. Without you, there would be no revolution.

50+

Introduction

Problems worthy of attack
Prove their worth by attacking back.
—Anonymous

I'm one of those lucky people who chased a dream and caught it. When I was appointed chief executive of AARP in mid-2001, I felt as if my whole career had been preparation for this one job. I had found my perfect opportunity to make a difference—to help combat those "problems worthy of attack that prove their worth by attacking back."

We have a saying at AARP that age is just a number and life is what you make it. For Americans who are age 50 and over, the number is 50+ and the life you can make at that age has infinite possibilities. There's a thing about that plus sign: It means a whole lot more than "fifty-something" or "in her golden years" or "heading toward retirement." That plus sign means that more people are living longer and that people turning 50 today have more than half of their adult lives ahead of them. In fact, more and more people are actually turning 50 every day at a rate that's the highest in the history of the United States. A boomer turns 50 every 7.5 seconds. The plus sign behind that 50 also means that people thinking about retiring now have the opportunity to create a better quality of life, leave a legacy to our country, and ignite a revolution that will change the way we think about aging in America. The 50+ generation just beginning to appear on the horizon will ignite this revolution and change the United States in the process.

I love where I work because I believe deeply in AARP's mission of enhancing our lives as we age. It's a mission that speaks to all generations, those that are younger as well as those that are 50+. We are beginning one of the most important societal changes of all time—the aging of America and the world. And with well over 36 million members in the United States and an international presence, AARP is in the forefront. This is an exciting period, an opportunity to be part of influencing events and social change in the unfolding drama of an aging population.

I've always had a deep interest in making a contribution to solving major social problems and creating positive social change. I'm talking about the big, tough issues that do "attack back" in many ways, which is what makes them so difficult for us to solve in the first place.

I didn't start my career with such lofty aims, though. My goal after college, and my parents' hope for me, was to get a good job at a big company that offered health benefits and the chance to climb the rungs of the corporate ladder. That was the era of the corporate man, with not much of anything taught in business and other college classes about becoming an entrepreneur or taking a different route. And I say "corporate man" because, for the most part, young women didn't go into business. They majored in education (like my wife, Fran) or nursing or perhaps became wives and mothers (again, like Fran) soon after graduation. I recall competing for job offers in the spring of my last year in school, and I don't think any of my competitors for those positions were women. Times have changed; as women have entered every walk of life, we've virtually doubled our talent in most sectors of our economy. That's real change.

My first job was in consumer marketing at Unilever, where I learned the fundamentals of business. But first I learned humility. Before the marketing began, there was sales training, understanding the business from the bottom up by working retail. After a quick week of sales orientation I was given a station wagon full of products and promotional materials and a sales bag (I still have it) and sent off into the Syracuse sales district in upstate New York. My territory was from Binghamton down into the Catskills. We had a large product line, but our Unilever mainstays were laundry detergents. I had only two business suits, which I alternated day by day throughout the weeks and months of my retail apprenticeship. By working the shelves in supermarkets and walking through warehouses, I collected a great deal of detergent powder in my pants cuffs and pockets, and when it rained, I "sudsed." This was not a good way to make a dignified impression, but it was a good way to learn the business.

Then, after completing the sales training program and joining the Unilever marketing operation in New York City, I realized just how competitive things really were. We assistant brand managers (mostly rookies) were seated along with the secretaries at metal desks in a kind of big bull pen on each marketing floor, and around the outside were the offices of the group brand managers and brand managers, with the corner office belonging to the division vice president. It was clear that the idea was to earn your way out of the bull pen and into one of those carpeted offices. I did, and in the process I learned my trade.

I left Unilever to go to what was then a hot New York ad agency, Wells Rich Greene, and from the agency side of the business I continued to work on packaged goods, with clients such as Ralston Purina and Bristol-Myers. It wasn't detergents and fabric softeners and toothpaste anymore; now it was hair cream, dog food, cat food, and kids' cereals. Not much of a difference there, but I was climbing the ladder.

Despite my progress, I felt that something was missing. Red Blaik, the great Army football coach, supposedly said, "You have to be smart enough to play the game, but dumb enough to think it's important." I knew that both my colleagues and my competitors were plenty smart, but I just didn't think the packaged goods marketing and advertising game was enough for me. I wanted something that I vaguely thought of as more socially relevant.

This was really driven home, and I think the turning point came, the day I returned from a client meeting with two test products in plastic bags. One was a kids' cereal and the other a new dog food. A young copywriter came into my office, said that he was working on ad concepts for the cereal, and asked to see the product. As a joke, I reached into my briefcase, pulled out the bag of soft, extruded dog food, and tossed it across the room to him. "Yeah," the copywriter said as he caught it, "we can sell that."

That did it for me. I was definitely ready to change direction. I don't mean to denigrate business; that's where America's wealth is created. It's the economic engine that drives the country. But I was determined to change course. As I began to explore how and where, I was assigned a new client, the Public Broadcasting Service. It was probably the first time PBS had used an ad agency to build viewership for public television. One of my first tasks was to attend a press conference that featured Joan Ganz Cooney, one of the creators of *Sesame Street.* I was fascinated by Cooney herself and by the *Sesame Street* approach to learning. The thought struck me that marketing tools and practices could be applied to ideas, issues, and causes just as effectively as to the laundry detergents, toothpastes, and pet foods I had been promoting. This was relevant, I thought, and socially important. I wanted to try it, but how could I go about making it into a career?

I soon read a business article in *The New York Times* that said the Peace Corps wanted to "reposition" itself, to attract more volunteers with job experience and work skills that were in demand among developing countries. They were looking for a marketing person, and I landed the job. The year was 1970. Fran, our three young children—Peter, Alex, and Sarah—and I set out for Washington, D.C., and I was on my way to realizing my new ambition.

Early on I was intrigued to learn that a huge number of Americans claimed to personally know a current or former Peace Corps volunteer. But that was hardly possible given the then relatively small number of volunteers who had served. My conclusion was that Peace Corps volunteers had become folk heroes. People wanted to know them—even felt they did know them—because they admired those willing to give part of their lives to a good cause.

I also discovered that many returned Peace Corps volunteers shared a common fear—that time and events would erase any evidence of the good they had done in the countries in which they had served. All of us carry a strong desire, I realized, to leave a legacy, to feel we have made a difference in other people's lives. Both of these ideas had an influence on the rest of my career.

Jack Porter, my boss at the Peace Corps, had also left a commercial marketing career to work at the Peace Corps, and he, too, was intrigued with the idea of marketing ideas and causes. We decided to start a firm for just this purpose. But first, the White House intervened. People there had heard about my marketing work in New York, and I was asked to help start and manage the in-house advertising and promotion agency for the reelection of President Richard Nixon. I wasn't particularly political or ideological at that point in my life, but I thought it would be a great experience, as a young person, to work on a presidential campaign. It was a fascinating time, and I was excited to have the chance to apply my marketing skills to national politics.

Jack and I put our idea on hold, and I spent nine months as part of the November Group, as we named ourselves, working on the Nixon reelection campaign. Somewhat later, the experience turned sour when the facts behind the Watergate episode and related activities came to light. Some of the people held to account, including G. Gordon Liddy, were among those we in the November Group had worked with.

Immediately after the 1972 presidential election, Jack and I and a third partner, Mike Carberry, founded Porter Novelli, a firm dedicated to applying marketing to health and social issues. We had lofty goals, but our realities were more down-to-earth—bringing in clients and money to meet our small payroll. Bob Druckenmiller, whom I had known from our marketing days in New York and persuaded to come to Washington, came over from the Peace Corps to join us.

Our first major assignment was to help the National High Blood Pressure Education Program, then in early planning stages at the National Heart, Lung, and Blood Institute (part of the National Institutes of Health), reach out to the medical profession and the public about the lifesaving advantages of treating high blood pressure. I learned a valuable lesson right at the start from the institute's director, Dr. Ted Cooper, who made an early decision that was critical to the program's success. He rejected the advice of his key planning committee, made up of physicians and other health providers, who wanted to delay the public education part of the program for up to a decade. They believed it would take that long to inform doctors and nurses about how to detect and treat the disease. But Dr. Cooper refused and said that we would communicate to the public and health professionals at the same time, so that the two audiences reinforced each other. He wanted to make high blood pressure control a normal part of life, with patients asking to have their blood pressure checked at the same time that doctors were recommending it and doing it. Cooper's approach worked; messages were delivered to both audiences, and behaviors changed as a result. Deaths and disability declined over time, and today the program is still considered probably the most successful national health education program in U.S. history.

In time, Porter Novelli became involved in many health and social issues, including environmental protection, cancer detection and control, and reproductive health and infant survival in developing countries. We also brought in commercial clients, which helped us grow, but social issues and ideas were what made me eager to go to work each day. I wanted more than ever to focus there.

I had a schedule in mind; when my son Alex reached his junior year, that would mark the midpoint in my kids' college educations. It was a sort of watermark, when I would change careers. And that's the way it turned out. Alex hit his junior year in college and I "retired" from Porter Novelli in 1990, at the age of 49, to pursue a full-time career in public service.

Porter Novelli continued to grow, and today it is a large, international public relations agency and part of the Omnicom Group, a global marketing communications corporation.

I went to CARE, at that time the world's largest private international relief and development organization. I had previously served on CARE's board of directors, and I was familiar with the agency's mission and the work it did in developing countries in disaster response and in long-term programs in such areas as agriculture, the environment, health services, girls' education, and microenterprise (providing small loans to farmers, women's groups, and others). But now my everyday work with CARE's management and staff brought me face-to-face with some of the most dedicated, committed people I'd ever encountered. Many had been Peace Corps volunteers. To a person, they wanted to make a difference in the world, which they did through development programs, as well as by managing refugee camps, helping victims of natural disasters, and risking their lives in dangerous settings. I recall jolting over a rutted road in Mozambique in 1993, not long after their revolution had ended. Fran was with me. The young CARE driver at the wheel of the Toyota jeep said, "Don't worry; this road's just been de-mined!" Many CARE staff adopted children from countries in which they served, so that a CARE summer picnic was like a kiddie United Nations.

After four and a half years at CARE, including work on the Somalia and Rwanda crises, my next role in public service was as a founder and president of the Campaign for Tobacco-Free Kids. I had learned about the enormous toll that tobacco takes while working with the National Cancer Institute in my Porter Novelli days. I also learned what a huge payout in lives and cost savings can be gained by reducing tobacco use among youths as well as adults. And I never forgot the comment of a young research staffer at the Leo Burnett ad agency, which handled the Philip Morris account for many years. I asked him at a conference how he could justify marketing tobacco; he said, "I just hope our advertising isn't too effective."

It was 1995 and the battle against smoking in the United States was heating up and moving much higher on the national agenda. The Food and Drug Administration (FDA) was trying to assert jurisdiction over tobacco (which it still does not have), more young people were smoking, and public health professionals were gearing up to respond. At an international meeting in Paris, several of them, including Matt Myers, today the president of the Campaign for Tobacco-Free Kids, Mike Pertschuk of the Advocacy Institute, and Nancy Kaufman of the Robert Wood Johnson Foundation decided that the powerful tobacco companies and their association, the Tobacco Institute, needed an aggressive counterweight—"a tobacco institute for the good guys," as they put it. And that's just what we created—the Campaign for Tobacco-Free Kids.

Funded by the Robert Wood Johnson Foundation, the American Cancer Society, and the American Heart Association, we plunged into action. State attorneys general, health organizations, religious groups, and many others banded together to fight the industry hard, and Big Tobacco fought back. We made a lot of progress, but unfortunately, we didn't win out in Congress. We failed to get our comprehensive tobacco control bill, led by Senator John McCain, through the Senate. The legislation would have established government regulation and programs, reformed tobacco industry marketing and other practices, and driven smoking down further and faster. We did all we could to support the legislation, with John Seffrin, CEO of the American Cancer Society, and Cass Wheeler of the American Heart Association and others out front with the Campaign. Although the bill didn't pass, we made a difference. Today overall smoking has declined, more and more cities and states are going smoke free, and the tobacco industry is no longer accepted as just another American business. Nor does it have the choke hold it once did on our legislative process. The tobacco war is far from over, but the Campaign for Tobacco-Free Kids and others are working hard, and things are changing for the better.

> All progress is precarious, and the solution of one problem brings us face-to-face with another problem.
> —*Dr. Martin Luther King Jr.*

From where I now sit at AARP, I see that, as a society, we have made great progress in making life better for all generations. But with the largest 50+ generation in history entering their mature years, life is about to get even better. With increased longevity adding vital and productive years to our extended lives, we have come to an important crossroads. In front of us is an unprecedented opportunity to make changes that will not only improve our own lives but also make our country stronger. The question we have to ask is are we going to lead that change or let that change lead us? I am an optimist. I believe that most people are like me. They want to make a difference in the world. They want to lead the change.

And the people who will lead this change are the people in the 50+ generation. The boomers who make up part of this group are savvier about technology, about keeping fit, and about planning for retirement. Most important, they have been more engaged in social issues than many generations before them, simply by dint of their growing up mostly during the 1960s, a time of incredible social change around the world. I'm going to be talking about 50+ people all through this book who are making changes in the current system to reinvent the way Americans think about and react to aging. For me 50+ is a state of mind that starts in one's late forties and goes on past one's nineties. Every bit of what I say in this book is directed toward the 50+ generation. All of the examples and suggestions are things you can do to take part in and lead this dramatic social change, which ranks with the Industrial Revolution and the Digital Revolution as the most significant in our history.

When people who are now 50+ were living through the 1960s, Bob Dylan was singing "The Times They Are A-changin'." And it's no less different now. As Bob Dylan suggested, everyone needs to be involved or the revolution will roll right over them. I think we can all be involved. This is our time—to seize the day and make the most of our extraordinary opportunities. We are at a unique moment in history when the need for change, the demand for change, and our ability to create change are coming together. For the 50+ generation, the time is now.

one

A New Vista in the Land of Opportunity

We are all faced with a series of great opportunities—brilliantly disguised as insoluble problems.

—*John W. Gardner*

A while ago, I spoke about health and aging to an audience in Lexington, Kentucky. When I finished my remarks, a woman raised her hand to ask this question: "Do you know that women live longer than men?" I said that I did, to which she replied, "Well, what are you going to do about it?" Even if I could do something about it (which I can't), the fact is, both men and women are living longer. For the first time in history, long life isn't a rarity. Two-thirds of all the people who ever reached the age of 65 are alive today. What's more, 65 isn't even old anymore—most of us can count on another eighteen years or so after that, and more than half of us will live past 90. The fastest-growing segment of the population is those 85 and older.

All of this is good news for America's 78 million baby boomers, the oldest of whom just turned 60 this year and the youngest 42. As the boomers age—one reaches the age of 50 every 7.5 seconds, which adds up to 4 million every single year—the cascade of those over 65 will double over the next thirty years to 70 million. The first boomers turn 65 just five years from now, in 2011. This age shift is having an enormous impact—from family life, work, and recreation to the economy, health care, housing, education, transportation, and technology. But we're beginning to realize—with a jolt—that society has not kept up the demographic shift, and we're certainly not ready for the onslaught ahead.

- *boomers have not prepared adequately for their long futures;*
- *companies are rapidly shifting financial risks and responsibilities to workers and retirees without adequate preparation and safeguards;*
- *government programs are not working as well as they should, and many need to be modernized, better financed, and more engaging to the public;*
- *we have a health-care system that is designed to pay bills but doesn't promote health and wellness; and*
- *we have a growing older population that by and large is vital and active and possesses great intellectual wealth. But we have not structured a social model to optimize their continued involvement.*

Many, in fact, fear this future. Who can blame them, given the alarmist tone of much of the discussion? We hear that Social Security is on the brink of collapse—that by 2020 each retiree will be supported by the payroll taxes of only two workers, far too little to keep the system solvent. Chicken Littles squawk that an army of "greedy geezers" will vote down school taxes but give themselves so many benefits as to bankrupt the country. Others imagine a nation of nursing homes filled with helpless, hopeless old folks.

In just one recent day's worth of articles from around the country I found these stories:

- *"Boomers to Overload Health System: Rising Costs of New Treatments, Fewer Resources Seen as 'Disastrous'"*

- *"Think Social Security Is Secure? Think Again"*
- *"How Bedrock Promises of Security Have Fractured Across America"*
- *"Companies Are Discarding Traditional Pensions"*
- *"Medi-Cal* Cut Threatens Poor, Disabled; More than 3 Million Patients Could Be Affected by a 5% State Reduction in Payments to Doctors, Who Say They May Phase Out Services"*

And to add insult to injury:

- *"Baby Boomers' Ears Paying for All Those Loud Rock Concerts"*

No question, these are challenging times. And although these pessimistic prognosticators go too far, it's certainly true that there is plenty of reason for concern. David Walker, the comptroller general, has said the United States faces a long-term budget deficit "that will only increase as the baby boomers retire," leading to a "financial imbalance [that] will test the nation's spending and tax policies." He describes it as "a retirement tsunami . . . that will never recede."

Clearly, our society needs to make some changes and we need to begin now. But I see that as a positive development, not a negative one, with boomers leading the way to a brighter future for all of us. At every step of their remarkable journey, they have transformed American life and culture.

The transformation began with the first wave of babies just after World War II. As hospital nurseries started filling up, schools were built, pediatricians were trained, and consumers bought the products and services they needed to cope with the deluge. In short, Americans rolled up their sleeves and did what they had to do.

* Medi-Cal is the state of California's Medicaid system.

When the baby boomers were still just that, babies, our leaders made a conscious decision to invest in research to develop vaccines and cures for childhood diseases. Consequently, afflictions such as diphtheria, whooping cough, smallpox, and polio—which once killed and maimed thousands of children every year—were all but eradicated. Vaccinations for chicken pox, measles, and mumps became standard practice in this country. And as the babies grew, we built whole new suburbs to house them, fast-food restaurants to feed them (a mistake, perhaps), and schools and universities to educate them. As a result of all this change, the United States became a better, more productive society.

Now even the youngest boomers have passed 40 and are moving into middle age. When they were kids, 50 was considered old. But perceptions have changed. It's a sure sign of progress when, instead of "old folks' homes," specially tailored recreation facilities and new communities are springing up across the country. And just as when the boomers were young, the research and medical community is focused on attacking their health problems, this time the ones associated with aging. This effort alone may make a huge difference. Disability among older people is already decreasing, and if successful treatments for Alzheimer's disease, arthritis, incontinence, and osteoporosis are discovered, the nursing-home population—which is already declining—could be cut even more, possibly in half. The millions of Americans freed from these debilitating diseases would enjoy a much-improved quality of life, to the great relief of their families and friends.

Nearly everyone agrees about the impact of the boomers and our increased longevity. What's lacking is a consensus on how we should adapt to the new realities. The collective "we"—individuals, institutions, communities, businesses, and government—don't share a common vision of the life we want or the changes we will have to make to achieve it. Many boomers are already experiencing the future by caring for aging parents. And, as they do, they're beginning to weigh in on what works and what doesn't. By and large, they're seeing a whole lot that needs to be changed.

So what some see as insoluble problems are, to my mind, great opportunities—opportunities, as this book spells out, to make us healthier and transform our health-care system, to rethink our retirement expectations, to extend our productive, creative lives, to build more livable communities, to change the culture so the country can actively profit from a still vital population, and to leave lasting legacies that improve the lives of others and strengthen the country for future generations.

OPPORTUNITIES FOR CHANGE

This increase in the life span and in the number of our senior citizens presents this Nation with increased opportunities. . . . It is not enough for a great nation merely to have added new years to life—our object must also be to add new life to those years.
—*President John F. Kennedy, special message to the Congress on the needs of the nation's senior citizens, February 21, 1963*

Many boomers approaching their landmark sixty-fifth birthdays dream of active, productive, and well-financed years ahead. Yet we know from the experiences of older people today that shortsighted public policies and private-sector practices coupled with imprudent personal behaviors threaten to smother these ambitions.

For example, our health-care delivery is based primarily on providing acute care, while more and more people are living with chronic conditions such as high blood pressure, diabetes, and heart disease. Over 45 million people are uninsured. Our society is aging, but our new doctors are not studying geriatric medicine. While the cost of health care goes up, the quality of care is going down. At the same time, people are being asked to take more personal responsibility for their own health-care costs. Yet the expense of health care makes it less affordable for many. Out-of-pocket spending on prescription drugs and long-term care represents the greatest health-related financial risk for older Americans.

Even many of those who have access to affordable health care are in danger, although largely through their own fault. While legions of fit and healthy people 50+ run marathons, swim, dance, garden, and beat younger opponents on the tennis court, a multitude of others are shortening their lives with sedentary lifestyles. In other words, being couch potatoes. Poor physical fitness (along with smoking) puts people at greater risk for potentially fatal diseases such as high blood pressure and heart disease. And the increasing incidence of obesity among all age-groups in this country threatens to reverse many of the strides made in health and longevity over the past decades. As chapter 2 points out, we must change our focus from providing acute care for long-established problems to intervening early, before people's health is compromised.

Meanwhile, retirement is being reinvented right before our eyes. As more people live longer and healthier lives, they are searching for ways to continue contributing to society while finding personal fulfillment in their own lives. Many are volunteering, going back to school, spending more time with grandkids, or caring for an elderly parent or relative. Regardless of their activities, they don't see life after 50 as a time to shift into neutral . . . it's full speed ahead toward an active lifestyle of involvement and engagement. But far too few boomers are saving enough to finance the lifestyles they want. For members of the so-called sandwich generation, the demands of raising their children even as they care for aged parents make it hard to put aside what they'll need for retirement. At the same time, businesses are scaling back traditional pensions in favor of tax-advantaged saving and investment plans that make retirement income less secure. They are also trimming or even eliminating retiree health care. Even people who have planned well for their retirement are only one major medical episode away from seeing it all go up in smoke. In short, as chapter 3 discusses, retirement planning has not kept up with the startling increase in longevity or the expectation of an active lifestyle.

Making it easier for older people to find and hold on to jobs is one part of the solution. Many people want to or need to work into their

so-called retirement years. And with all the hand-wringing in antici-
pation of the baby boomers' retirement, it's seldom mentioned that
just six years from now, in 2012, the "baby bust" generation that follows the boomers will, in all probability, be unable to fill all the available jobs. Some enlightened companies, aware of the looming shortfall
and eager to retain the skills and experience of their more mature
workers, are encouraging the 50+ generation to stay on the job. But,
as chapter 4 indicates, others are still pushing the notion of early retirement or simply saying good-bye to older employees. This myopia is
bad for all those who want to continue working, contributing, and
earning the money they need to live comfortably in the next stage of
their lives, and it's detrimental to the well-being of our country as a
whole. Fortunately, change is afoot as self-interested employers increasingly understand the folly of denying themselves the value that
older workers add to the workplace.

"Aging in place" is the dream of most people—and enabling older
people to remain in their communities as they age can benefit the communities as well. The wit and wisdom that comes with a lifetime of
experiences enriches life for everyone. To help 50+ Americans achieve
their dream, chapter 5 explains, we must design age-friendly living
arrangements and better transportation options.

The way the members of the 50+ generation are portrayed in the
media and other parts of society often bears little or no resemblance
to the healthy, active, fun-loving people most of us know and interact
with every day. Many people have enough disposable income to enjoy
travel, dining out, new learning experiences, and wide-ranging entertainment options. The economic power and vitality of those of us 50+
gives us an opportunity to change the culture of the marketplace and
propel an economic boom. Moreover, great rewards await those businesses that have the ability to see through the misconceptions and
take advantage of the opportunities, as chapter 6 demonstrates.

The active lifestyle that people 50+ want also encompasses being
active citizens. Chapter 7 explores the role that people play as
advocates for national, state, and local causes. We know that people

50+ vote in large numbers, but most don't view their duties as citizens as just a one-day commitment. As youth, they led a revolution to change America by becoming citizen activists and advocates. Now they have that opportunity to do it again . . . to lead another revolution to reinvent America as our population ages.

One of life's greatest satisfactions comes from giving back to society. For the boomer generation, as well as for people already in their later years, the opportunities to leave a legacy and enrich their communities and country are limited only by their imaginations. The idea of service is nothing new. Many years ago, my mother took me along when she taught handicrafts in a Boys Club in Carnegie, Pennsylvania. I've never forgotten it. The challenge is to multiply the joy of serving others by enlisting greater numbers of people and getting them thinking about the innumerable ways in which they can give back, as chapter 8 makes clear.

REALIZING A NEW VISION

If I'd known I was going to live this long,
I'd have taken better care of myself.
                              —*Eubie Blake*

I hope the prospect of increased longevity will cause us to view our lives differently from an earlier age and influence our decisions along the way. As Eubie Blake suggested, maybe if we know we are going to live so long, we'll take better care of ourselves.

This, however, is a book less about aging than about social change and what each of us can do to advance it. It's a call to action about you and your life and this country. By seizing the opportunities that accompany aging, I believe we can begin to shape a common vision of the lives we want for ourselves and for future generations. After all, as the ancient proverb says, "Where there is no vision, the people perish." We can engage people in the quest to realize their own goals and dreams and to make life better and society stronger for everyone in the years ahead.

Congresswoman Barbara Jordan once said, "What the people want is very simple—they want an America as good as its promise." And achieving an America as good as its promise depends on the balance between what society can do and what we must do ourselves as individuals, exercising personal responsibility. We may have to pay a little more; we may have to exercise a little more; we may have to save a little more; we may have to work a little longer. But we can do it. We can make our lives, our communities, and our country better.

And now is the time to do it. The longer we wait, the harder these problems worthy of attack will fight back. And the sooner we take on our problems and challenges, the less likely it is that we will leave them for the next generation to solve.

George Bernard Shaw put it this way. He said that "we are made wise not by the recollection of our past, but by the responsibility of our future." The responsibility of *our* future tells us that we must all join together to create a country

- *where government stands sentry over vital social programs such as Social Security, Medicare, and Medicaid and takes reasonable and responsible steps to strengthen them for generations to come;*
- *where corporate giants and small businesses alike prize the experience of older workers and reject age discrimination as bad business;*
- *where people of all ages can receive quality health care that they can afford;*
- *where older people can remain in their homes for as long as possible and continue to be active in their communities; and*
- *where all Americans can achieve independence, choice, and control in ways that are beneficial and affordable for them and society as a whole.*

We can make our lives and our families' lives richer. And we can create a society where all people can afford to grow old with dignity and purpose and have the opportunity to continue chasing their dreams. Our ability to achieve all this is limited only by our lack of imagination and creativity. Two hundred years ago, if a farmer were asked what could be done to improve his life, he might have said, "Give me more horses." He would not have thought of a tractor or a combine. Today when we ask, "How do we capture, as AARP's founder, Dr. Ethel Percy Andrus, put it, 'the accumulated experience, the knowledge, wisdom, and skills of all older adults and the increased longevity of our population'?" the answer is not to put up more nursing homes or build a better wheelchair. We need to think about changing ourselves, the environment we live in, and how we interact with it.

Back when I was working at Porter Novelli on health and other social programs, a man who believed that I knew something about social change came to my office and asked me, "How do you start a groundswell?" I didn't have a good answer then. But today I would respond by saying this: "Watch us and join in, because that's just what we're doing, creating a powerful groundswell on behalf of 50+ Americans."

We can't leave the future to chance. We must learn, educate, and create change. This book aims to jump-start the process by getting everyone started thinking and talking about living long, healthy, and engaging lives. After all, from the day we are born we become a part of the aging population. And when people of every age understand what it means to grow older, we will be on our way to changing society. We will improve our own lives and those of generations to come. And we will not only fulfill our responsibility to future generations; we will also create an America as good as its promise.

two

The Opportunity to Transform Health Care

The health of a nation is measured by the health of its people.
—*Anonymous*

It's a wonderful world we live in. Thanks to advances in public health and hygiene, medical breakthroughs in antibiotics, vaccines, and surgeries, plus new treatments for old killers such as diabetes and cancer, people are living longer and healthier lives than ever before.

The 50+ generation and their older brothers and sisters do more desk work, which is less grueling than many of the jobs their parents held. They smoke less, get more and better medical treatment, have less heart disease, and suffer fewer strokes and disabilities. Prescription drugs have largely replaced hospitalizations and surgery as first-line treatments.

But there's a darker side to this story. The delivery of costly medical treatments is straining our health-care financing structure, as many people grapple with chronic illnesses and disabilities in a system that is not built to handle their problems. And the growing needs of the vast tide of aging boomers will only worsen the strain and potentially overload the system.

We like to think that the United States has the best health care in the world, but how can that be true when you consider that:

• Our health care is outrageously expensive and getting more so every day. The United States spends $1.9 trillion a year on health care—some $6,280 for every man, woman, and child in the country. That's 16 percent of the economy, well above what any other industrialized nation spends. And yet we trail these countries in health outcome measures ranging from infant mortality to life expectancy. Not to mention that the wealthiest nation on earth is the only developed country that has not figured out how to make health care available to all its citizens.

Medical costs have been rising far faster than the cost of living in recent years, and the already-high prices of brand-name prescription drugs, which are essential to the practice of modern medicine, are increasing even more rapidly than health-care costs in general. In fact, out-of-pocket spending on prescription drugs and long-term care represents the greatest health-related financial risk for older Americans. Drug price controls like those imposed in other countries are probably not the answer, but neither do we want medicines priced out of the reach of average Americans. The Medicare prescription drug benefit is a good step toward making drugs affordable, at least for those 65 and older. It can certainly be made better, but at long last we have drug coverage in Medicare. But what about everybody else, especially those without adequate coverage from their employer plans?

• The numbers of uninsured or inadequately insured are rising. Some 45 million people are without health insurance in this country. In some cases, employers have stopped offering it; in others, the working poor and even some moderate-income families can't afford insurance when it is available. The lack of insurance leads to large disparities in health status between the haves and the have-nots. And it's expensive for all of us.

People 50 to 64 years old account for about 11 percent of those without health insurance, and 45-to-64-year-olds make up about 14 percent. The higher incidence of medical problems as people age makes it difficult to insure these groups. Those who have been down-sized out of the workforce find themselves scrambling to prepare for retirement and hoping that serious illness won't strike before they turn 65 and qualify for Medicare.

• Inefficiency and poor-quality care plague the system. An enor-mous share of the care we do provide is wasted. A study by the Dart-mouth Medical School found that as much as one-third of all our medical spending—about $600 billion a year—is probably unneces-sary. And shocking though it may be, the health-care system itself is actually a leading cause of death in the United States. The Institute of Medicine estimates that medical errors—misdiagnoses, medica-tion mistakes, preventable infections picked up in the hospital, and other mistakes—kill as many as 195,000 people a year; only heart dis-ease and cancer take more lives. Up to half those errors occur in hos-pitals, and a person has more than twice the chance of dying in a hospital than in an auto accident. As some people like to say, a hospi-tal is no place for a sick person.

• More and more of the rising costs of health care are being shifted to the individual. There are many reasons, including the growth in the numbers of uninsured seeking care they cannot pay for. These numbers, in turn, are rising in part because companies struggling to compete in a global market are requiring employees to shoulder more of the health-care burden, sometimes charging current em-ployees and retirees higher premiums, sometimes doing away with health plans altogether. Recent news stories about the financial problems facing U.S. automakers point out that foreign competitors enjoy a big cost advantage because their countries provide universal health coverage.

The soaring price of health care and the shifting of costs also carries over to Medicare, which provides for those 65 and older, and Medicaid, the shared federal and state effort to provide a health safety net for children living in poverty, older Americans needing long-term care, the disabled, and others among society's most vulnerable. Both Medicare and Medicaid are already under financial stress; the needs of the boomers could soon swamp these programs.

Medicaid, in particular, exemplifies how costs are being shifted. Many of those who lose health insurance become eligible for Medicaid. Yet most people who lose their jobs can't qualify for Medicaid. Only mothers with children can, and even they must pass an asset test. Still, Medicaid has become the nation's largest health insurance program, covering one in every six Americans. Between 2000 and 2003, Medicaid's costs grew by one-third, with much of the spending explosion due to the shift from private to public responsibility for insuring Americans, not to the expenditure of additional dollars on health care overall. Clearly, doing away with private health insurance doesn't solve the problems; it only transfers them. Nor does the chain reaction stop there.

Medicaid is funded jointly by the federal government and the states, most of which are financially strapped. To slow the soaring federal deficit, some of our government leaders favor cutting or capping Medicaid dollars or changing Medicaid from an entitlement program to a discretionary program funded by block grants. These are set amounts of money that states can use pretty much as they see fit. Because many states are also facing fiscal pressures, they like the flexibility a block grant offers. The problem is, block grants are based on preestablished funding levels, which means that the rising costs of health care would thus force the states to scale back or eliminate many currently mandatory Medicaid services. Doctors, hospitals, and other providers would be saddled with more instances of uncompensated care. This is already a big problem, and it would force them to try to offset their increased costs by raising the price of treatment for those who do have insurance. In turn, insurance companies would charge higher premiums and co-pays in a never-ending cycle of rising medical costs. In short, funding for the largest, and perhaps most needed, of all government programs would become, in essence, little more than a game of "hot potato."

Medicaid can certainly be made more efficient, including reductions in fraud and waste. But the only long-term, sustainable solution is to attack the problem at its root: our dysfunctional health-care system.

• Detrimental behavior and poor lifestyle choices pose a growing threat to our nation's health. Far too few Americans of every age get enough exercise, and unhealthy eating habits increase the risks. Obesity in those 50+ has doubled since 1982, and it is increasing rapidly among children as well. Diabetes is also on the rise, with an estimated 14.6 million already diagnosed and another 6.2 million unaware they have the disease. The American Diabetes Association puts the financial toll at $132 billion annually, a cost that is sure to soar if the Centers for Disease Control and Prevention is correct: The CDC expects one in three 5-year-olds in this country to become diabetic. In New York City, the disease has already reached epidemic proportions and affects more than one in eight adults.

More than half of all people 50+ have diabetes, high blood pressure, heart disease, or some other chronic condition. As the 50+ segment increases, so will the need for health services. But our system is not geared to deal with chronic illness, and few new doctors are specializing in geriatrics. Nor can we expect future doctors to choose this specialty, since Congress, in a moment of shortsightedness, chose in late 2005 to eliminate the budget for geriatric training in American medical schools.

In sum, dangerous trends are converging: rising health-care costs, a rapidly expanding population of uninsured or inadequately insured Americans, inefficient and sometimes poor-quality care, the shifting of health-care costs to the individual, and the growing incidence of behavioral and lifestyle-related disease. None of these issues is really new, but as the situation becomes more acute, it is putting even more strain on an already-dysfunctional health-care system.

The American system is focused on disease care rather than health care, on paying bills and shifting costs for acute illnesses rather than on preventing disease and dealing with the chronic conditions that are affecting more and more of our population. We fund remarkable medical research, primarily through the National Institutes of Health (NIH) and other institutions, but much of it is aimed at understanding disease rather than promoting health. We need a better balance.

The same can be said for the pharmaceutical industry. Its innovative, privately funded research mainly seeks to find profit-making cures for disease and disorder rather than less lucrative vaccines and other preventive care. For those who can afford them, the industry's advanced therapies, wonder drugs, and medical devices function extremely well after illness strikes. This is a vitally important health-care industry, and pharmaceutical companies should make a reasonable profit. But we are in desperate need of ways to prevent disease, better manage chronic disease, and promote overall good health.

The dysfunction is obvious once a patient enters the health-care maze, usually via a doctor's appointment. Misdirected incentives built into the system often lead to a battery of diagnostic tests done not only for diagnosis but also for "defensive" purposes, just in case legal problems pop up later. Diagnosing via a battery of tests is far more costly than the old-fashioned way of listening to a patient describe complaints and symptoms. Sure, modern diagnostics are needed, but a $45 bill for a thoughtful thirty-minute conversation with a doctor can easily turn into a $750 bill just for the lab tests ordered in a routine physical examination. The overwhelming majority of physicians want to help people, but the system isn't helping them to help us.

Part of the dysfunction stems from the fact that physicians believe, and rightly so in some cases, that they are being undercompensated by Medicare and other health insurers. It is important that fair fee schedules, based on the widely varying costs in different parts of the country, be implemented. But it is equally important, critical really, that the system begin rewarding preventive care to avert costly medical problems before they begin. A cardiologist, for example, receives thousands of dollars for open-heart surgery but a tiny fraction of that for counseling and persuading a patient to stop smoking.

In Japan, where incentives reward outcomes rather than procedures, doctors perform approximately one-tenth the number of surgeries per capita than in the United States. Yet, by most measures, the Japanese are at least as healthy as Americans. The idea of paying for treatment based on proven practices, sometimes called pay for performance, is advocated by many, including Dr. Mark McClellan, who directs the federal Centers for Medicaid and Medicare Services. But we are a long way from turning this idea into law and putting it into widespread practice.

Promoting health has simply not been a high priority on our national agenda. When nothing is particularly wrong and when taking a few precautions could stave off future problems, the system comes up short. Tilted toward the view that, sooner or later, many, if not most, people will get sick and require expensive treatment, our system's lack of interest in preventive care turns that pessimistic view into a self-fulfilling prophecy.

It can be scary just to think about the rocketing cost of medical care, especially for the millions of people with no insurance, and tales of deadly mistakes and misdiagnoses make things worse. Many people live in fear of losing their health-care insurance or of not being able to pay for the insurance they have. Trying to fix the many problems in our complex system is akin to wrestling an octopus. Every time we make a little headway solving one aspect of the health-care crisis, another tentacle reaches out to wrap itself around our necks.

But we can beat this creature. Fixing America's dysfunctional health-care system and improving the health of our citizens is not beyond our grasp. But the fix will take more than just a little tinkering around the edges. To make health care work, and work well, in today's world will require a national commitment to a transformative vision, one that expects nothing less than a healthier America in which people of every age and every social class can look forward to long and vigorous lives and top-quality care. To bring the dream to life, all of us—government officials and other decision makers, business leaders, and academic experts, the not-for-profit sector (parts of which are now delivering health and long-term care), and individual citizens—have to think differently about health and take on new responsibilities to bring about the change.

It's a huge change on all fronts, including the financial one; initially, some serious spending will be required. But the potential payoff is even bigger. An efficient, best-in-the-world health-care system that emphasizes staying healthy and preventing illness will benefit all generations and all segments of our society. And over the long run, it will save money, too.

The experts already know what needs to be done. Much of what they recommend can be captured in the following seven steps:

- *improving the use of information technology to cut waste and achieve efficiencies;*
- *reducing the toll of medical errors;*
- *promoting health and healthy behavior from infancy through old age;*
- *preventing disease, not just curing it;*
- *sharpening our focus on the growing problem of chronic diseases;*
- *dealing with the escalating cost of prescription drugs; and*
- *making sure that all Americans have access to the health-care system.*

The remainder of this chapter will discuss these seven steps in turn.

HEAL WITH TECHNOLOGY

I do not fear computers. I fear the lack of them.
—*Isaac Asimov*

Today virtually every aspect of our lives is based on information technology. IT is everywhere; it is central to almost every industry. But the health-care sector is behind the times. People with widely differing views on many issues—Senator Hillary Rodham Clinton and former Speaker of the House Newt Gingrich, for example—are in full agreement on the need to bring more and better IT to health care.

Just how far behind is the health-care sector? Well, many, if not most, medical records are still kept on paper, and they must be mailed or faxed among health-care providers. The exchange of information is thus painfully slow and costly; as a result, tests and medical histories are often duplicated unnecessarily. Prescriptions, too, are still usually written on paper, at the expense of the speed, accuracy, and savings that could be realized if doctors' orders were "e-prescribed."

As patients, we often feel uneasy about the mass of handwritten notes, blurred faxes, and bits of paper of varying sizes that we accumulate in our dealings with the current health-care system—paper that gets stuffed into yet one more file folder. Can doctors and nurses and technicians and pharmacists actually make sense of all these things? I hope so, but we really have to wonder.

I remember that a few years ago, when my parents spent winters in Florida and came back to Pittsburgh in the summer, they had doctors in both places. But the records didn't travel back and forth with them. There was a great deal of duplication and lots of family discussion over whether one set of physicians knew what the others were doing.

Attempts by the health-care system to enter the computer age have not gone very well. During the 1990s, a decade of booming productivity in the U.S. economy, productivity in health-care services actually declined. And today, even though health spending is increasing more than three times faster than the overall economy, there is no evidence that productivity is keeping pace. Hospitals that did invest in IT and Web technology often spent their money on systems that didn't work or couldn't talk to each other. Some hospitals and doctors' practices now have good internal IT systems, but they aren't often connected, which means your primary care physician and your orthopedist or your cardiologist or your rheumatologist can't be on the same virtual page at the same time.

But things are beginning to change. In 2004, the Bush administration launched a sweeping project to create a complete electronic record of every American's health care and to link all the records into a giant medical server called the National Health Information Network (NHIN). When it gets up and running (2014 is the target date), all the appropriate professionals treating a patient in the health-care system will supposedly have access to any patient's file—with safeguards to protect privacy. The internist and the orthopedist will be able to view the same MRI results at the same time on their own screens. The emergency-room nurse will know if a new prescription might interact badly with the medications a patient is already taking. A brain specialist in California will be able to retrieve with a few clicks of her mouse the records and all current tests of a new patient from New York.

Setting up such a system won't be easy. Skeptics doubt that such a vast, intricate network will work or that it can be successfully instituted from the top down rather than built up from insurers and other institutions in loose collaboration. Will it be free of glitches? Patient advocates fear hackers will break in and abuse the system for mischief or commercial gain or even for blackmail. Perhaps the biggest obstacle is that hospitals and doctors, many in small practices, will be expected to bear a large share of the estimated $150 billion cost of the system, while the bulk of the savings will go to Medicare, Medicaid, and private insurers.

As part of the initiative, some lawmakers want to legislate incentives encouraging health-care providers to set up electronic medical-records systems that are compatible with the network. Medicare is offering its own system, called Vista, to doctors free of cost, but maintenance may be a problem. Uncertainty prevails. And in the long run, competing commercial systems may win out as easier to use when doctors weigh all the pros and cons—if they can be persuaded to make the switch in the first place. Clearly, an attractive set of incentives is needed. The complexity and challenge of building the health network resembles that of the first transcontinental railroad, with different and sometimes competing interests, varying gauges of track, environmental and other hurdles to be overcome, and only a distant promise of success.

But despite all the obstacles, the project has built up a head of steam, because the benefits of bringing American medicine into the twenty-first century are so enormous. Proponents say the network could be the biggest advance in medicine since the discovery of penicillin. The network has the potential to save tens of thousands of lives every year and, by some estimates, cut up to $120 billion a year from health-care costs by eliminating duplicate tests, shortening hospital stays, and improving care for chronically ill patients. Eventually, some optimists believe, the savings could add up to as much as $600 billion a year. The project has bipartisan support in Congress; nearly a dozen e-health bills have been introduced.

The benefits to be gained from bringing hospitals fully into the computerized world can be seen at Hackensack (New Jersey) University Medical Center. Since 1998, the hospital has poured $72 million into IT improvements, creating something of a central nervous system for the entire hospital. Nurses use wireless laptops on wheels to enter each symptom, medical order, and prescription for every patient. Doctors keep current on their patients' progress, consult with specialists who can call up the same data online, and send in new prescriptions as needed. If a prescribed drug might interact badly with a medication the patient is already taking, the system flashes a warning. Virtually every department of the hospital is linked, from the automated pharmacy to the X-ray room, eliminating much of the previous paperwork. And if a doctor is unable to be present in person at the hospital, he can use "Mr. Rounders," a life-size robot, to make virtual rounds of the wards and "visit" with his patients. The robot—whimsically dressed in a white coat, stethoscope dangling from its "neck"—has a two-way video system that doctors can control from their laptops to talk with patients while consulting their electronic records.

The robot may strike some as too much automation, but overall, Hackensack's investment of attention and money is paying off. The hospital's mortality rates have dropped by 16 percent in just four years, while productivity and quality of care are rising. And in a Medicare-funded study of innovative techniques, Hackensack was one of only two hospitals that scored in the top 10 percent in four out of five categories being studied.

REDUCE ERRORS

> Victory often goes to the army that makes the least mistakes, not the most brilliant plans.
>
> —*Charles de Gaulle*

Any medical error is one too many, and the high number of errors in America's health-care system is a shocking symbol of much-needed change. In addition to as many as 195,000 deaths a year, these mistakes cause an even greater number of injuries, medical complications, adverse drug reactions, and permanent handicaps that spread pain and misery to patients and their families across the country. Lawsuits often follow.

Technology is part of the solution. IT has been shown to reduce some kinds of medical error—such as delivering the wrong medication or incorrect dosages—by as much as 90 percent. Hospitals around the nation are working to establish online patient-safety programs that combine many of the IT improvements already under way.

Documentation systems, for example, can ensure that every symptom, treatment, and prescription will be part of a patient's permanent record and accessible to the patient's entire medical team. Computerized document systems put doctors' instructions on record. New-patient identification systems, ranging from bar-coded wristbands to implantable chips, guard against mix-ups.

But technology alone can't end medical mistakes. In fact, if the technology is poorly designed or used in sloppy processes in a system not attuned to patient safety, technological safeguards can backfire and cause errors to cascade. In the end, technology is only part of a solution that also requires new processes, better communication and teamwork, patient and family involvement, and a culture that gives patient safety and well-being top priority.

There's no point in having an IT system that tracks physicians' orders if a doctor neglects to use it. Training nurses and technicians to accept orders only through the system will force doctors to get onboard. In addition, detectors must be built in to show whether a medication has been properly prescribed, to check that the dosage is correct for the patient, and to verify that the right patient got it. In an emergency, it must be possible to override the system, but also to devise procedures to backtrack and record what was done during the crisis and to explain why.

Communication with patients and families is equally critical, and this is where you and I come in. As patients and family members, we need to be sure that we are heard, that we ask the right questions, and that we understand the answers. Studies show that what patients have to say, especially older patients, is given short shrift by most health providers. Instead, diagnostic tests often trump patients' complaints, especially if those complaints are never heard. And when multiple specialists are called in, all too often communication worsens. Some experts say the odds of a mistake double with each professional team added to the case.

When I go to the doctor, I like to have my wife, Fran, along, because it is hard for me to remember everything that is said. When she isn't there, I take lots of notes. This may make the visit a little longer, but when I leave, I have a better understanding of the situation and what I'm supposed to do.

Both professionals and patients and their families can help cut down on errors by following the advice of Dr. Donald Berwick, a medical professor at Harvard and the president and chief executive officer of the Institute for Healthcare Improvement in Cambridge, Massachusetts, which recently launched its "100,000 Lives Campaign."

Dr. Berwick and other physicians at the institute have identified several critical steps hospital professionals can take to reduce patient deaths. Some are technical, like the rapid response procedures used in a cardiac arrest and the ways of making sure a patient's medications are kept straight when he or she is transferred from one hospital to another. Other, surprisingly elementary precautions include hand washing before surgery. Dr. Berwick and his colleagues estimate that 100,000 lives could be saved each year if 2,000 hospitals complied with the institute's recommendations; they are well past their hospital participation goal at this writing.

Patients and families are urged to get into the act by asking doctors if they've washed their hands, for example. It's hard to imagine most patients asking doctors if they've washed, but who knows? Maybe the growing awareness of the need to prevent errors will give patients (or family members) the courage to ask before the doctor examines them. Dr. Berwick's involvement does emphasize the need for patients to protect themselves and to take personal responsibility for not becoming a "medical error."

Another essential step in preventing mistakes is to change the incentives built into American health care. As it is, insurers, beginning with Medicare, pay doctors and hospitals for the procedures they perform regardless of the results. In fact, poor care can actually be more profitable than good care, since health providers can be paid again for fixing their own mistakes.

Say a patient goes into the hospital for heart surgery and, while there, contracts a staph infection. Either the patient's initial stay is lengthened or she is readmitted in order to treat the infection. Either way, the hospital gets paid both for the heart surgery and for treating the infection. So, mistakes are often rewarded, and that needs to change. Not long ago, Congress drew up legislation that included pay for performance measures as a trade-off for physicians receiving higher Medicare payments. But when the physicians' lobby objected, the measure was scuttled.

In an experiment in paying for performance rather than procedures, Medicare recently enlisted 277 hospitals to accept fees that depend on carefully measured results for five kinds of procedures. Preliminary data showed the quality of care rose by 6 percent after that change. The previously mentioned national IT network could help take us to performance-based pay—measuring the quality of care by tracking infection rates, surgical complications, recovery times, and other factors in treatment. Doctors and hospitals would then be rewarded based on their results.

In another step toward reform, the network could be used to identify the treatments that work best, after which doctors would be encouraged to use those treatments. Such evidence-based care not only improves quality; it also saves money. But just as with performance-based pay, evidence-based care raises hackles among some medical professionals, who disparage it as "cookbook medicine" and prefer to rely on their own judgment about patients' needs. Some also argue that being limited to certain treatments would stifle medical progress. These arguments seem weak, since doctors would still be able to override the recommended treatment, regardless of the evidence, if they think it is warranted.

A major proponent of evidence-based care is UnitedHealth Group, the nation's second-largest private health insurer.* Twice a year, its foundation distributes free to doctors and other health-care professionals in the United States more than 500,000 copies of *Clinical*

---

* In the interest of full disclosure, I should point out that United and AARP work together in offering health-care products and services.

Evidence, a *British Medical Journal* publication that reports the latest evidence-based treatments and protocols for a wide variety of conditions and ailments. Busy doctors who can't hope to keep up with all the research, new drugs, and other treatments use the publication as a quick, authoritative reference to save time and improve the health outcomes of their patients. UnitedHealth has also mounted a public education campaign to encourage and support people's use of evidence-based information in making wise health-care choices. The company runs humorous ads in popular magazines that tell people how to get the most out of a visit to the doctor, how to take charge of their care, and how to use antibiotics appropriately. UnitedHealth's Web site also includes information about how to be healthier and prevent disease. One of its best features is a real-time health chat line that allows people to obtain individualized information and one-on-one advice from a nurse at any time.

Earlier I mentioned the importance of making the culture of safety a top priority. It needs to be embedded in every place that medical care is delivered—hospitals, doctors' offices, clinics, pharmacies, anywhere patients are treated. Physicians and other professionals must feel not just permitted but required to admit mistakes, so that errors can be openly discussed and ways found to avoid repeating them. The system must stress correcting flaws rather than punishing them— which, in turn, may require finding a way other than lawsuits to compensate victims of malpractice. When a health-care professional does report an error, it should not be an automatic ticket to a lawsuit. Before medical errors can be corrected, they must be understood. And before they can be understood, they have to be reported and researched. An Institute of Medicine report suggested a nonjudicial approach—some means of alternative dispute resolution—to take most malpractice claims out of the courts.

No one in helping professions such as medicine wants to make a mistake. Yet everyone in the system must be acutely aware of the human damage their mistakes can cause. At Sharp HealthCare in San Diego, the patient-safety program regularly invites its former patients to tell the hospital staff of the consequences of medical mistakes. In one example, a patient described "in excruciating detail," according to Nancy Pratt, R.N., senior vice president for clinical effectiveness, what happened after a sponge was sewn into his abdomen. The story had the staff members' complete attention. "You could hear a pin drop," Pratt said.

GET HEALTHY

> As I see it, every day you do one of two things: build health or produce disease in yourself.
>
> —*Adelle Davis, nutritionist*

The third requirement for improving health care is more about ourselves than it is about the system: It is about promoting health and healthy behavior from infancy onward. Not a lot can be done about the health effects of things such as genetics and accidents, but we *can* affect the majority of health outcomes by taking responsibility for our own health and that of our children and grandchildren.

A good place to begin is with our eating habits. Obesity is a major killer. Americans eat too many carbohydrates, too much fat, too much sugar, too much of everything—to the point where one-third of all adults, plus increasing numbers of children and teenagers, are clinically obese.* Most Americans need to adjust their diets to reflect their actual roles in a society that relies more on brains than brawn.

The obesity problem has been creeping up on us for a long time. I remember years ago, in my Porter Novelli days, when we discussed

---

*Being clinically obese means having a body mass index (BMI) over 30. To calculate your BMI take your weight in pounds and multiply it by 703, then divide that figure by your height in inches and divide that result again by your height in inches. It sounds complicated, but a simple calculator can help. Alternatively, there's a calculator online at http://nhlbisupport.com/bmi/ where you can just type in your numbers and come up with answers.

doing an exercise and nutritious eating program with the U.S. Navy. The officer in charge said the Navy had a problem keeping highly trained personnel, because once they reached a given point of over-weight, they weren't allowed to reenlist. When I asked what the Navy had done about the problem up to that point, the officer responded, "We've been changing the records to make 'em taller." Obviously, not a good long-term solution.

Essentially, we've got to stop supersizing ourselves, our kids, and our grandkids. The food and restaurant industries can help by cutting portion sizes and offering healthier choices. But no one force-feeds Americans with french fries, giant, high-fat hamburgers, and sugary soft drinks. No one orders us to bulk up our children. Ronald Mc-Donald is a seductive guy and, reportedly, second only to Santa Claus as the most-recognized fictional character in the country (at least Joe Camel is out of the picture). Sure, kids are susceptible to fast-food temptations, but it's the job of all adults to steer them right. We have a double responsibility—first for our own eating habits and then for those of our families, especially the youngsters. Fortunately, my four grandkids—Juli, Nathan, Christopher, and Dominic—are slim and healthy, and I want to do my part to help keep them that way.

Government has a role to play in promoting standards, but it is parents and teachers who must demand more nutritious meals in schools. We need a strong national campaign against childhood obesity, and I have a good slogan to kick it off: "Leave No Child with a Big Behind."

As dangerous as obesity is, there is an even greater threat to our health. The most accurate predictor of premature death—more than a history of smoking, a high cholesterol level, or even obesity—is poor physical fitness. As the demand for physical activity has waned in the workplace and in American life in general, we have become more and more a nation of couch potatoes.

The problem begins early: Television and computer games have replaced outdoor play, and many children no longer walk to school and other activities. Instead, buses and/or parents drive them. How sad to see kids who live only a short distance from school loaded on buses for the morning and evening "commute." My grandson, Dominic, has to ride a bus the half mile to and from his school because there are no sidewalks. A lack of sidewalks in suburban neighborhoods and other safety concerns keep kids from enjoying the multiple benefits of walking.

Today, all across America, only a small percentage of trips to school are made on foot or by bike. Except for the minority of kids in organized sports, most students find little in school and college to keep them moving.

The pattern persists on the job in most urban and rural areas and certainly in the suburbs, where the car is king. Even yard work no longer requires much physical activity; there's a power tool for every chore, and the owner of every postage-stamp-sized lawn has a garage full of them.

I remember as a kid reading comic books with ads for Charles Atlas's famous physical-fitness program. I wanted muscles just like his, and I even sent away for his guaranteed strength and muscle-building kit. I was disappointed to receive a bunch of rubber bands with a dinky instruction booklet showing me how to press against my closet door to build my physique. Now I realize that rubber bands and other simple techniques are better than nothing, especially for people who travel constantly and spend so much time in hotel rooms.

I left Charles Atlas and his rubber bands behind for competitive sports. But even though I no longer compete on the playing field, I still work out to stay in shape for the biggest competition—life. And believe me, I know just how difficult it is to carve out time from a busy schedule to go to the gym or engage in other activities to keep fit. But staying strong and in shape is a personal lifetime requirement.

I was reminded of my own responsibility on a trip to New York, when I accidentally locked myself inside an office pantry. People on the other side of the door were saying, "He's trapped," and urging me to "hang in there." I'm a bit claustrophobic, so I was thinking to myself, Be calm and breathe deeply—and wondering if I could use the fire extinguisher on the wall to break down the door. Then I thought, How would Arnold Schwarzenegger handle this? The next thing I knew, an employee of the firm, a former football player, was kicking down the door. I walked out as nonchalantly as I could, thanked the guy, and told him I was glad he had stayed in shape.

My dad always tried to stay fit, and golf was his favorite activity. A couple of years before his death, he told me that he had shot an 88 on his local course in Florida. That didn't sound so bad to me, and I wondered why he was unhappy about it. Turns out that he had lost a few bucks on the round and just missed shooting his age—he was 87 at the time. Dad started golfing when he was a kid, mostly on public courses, where he caddied during the Depression. He continued to enjoy golf nearly his whole life.

We try hard to get our people at AARP into fitness regimens they will enjoy, offering a gym, a physical-fitness boot camp, fitness-center discounts, and other inducements. More and more of our employees are getting involved, but not everyone. To get more people into thinking about physical fitness, I pulled an April Fool's joke by announcing that the elevators in our ten-story national office would be shut down for two weeks. Everyone would be forced to walk the stairs. Some people said okay, some laughed (the ones who figured out it was a joke), and some were outraged. But a while later, I received a gratifying e-mail from a woman who said:

> I haven't made exercise a priority since high school. I had a million excuses: student, career, mom, etc. I realized this summer that if I didn't build exercise into my day, it just wouldn't happen. I started riding my bike to the metro in September, when traffic delays made commuting by bus frustrating. I ride three or so times a week. Just 15 hilly minutes to and from, I've lost 15 pounds without modifying my eating habits. More important, I have a built-in release at the start and end of my day. I get to work without waiting for a bus and sitting in traffic. I always heard about how addictive working out, running, or cycling could be. Now I believe it. Thanks for encouraging staff

and giving us benefits that, if we choose, will change our lives . . . pass this along.

Staying healthy and independent is a lifelong job. And with more of us living longer, life itself has definitely become a marathon. If we want our lives to be not just longer but also better, we have to keep to a steady, endurance-building jog for most of the race, with the ability to sprint when circumstance demand. The reason is simple: What we do in the short term can have a tremendous effect on the quality of our lives in the long run.

It seems obvious, except perhaps to the young, that the behaviors and habits we develop as kids have a direct impact on our lives as we get older. For instance, Duane Alexander, director of the National Institute of Child Health and Human Development (part of the NIH), calls osteoporosis "a pediatric disease with geriatric consequences." But trouble may strike well before old age. The largest increase in chronic diseases, including obesity and diabetes, is among people in their thirties, and nearly all these problems are caused by behavior—eating too much and exercising too little.

The remedy for this epidemic is both simple and complicated. Americans of all ages should get enough regular exercise. If you've got a moving part, move it. Starting physical activity is much easier than keeping at it over time. Older people are the most sedentary of all, so AARP works to promote physical activity among the 50+ population. We want to take our campaign to a national level, but first we have to figure out how to persuade large numbers of men and women to stay with an exercise program over the long haul. Too many stop after eight or ten weeks.

In reality, we don't know just how unfit Americans actually are because no one measures it. The President's Council on Physical Fitness and Sports stopped surveying the fitness of U.S. schoolchildren back in the mid-1980s. We do know that the average American adult takes about 5,000 steps every day, which sounds like a lot until you learn that about twice that number is recommended. Tommy Thompson, the former secretary of the U.S. Department of Health and Human Services, is devoted to his pedometer. He uses it to make sure he gets in his 10,000 steps a day, no matter what. When Thompson came to address our AARP board of directors, he said to me as we met in the hotel lobby, "Let's take the stairs. I've got to get my steps."

The experts tell us that walking is the best all-round exercise for most people and that, at a minimum, we should walk at a pace of three miles an hour for ninety minutes a day, most days a week. How many of us do that or the equivalent? Somewhere between a quarter and half of Americans surveyed say they do—but many of them surely don't. In fact, according to a study by the Environmental Protection Agency, walking may even be on the decline.

One way to promote exercise is to build walking into daily life—in other words, to change our current American lifestyle. To meet this goal, a group of urban planners, fitness experts, and others have teamed up to promote the New Urbanism, a movement to replace the suburban model with compact, walkable communities that encourage not only exercise but also neighborliness, reduced auto traffic, and community involvement.

Health-care insurers, who have a major stake in keeping their members fit and healthy, are also taking a hand in promoting exercise. Minnesota's HealthPartners and Blue Cross and Blue Shield now offer their members discounts to local gyms. Elsewhere, Britain's Virgin Group, in partnership with Louisville, Kentucky–based Humana, is launching Virgin Life Care. Members who work out will receive points they can use to lower their premiums—or to get discounts on travel, sneakers, DVDs, and the like.

Some employers, who want to pay lower insurance premiums and have a healthier workforce, are designing workplaces that encourage employees to exercise. Sprint Nextel, the communications company, built its 200-acre headquarters campus in Overland Park, Kansas, with parking garages far from office buildings. The buildings themselves, which are as much as a half mile apart, have attractive, well-lighted staircases that people tend to use because the elevators are made to run slow. This is personal responsibility with a bit of a boost from the boss. The GlobalFit Network, consisting of more than 1,500 fitness clubs, offers members reduced fees up to 60 percent off regular monthly dues.

EMBRACE PREVENTION

He who cures a disease may be the skillfullest,
but he that prevents it is the safest physician.
—*Thomas Fuller*

The fourth step in healing the system requires that we move toward a prevention model of health care. As the boomers age, they will demand it, because they want to remain active and productive. It's an old idea, expressed most memorably by Ben Franklin when he said, "An ounce of prevention is worth a pound of cure." But it's an idea that has never made more sense than it does today.

We can't prevent all disease, of course, but we can do much more to keep people out of doctors' offices and hospitals. Medicare is doing its part by offering a free physical exam when a person turns 65 and joins the program. Medicare also now screens for diabetes and heart disease, a critical step in prevention and early detection.

To further advance the idea of prevention, we need to change, as mentioned earlier, the incentives built into the health-care system so that medical professionals are rewarded for good outcomes and healthy patients. As it is, the fee-for-service system gives us lots of choice, but it is an open invitation to schedule more office visits, more tests, and more surgery. The Health Maintenance Organizations (HMOs) have long stressed prevention, but with less success than hoped. Some analysts believe that most HMOs (and companies) don't take prevention seriously enough, because they know most patients and employees don't stay with them long enough for the necessary investment to show positive results on their bottom lines.

The performance-based-pay and evidence-based-care experiments mentioned earlier point the way to genuine reform, but they still would not reward true prevention. Another idea to shift the focus to prevention is to give health-care professionals salaries and bonuses based on how many of their patients remain healthy. It's a model, though, that has not won much acceptance in the United States, and it's hard to see how it could get through the American political process. Even if such a prevention model did clear the political hurdle, making it standard practice would be a radical change requiring a long, complex transition.

Nevertheless, Kaiser Permanente, the Oakland, California–based health provider and insurer, has taken a major step toward making the transition. Kaiser typically charges employers a fixed annual fee for every member enrolled, thus giving its doctors and other employees a strong financial incentive for keeping members healthy and preventing any condition that would require costly treatment.

As one measure of the incentive's possible effectiveness, Kaiser reports a death rate from heart disease among its members that is 30 percent below the rate in the general population of northern California. Members who do suffer heart attacks are enrolled, while still in the hospital, in a yearlong program to prevent another attack through healthy diet, exercise, blood pressure and cholesterol control, and help quitting smoking if needed.

UnitedHealth Group uses a different approach, directing targeted information and tips to members. It partners with the American Diabetes Association, the Kidney Foundation, and other national organizations to send people specific, confidential information about health promotion, disease prevention, and current treatments based on the recipients' health profiles.

To bring about a real revolution in health-care incentives, we might consider a system modeled on Japan's, where prevention takes precedence over treatment. Japan provides health care for all its citizens at a cost, measured as a percentage of the economy, that is about half what we spend in America. What is more, the Japanese have a lower infant mortality rate and a higher life expectancy than Americans.

Technology, too, has a role to play in prevention, just as with so many other elements of health-care reform. We must work toward the day when patients store their own medical information so that it is readily available to any authorized health-care professional. Personal medical data might be stored on a smart card carried in a purse or wallet or in one's body (yes, get used to it!) on an implantable chip that could be read by technicians in an emergency even if the patient were unconscious.

Doctors could also conduct consultations over the Internet ("mouse calls"), viewing patient records on a computer screen while the patient describes ailments, asks questions, and receives advice. Fees for this kind of service would be lower than for office visits and would provide an incentive for people to get medical advice before conditions develop into more serious diseases or ailments that require more extensive—and expensive—treatment.

Prevention is everyone's business, ours as well as the system's. Since the 50+ generation is one of the most health-conscious ever and is savvy about the use of technology, we can lead the change toward prevention. By asking for more preventive care and practicing what is preached we can go a long way toward reducing the incidence of costly treatments and hospital stays.

MAKE CHRONIC CARE CENTRAL

All interest in disease and death is
only another expression of interest in life.
—*Thomas Mann*

The fifth prescription for transforming our ailing health-care system is to greatly increase the focus on chronic-care management. As I've noted, chronic conditions such as heart disease, obesity, and diabetes are becoming more and more common, yet our caregivers and the system itself continue to concentrate on acute and episodic disease and treatment.

Cass Wheeler, chief executive at the American Heart Association (AHA), is trying to change that. AHA set a long-term goal in 1998 to reduce deaths from coronary artery disease and stroke—and the prevalence of key risk factors—by 25 percent by 2010. As of October 2005, deaths from heart disease were down 17 percent and deaths from stroke were 12 percent lower. Wheeler also reports significant progress in reducing the prevalence of a number of risk factors, including high blood pressure, high cholesterol, and smoking. When and if this goal is reached, it will mean 146,000 fewer deaths from heart disease and 46,000 fewer deaths from stroke.

Even cancer is becoming a chronic disease. John Seffrin, the head of the American Cancer Society and an effective crusader for cancer control, lists the society's goals over the coming decade as reducing cancer deaths by 50 percent and cutting incidence by 25 percent, while measurably improving cancer patients' quality of life. These goals won't be easy to achieve, Seffrin admits, but they point up a critical fact: More and more people are living with (and after) cancer; hence they require chronic-disease care.

Too often, people with chronic diseases get little or no care until a crisis lands them in costly emergency-room settings, hospitals, or nursing homes. In fact, chronic patients—sometimes known in hospitals as "frequent fliers"—soak up a huge share of the nation's medical spending. Chronic patients make up only 5 percent of Medicare beneficiaries, but they account for 43 percent of the program's outlays. Senator Kent Conrad of North Dakota had it right when he said, "We need to focus like a laser on that five percent."

Many chronic-disease patients have multiple problems. They may be bed-bound, unable to drive, and out of the loop of regular visits with a doctor who knows them; they show up in a medical facility only after their problems have become critical and require the costliest care. To change the health-care system for the better, we must stop that cycle.

Organizations such as Kaiser Permanente are showing the way. Kaiser spends $55 million on chronic-care programs in northern California alone and considers it money well spent. "What's really expensive is if we don't take care of these people and manage their chronic conditions," says Dr. Robert Mithun, chief of internal medicine at Kaiser's medical center in San Francisco.

UnitedHealth Group's EverCare Program is one of the more innovative models for effective chronic-care management. It is an evidence-based model that uses teams made up of doctors, nurses, nurse-practitioners, and other health-care professionals, as well as the patient and his or her family members. The goal is active management of those with chronic conditions, many of whom have three or more problems such as diabetes, heart disease, asthma, and high blood pressure. EverCare's nurse-practitioners identify the early signs of an acute episode and teach family members and caregivers those signs in order to enable them to prevent crises.

The result is fewer hospitalizations and much happier families and patients. Fewer hospitalizations also saves federal and state government dollars. In short, the program is producing better outcomes and better health for less money among a population that is costly to treat. Patients and their families have given EverCare a 97 percent satisfaction rating in each of the past three years. Listen to Marilyn Dachman's story to understand why.

Marilyn's daughter enrolled her in EverCare Select after she qualified for Arizona's Medicaid program. At 60, Marilyn had been in and out of the hospital for a ruptured spleen, a triple bypass, and repair of a hernia. She had also struggled with bouts of pneumonia. While Marilyn felt comfortable living independently, her doctors advised her family otherwise, saying Marilyn would need someone to care for her because, as she herself put it, she had "died three times and been brought back."

At that point, Marilyn became eligible for Arizona's Medicaid managed-care program and she moved into an assisted-living facility. Shortly afterward, Marilyn's daughter enrolled her in EverCare Select.

Jennifer Butler, a care manager in the program, assessed Marilyn's total care needs and arranged medical and in-home support. Jennifer made sure that hospital bills and prescription drug costs were not Marilyn's primary concern. Rather, Marilyn explained, "I could concentrate on getting well."

After her hospital stays, Marilyn had trouble showering alone and handling other grooming needs. So Jennifer arranged for caregivers to help Marilyn bathe and regain her confidence in her ability to groom herself.

Innovative health-care professionals are attacking the chronic-care problem from another front by challenging conventional wisdom and reaching into the medical bag for an old remedy: house calls. When was the last time you heard of a doctor making a house call? Out-of-date for half a century, house calls are making a comeback with the advent of new technology such as pocket computers and portable X-ray and cardiogram equipment. Costly though it may be to visit a patient at home, on average, it is actually cheaper than having chronically ill patients come to a doctor's office, and home visits are definitely cheaper than emergency rooms. "If we don't have a better chronic-care management system—with house calls—for the frail elderly who are the most expensive [to treat], we're going to bankrupt the Medicare program," says Constance Rowe, executive director of the American Academy of Home Care Physicians. "It's not only cheaper; it's what people want. They don't want to be hospitalized."

C. Gresham Bayne, a 50+ San Diego physician, pioneered the modern house call in 1987, starting a full-time home-care practice. He also began a campaign that persuaded Medicare a decade later to raise its fee for home visits, from $60 to what is now $100 per call (still far less than the average cost of a visit to a doctor's office). Bayne's Call Doctor Medical Group now makes about 800 house calls every month.

California-based Care Level Management contracts with insurance companies to provide home care for selected chronic patients in exchange for a portion of what the insurers save in hospital fees. That can be an attractive arrangement for both the doctors and the insurers. If a patient with heart problems develops pneumonia, for instance, an emergency-room visit can cost up to $6,900. A Care Level doctor can come to the patient's home, order an in-house course of intravenous antibiotics, and make a follow-up visit, all for just $750. Care Level's doctors have a 24-7 job, since they are on call any time a patient needs them, but they say it's a rewarding way to practice medicine.

A study found that one company saved $7 million in six months after signing up Care Level to visit just 318 patients. And Medicare has been impressed enough with that record to hire Care Level for a three-year demonstration project serving 15,000 patients in Arizona, California, and Texas. "If this works, we can structure other things . . . in other parts of the country," explains Jeff Flick, Medicare's Western Region administrator.

CUT DRUG COSTS

> . . . a focus on cost does not mean "don't spend"—
> it means "spend wisely."
> —*John J. Brennan*

The sixth essential step in redeeming our health-care system and improving the nation's health is to bring down the high costs of prescription drugs for all Americans. Today's sophisticated pharmaceuticals are increasingly replacing surgery as first-line treatment for serious illness. In addition, they keep people independent, working, and out of hospitals and nursing homes. But miracle drugs can't perform miracles if people can't afford them. I've made that point many times over in discussions with members of Congress, other policy makers, AARP members, and concerned citizens, not to mention leaders of the pharmaceutical companies themselves.

This is not about decimating the U.S. pharmaceutical industry, nor do we want it to take its research and development offshore. We need a strong American industry, one that will innovate and create new drugs to improve our lives. Parkinson's, Alzheimer's, diabetes, and other diseases not only destroy lives; they also cost billions of dollars that could be saved and directed to other needs if effective treatments can be found. In addition, we must give full support to our National Institutes of Health, the world's greatest health-research institution and the source of many of the medical breakthroughs that the drug companies go on to utilize in developing useful pharamaceuticals. As citizens with a stake in all this, we need to advocate for expanded budgets for the NIH.

That said, we have to face facts: Prescription drugs, especially brand-name varieties, simply cost too much in this country. Our prices are so high that, essentially, we are subsidizing lower costs in other countries.

There are ways to reduce consumer spending for prescription pharmaceuticals, and people 50+ are leading the charge:

• Invest in evidence-based drug research. Evidence-based research, as defined earlier, works particularly well in evaluating prescription drugs, because drugs within specific classes (statins to lower cholesterol, for instance) can be compared for both efficacy and cost. Results can help doctors (and patients) determine, among other things, whether a less expensive drug is just as effective as a more costly one or whether superior results justify using the more expensive product. Comparative-based-care results would likely spur competition as well, lowering prices for consumers. Physicians, of course, would have the last word on which drug to use. They could override the general research findings and directives if they decided a specific patient needed a specific drug.

• Expand the use of generic drugs. Generics are functionally equivalent to brand-name drugs, but they sell at markedly lower prices. In addition, annual price increases for generics have, on the whole, been far less than for comparable brand-name prescriptions. In 2005, the federal Government Accountability Office reported that retail prices for brand-name products jumped by 5.5 percent the previous year, while generic prices inched up only 1.8 percent. In the first eight months of 2005, the increases were 5.7 percent and 2 percent, respectively.

• Encourage innovative strategies like group purchasing among states. A number of states—including Michigan, Kentucky, Hawaii, and Maine—are already reducing drug prices by pooling their purchases. More states should follow suit. Pooling increases the size of orders to pharmaceutical suppliers, and larger orders mean more market power, greater negotiating clout, and, ultimately, lower prices.

• Educate people to use prescription drugs more wisely. Even though people 45 and over—but especially those 65 and older—take lots of prescription drugs, they often don't realize the full benefits because they aren't taking the drugs as directed. Moreover, many people avoid generics despite their comparable efficacy and lower cost. Consumers need to know how to purchase medications more cost-efficiently and how to use them wisely. When all consumers, but especially older people who take the most drugs, are adequately informed about and properly using the drugs they are prescribed, health-care costs will drop substantially, as will the number of adverse interactions and negative side effects that people experience.

• Import safe prescription medications from Canada and elsewhere. Brand-name drugs in Canada and many Western European countries generally cost 20 percent to 50 percent less than their American counterparts. U.S. law prohibits the importation of drugs from foreign countries, but hundreds of thousands, perhaps millions, of Americans defy that prohibition annually to fill prescriptions at more affordable prices.

It is a controversial idea, one that the pharmaceutical industry adamantly opposes. Neither the Clinton nor Bush administration would certify the safety of pharmaceuticals imported from Canada, Australia, England, or other countries where drugs are cheaper. Part of their reluctance was a concern about safety, and partly it was due to the clout of the drug industry. But the idea is gaining momentum in Congress, and if the leadership would allow a vote, importation would almost surely pass with bipartisan support. Lifting the ban and enforcing safety standards to prevent adulteration and counterfeiting would not only make drugs more affordable for Americans; it would also put pressure on U.S. pharmaceutical companies to compete by lowering their prices.

As discussed earlier, Congress took a major step toward making drugs more affordable and available in 2003, when it passed the Medicare Prescription Drug Improvement and Modernization Act (MMA), which contained a major new prescription-drug benefit called Medicare Part D. The drug benefit began January 1, 2006, and, at this writing, many beneficiaries, their adult children, and others assisting them are still uncertain about which, if any, plan to join. Criticized as being too complex and difficult to navigate, the new drug program drew this response from a woman I talked to in New York in late 2005. "I have a Harvard MBA," she said, "and I can't understand this thing, and neither can my mother."

Among the problems that arose as the new program unfolded were those involving the so-called dual eligibles, people eligible for both Medicaid and Medicare, who had been getting prescription drugs at very low cost. Several states stepped in to guarantee that these people, many of whom were falling between the cracks and unable to get needed medications at affordable prices, would continue to get their low-priced medications until the Medicare snags were ironed out.

The Harvard MBAs and their mothers, along with millions of other middle-income Medicare beneficiaries, appear to be making their way through the maze of more than forty different competing plans with different premiums, co-payments, and lists of covered drugs. At this point, more than 31 million out of 42 million have enrolled in a plan, which means that more than 37 million beneficiaries now have drug coverage from a reliable source. (See chapter 7 for more on the MMA.)

MAKE INSURANCE AVAILABLE TO ALL

Don't duck the most difficult problems.
That just insures that the hardest part
will be left when you're most tired.
Get the big one done—it's downhill
from then on.
—*Norman Vincent Peale*

There is one more, absolutely essential step needed to transform America's health care. None of the other reforms I've talked about can fix the system unless all of our citizens have access to insurance. Today one out of six Americans, more than 45 million people, lack any health insurance at all. Many of them are working people or they are children in families with at least one parent employed outside the home. Some of the uninsured are young and healthy and don't want, or can't afford, to pay the cost. Others are older individuals between 40 and 64, still too young for Medicare, which kicks in at 65, who are unemployed, don't have health insurance at work, or are uninsured for some other reason. They are in a difficult and precarious situation.

As health-care costs have continued to soar, more and more employers have decided that they cannot afford the premiums, so they've stopped offering medical insurance to their workers. Likewise, more and more employees who do have insurance available to them can't afford the premiums and co-pays, so they don't take it. As a result, the number of uninsured has been growing by roughly 1 million a year.

The expanding number of uninsured increases the health-care burden for all of us. Why? Because people without health coverage tend to avoid doctors until an ailment becomes serious or life-threatening and then they go to the emergency room—the most expensive and least efficient way to deliver medical care. This is also beginning to cause overcrowding in many emergency rooms, hampering the ability of emergency-room personnel to deliver quality care.

One of the system's great ironies is that only the uninsured, those least able to pay, are charged the full sticker price for medical care.

For insurers, including the government, the doctors' and hospitals' posted fees are merely the starting line for negotiating discounts that increase in proportion to the payer's bargaining power. For instance, a Medicare patient who is billed $955 for an echocardiogram eventually finds that the bill has been settled for less than 60 percent of the stated price, with Medicare paying $438.94 and her secondary Medigap insurer kicking in another $109.74. But an uninsured patient will be charged, and perhaps hounded for, the full amount. This policy is counterproductive and often futile, since a great many uninsured people don't or can't pay their bills. In the end, health-care providers scramble to make up for the uncompensated care by raising prices for employers and everyone else.

Some 17.5 million Americans have bought health-insurance policies on their own, without the benefit of employers or labor unions or other middlemen bargainers, and they pay a high price. A few of these policies turn out to be outright fakes from people peddling worthless paper or counterfeit Medicare drug cards. Others are legitimate policies, but with obscure clauses that cap benefits or narrowly define eligibility in order to deny service when it's needed. The U.S. Department of Labor has opened more than 700 investigations of health-insurance frauds, finding violations of $139.5 million, and state regulatory loopholes leave room for even more creative scams. A Texas law, for instance, bans insurance fraud, but peddlers of fake discount cards can't be prosecuted under it because they aren't selling insurance.

The problem of the uninsured has been studied, debated, and argued about for years. Many advocates favor a single-payer, tax-based system like Medicare, meaning national health insurance for everyone. But national health insurance has been a political nonstarter. The Clinton administration tried and failed to work out a comprehensive plan in the early 1990s that would have been paid for using an employer mandate approach. Another possible solution is to require individuals to purchase insurance, which hasn't caught on, either.

This standoff simply can't go on. We absolutely must repair our broken health-care system—and not by simply shifting costs from one sector of the economy to another. When industries, for instance, have to pick up more of the cost, they are handicapped in competition against foreign companies whose governments cover the cost of health care. In the end, U.S. companies routinely pass much of their health-care costs on to employees and consumers, resulting in higher prices for goods and services. The impact of this malfunctioning system, both on the economy and on individual citizens, is much too damaging to be endured.

The path toward a solution lies in transforming the health-care system by following the seven steps I've discussed in this chapter. Each is very difficult, but none is impossible. Together they will improve the quality of care for all Americans and give us much better value for our money. They will help make Medicare and Medicaid sustainable over the long run. They will make it easier for us to age in good health, without fear that illness will wipe out our savings or endanger our children's financial well-being.

The obvious question, and one I hear repeatedly, is this: If we know what needs to be done, why don't we do it? After all, isn't this a country that gets things done? Why don't we take all necessary steps to transform the health-care system? We should and we can, but there are some major roadblocks along the way, including:

1. The enormity and complexity of the problem. Transforming the health-care system isn't like putting a man on the moon; it's like putting a whole city on the moon. It's a daunting task, partly because of the size and complexity of the system and partly because of the challenge involved in getting people to take personal responsibility for changing their own behaviors and health outcomes.

2. The large number of organizations, professions, and special interests that have a stake in the system. Many of the stakeholders are effective and powerful lobbies in their own right, and they surround themselves with even more lobbyists and the equally powerful voices of advertising agencies, law firms, and public relations experts.

3. The divisiveness wrought by fierce, intense partisanship among our national leaders and the rank and file in Congress. This partisanship has soured our national discourse and threatens the ability of our political system to function and to find solutions to the serious problems we face. It's easier to criticize and block complex legislation than it is to construct a workable plan and achieve consensus to get it passed. When it comes to politics, defense often trumps offense. In short, the divisions in our political system have reached an unacceptable and corrosive extreme.

4. Finally, as a nation, we seem to have a collective unwillingness to shoulder the shared responsibility necessary to address the problem. As long as it's perceived as affecting others and not ourselves, it will be difficult to ask for shared sacrifice to solve it.

What will it take to overcome these barriers and achieve the goal of a better, safer, more affordable health-care system? My discussions with members of Congress, the Bush administration, other policy makers, and senior business executives have convinced me that most of these leaders see the problems clearly. They aren't blind to the current system's economic and social costs. But they also recognize the enormity of the obstacles, and many don't like the odds in favor of reform. They have been down this road before (think of the Clinton administration's ill-fated attempt at health-care reform and the huge difficulties of getting drug coverage into Medicare). These realists survey the landscape and understand full well how hard it will be to overcome powerful special interests and intense partisanship. And some members of Congress think there is insufficient interest among their constituents for transformational health-care reform; they may be right.

So what can the 50+ generation do to overcome the inertia? I'll tell you what we can do . . . three things, at least:

1. Build public demand. It will be a tough sell because many people, especially the relatively well-off, are still getting their health-care bills paid. They may be feeling mounting frustration, but they don't yet perceive a crisis. Nevertheless, with enough education and an honest recounting of the facts, I believe we can start a groundswell.

2. Create more pressure from corporations. Business leaders certainly understand—as does the public—that it's in everyone's best interest to support a healthy, competitive corporate America. But many of these executives seem wary of reform because they don't trust government and they fear that botched reform might make things worse than they already are. Politics and special interests also play a part, and tax policy may well take precedence in the business community over health-care policy. Can we get corporations large and small to pound harder on our political leadership for health-care reform? Right now, it's uncertain. Business leaders may decide that their best interests lie in major changes, or they may opt to continue shifting costs, or they may simply choose to eliminate their health costs entirely by ending coverage. Of course, in the long run, businesses and everyone else pay when coverage is dropped, but that concept may seem too remote for people to get their arms around at this juncture.

3. Keep pressing politicians and policy makers. We need to tell them over and over that health-care costs are at the root of many of the problems and challenges we face, from mounting deficits to the competitive pressures American business faces in the global marketplace. Recently President Bush has elevated health care on the list of national priorities. But in Congress progress remains uncertain. Comprehensive system-wide change is probably beyond our elected leaders at this time. So perhaps we need a step-by-step approach that will yield more immediate benefits and eventually lead to transformation.

First we have to make more progress on agreeing what the problems are. When I was talking with the chairman of a key House committee about health-care reform, his chief of staff said that the real concern was Medicare and Medicaid, which he believed are the reasons for our soaring health-care costs. I disagreed, saying that Medicare and Medicaid costs actually reflect the high costs of health care generally—from pediatrics to geriatrics. The problems are systemic.

It's often been said that it takes a crisis to get problems fixed, and we may be headed in that direction. Some of the major problems we face could actually improve the chances for health-care reform. Take the budget deficit; enormous revenue and spending changes are needed to get the deficit under control. What better place to find savings than in the waste, fraud, and inefficiencies of the health-care system? Or how about the rapidly growing costs and problems of long-term care, brought about by a fragmented system? Finally, the health-care system itself could be headed for a meltdown, which would demand the immediate attention and action of those government and business leaders now straddling the fence.

While Washington thinks it over, many states are taking leadership roles in transforming health care. Maine's reform policy, known as Dirago, has been in effect for two and a half years. In its first phase, Dirago is providing health coverage to all the state's uninsured; its longer-term goal is universal coverage. Maine's reform legislation has become a model for other states.

Hawaii's prescription drug program offers broad coverage to residents with both low- and middle-range incomes. The Minnesota Medical Association approved a bold new approach, partly financed by tobacco taxes, that would require all insurers to offer the same benefits and compete on the basis of cost and quality, as well as concentrating on chronic-care management rather than treatment of episodic problems. They are now forming a steering committee to get their "Physicians' Plan for a Healthy Minnesota" implemented.

At least a half-dozen states, including Illinois and Wisconsin, are challenging the federal government's prohibition on importing drugs from Canada. Vermont has been on the front line of health-care-reform policy debates. Its legislature passed a universal coverage bill that directs payments to providers based on outcomes and quality. The governor vetoed it. Nonetheless, the veto is likely to be the beginning, rather than the conclusion, to a spirited, ongoing discussion of reform proposals. Oregon pioneered efforts in evidence-based reform, and its program is a model for other states. Likewise, Rhode Island has been a leader in providing universal coverage for kids. And several states, including Michigan, Kentucky, Hawaii, and Maine, have formed an interstate pool to enhance their market power in purchasing prescription drugs for state programs. And now Massachusetts is moving toward a plan of virtually complete health-care coverage. A mainstay of the plan is to require people to purchase health insurance, just as they must have car insurance.

State initiatives can also teach us what doesn't work. A few years ago, for example, when New Hampshire tried to contain costs by capping the number of prescriptions written for Medicaid beneficiaries, the Agency for Healthcare Research and Quality reported that hospitalizations increased 35 percent, resulting in utilization costs seventeen times greater than the savings in drug expenditures. New Hampshire abolished its prescription cap, and according to AHRQ, nine other states followed suit.

One controversial test case revolves around a Maryland law requiring companies with more than 10,000 employees to spend the equivalent of 8 percent of their payrolls on health care. The law is essentially aimed at Wal-Mart, a number of whose workers are receiving their health benefits through Medicaid, which means that the government picks up the tab for insuring Wal-Mart's employees. The law is being challenged, but in the meantime unions and others are lobbying for other states to follow Maryland's lead.

Dr. Henry Simmons, a 50+er, leads the National Coalition on Health Care, a large group of companies, insurance plans, pension programs, not-for-profits, and other organizations, including AARP. He believes that while incremental steps have merit, in the end we still have to confront the need for comprehensive reform that leads to universal and affordable coverage. The "perfect storm"—as he describes the interwoven crises in health-care costs, access, and quality—demands a total remake of the entire system.

The conundrum is that in spite of the necessity of transformational change, political realities may permit only the type of smaller steps the states have been trying. With the federal government facing large deficits and Congress in a budget-cutting mood, the larger vision and structural changes will be tough to achieve.

Each of us in our own way, from adopting healthy personal and family behaviors, to protecting ourselves from medical errors, to speaking out, can be a catalyst for change, for moving health-care reform forward. The pressure is growing. We need to focus it, intensify it, and encourage, even demand, bipartisan support for it. It will take all of us—government at all levels, corporate America, the nonprofit sector, community groups, and individual citizens—to wrestle this octopus into submission. We absolutely must get on with it.

three

The Opportunity to Reinvent Retirement

Only through time time is conquered.
—*T. S. Eliot*

Increased longevity is one of the greatest accomplishments of our time. A child born today can expect to live thirty years longer than a child born a century ago. And if the trend continues, my four grandchildren, the oldest of whom is 6, will, in all probability, live to see the turn of the next century.

For better or worse, the increased longevity will hugely affect the period of life we call retirement. It's no wonder the boomers are pondering the twenty, thirty, or forty more years they have left and asking: What do I want to do with the rest of my life? How will I make it significant? And not least: How will I pay for it?

Retirement is of fairly recent origin. Well into the twentieth century, most people never retired in the sense of that word today. Relatively recent health and economic changes, coupled with programs such as Social Security and Medicare, have made it possible to stop working while we still have some life left to live. The majority of Americans today are far removed from the kind of manual labor that has defined life through most of human history—and still does for at least a third of our neighbors in other countries.

In times past, retirement existed only for that very small number of people who survived life's demands and also had enough wealth—in either money or children—to keep body and soul together without continuing working. Most people dropped dead on the job. Those who survived but were unable to work were lucky if their families could support them.

Then, some eighty years ago, Henry Ford and other industrial employers instituted pension plans, which helped to fill the gap. But the creation of Social Security in 1935 was the watershed. Initially, the benefits were modest—and, by most standards, still are—but Social Security marked a turning point because it embodied the modern ideas of greater longevity, retirement from gainful employment, and income even when work stopped. Social Security changed the American mind-set. We came to accept and rely on the notion that you could expect to live decently after you stopped working.

The concept of leisure came to be associated with retirement after World War II, as communities with names like Sun City and Leisure World sprang up to attract the first sizable wave of fairly prosperous retirees. Leisure is still used to sell "the golden age"—and there's nothing wrong with that. But for more and more people, endless play does not satisfactorily conquer time or make good use of their longevity bonus. And for those who do retire to leisure, it's often later in life than it used to be. Most of us are neither burnt out nor worn-out.

To the contrary, we have a third or more of our adult lives ahead of us—about the same number of years many people spend working—and most of it can be lived in good physical and mental health. So, the longevity bonus may go into another career. It can be spent giving back to society through volunteerism. It may be time used to enjoy and build bonds with grandkids or to learn new things and pursue old hobbies. And, for many people, it's also the time to care for older relatives.

What most people today don't want is to be shoved off to the sidelines of society. Whether they change careers, start a new business, learn a new discipline, or phase into part-time work before packing it in altogether, the 50+ generation wants to be part of the action.

DISCOVERING THE OPPORTUNITIES OF RETIREMENT

> For age is opportunity no less
> Than youth itself, though in another dress,
> And as the evening twilight fades away,
> The sky is filled with stars, invisible by day.
> —*Henry Wadsworth Longfellow*

When I retired from Porter Novelli in 1990 at the age of 49, I had no intention of beginning a life of leisure. I wanted to pursue my goal of making a difference by beginning a new career in public service. For many of us, finding purpose in life is an adventure. We may think we want some version of a peaceful garden idyll only to learn that helping others to realize their dreams is our real calling.

Life in a garden never crossed the mind of Michael Holmes, the former head of human resources at Edward Jones, a Saint Louis–based investment firm. Michael, says his wife, Gail, is a 110-miles-an-hour kind of guy.

Michael left his lucrative corporate job for "retirement" at 46, an age at which many people are reaching their peak earnings. In Michael's case, time for reflection after open-heart surgery in 2004 made him realize he "had all the money" he needed, Michael told author Lee Eisenberg. "I wanted a more meaningful way to make a contribution." Helping nonprofits work smarter was his answer.

In some ways, Michael's second act was a natural. He'd long been in training—as a board member of the Sickle Cell Disease Association of America and the United Way, among other nonprofits—and had been thinking about his next move for more than fifteen years. Michael concluded that successful retirement required serious reflection about what really mattered to him, followed by a test-drive of the new life before leaving the old one. Michael loved his new role as a nonprofit business consultant, working with organizations such as the National Institute for Youth Entrepreneurship and a local Saint Louis chapter of 100 Black Men of America, but he also found that he missed the corporate life. So, earlier this year, he went back into the corporate suite at Express Scripts as chief human resources officer and senior vice president. Michael's odyssey demonstrates that the road to retirement is not a straight path but can be filled with twists and turns, which is what makes the journey exciting. And while he has gone back to full-time employment, Michael still finds time to indulge his passion of helping nonprofits to succeed.

My boyhood friend Mike Ferris has his own version of retirement. After a career in engineering at Westinghouse, he moved to Ocean Isle Beach, North Carolina, with his wife, Pat, partly to be near their daughter and her family and partly because of the longer golf seasons. Soon Mike got involved in the AARP Tax-Aide program, a free program that recruits and trains volunteers to help taxpayers, especially older ones, do their tax returns. He now manages two AARP Tax-Aide sites in Brunswick County and four other Tax-Aide volunteers. He likes helping people and working with other volunteers, and it still leaves him plenty of time for family and golf.

Finding purpose in life is an ongoing activity for retired veterinarian Bob Perry and his wife, Ione. At 70, Ione embarked on her third career, selling real estate. Meanwhile Bob, who had sold a successful animal hospital and retired in 1999, was playing a lot of tennis when he got the call to help stamp out a foot-and-mouth epidemic in the United Kingdom. So he jetted off to Britain to work seven days a week with vets from around the world to keep the deadly disease from destroying the U.K. cattle industry. Bob came home to Omaha only to be called on again, this time to fight a poultry disease in California.

Ione, whose first career as a high-school home economics teacher ended nearly twenty-five years ago, had wasted little time in moving into a second line of work: She began a fashion accessories business. So successful that her belts and scarves made it into New York department stores, Ione nevertheless decided to give traditional retirement a try and turned the business over to Goodwill Industries. But that didn't last long. Soon she jumped into the real estate game.

Ione insists that she's not in business for the money, although she does quite well. No, it's all about the people she helps to find the perfect home. They're "practically family," says Ione.

Michael Holmes, Mike Ferris, and the Perrys believe that having happy, successful lives as we get older depends on remaining engaged with the world around us, taking part in healthy, spirit-enhancing activity, and finding a purpose that satisfies our inner drive. Author and entrepreneur Bob Buford would not disagree; he describes the transition from our first careers as a journey from success to significance. Most people approaching the age of 45 or 50, he explains, want to move from a time when they had to prove themselves (what he calls Life I) to a time when they can begin to give back and make a difference (Life II). The problem is, many don't know how because they have no role models. The opportunity didn't exist for most of our parents and grandparents.

In his most recent book, *Finishing Well: What People Who REALLY Live Do Differently!*, Buford tells the stories of sixty "second-season trailblazers" who have pioneered the art of finishing well in these modern times, focusing specifically on what they are doing to find meaning.

Buford might have used his own career as an example of finishing well. After selling his network of cable-television systems, he began investing in the lives of others. He started a foundation to identify and provide resources for people and organizations with ideas that have the potential to return a hundred times the initial investment. He also launched the Leadership Network to support senior ministers and their staffs in large churches and is the founding chairman of the Peter F. Drucker Foundation for Nonprofit Management.

I first met Bob at a conference called an ideas festival, and ideas are his passion. Attaining significance, Buford writes, is not some kind of separate career for which people need academic preparation. Maturity and experience are what's essential. Just the qualities that boomers and their older brethren have in quantity.

RETIREES AS VOLUNTEERS

Volunteerism is what makes the world go round.
—*James Trammell III*

Volunteering is a kind of civic windfall in which vibrant men and women, retired and not, can apply their experience and talents to help revitalize America. Volunteering is not new to our country. We are already champion volunteers: 83.9 million adults—56 percent of all adults (and 65 percent of AARP members)—give of our time. This represents the equivalent of over 9 million full-time employees at a value of $239 billion.

What is new is the depth of the need. The call to help our fellow citizens in one way or another is greater than ever before. At the same time, we have a growing and underutilized population of people with the time and the capacity to serve. Energetic members of the 50+ generation offer an ideal source of dedicated volunteers. The convergence of these two facts offers us the chance to make a profound difference in American life.

Mike Mulligan, of Annapolis, Maryland, is one of those leading the charge. Mulligan did so well running MapQuest that he could afford to retire at 50 and indulge his passion for flying his Socata TBM 700 turboprop and Bell Jet Ranger helicopter. But his life changed when he discovered that he had prostate cancer. "That made me wake up and think about what I was doing with the rest of my life," says Mulligan.

A year and a successful surgery later, he decided to join Angel Flight as one of thousands of volunteer pilots who are on call 24-7 to fly patients and family members at no charge to distant medical facilities for life-sustaining treatments, organ transplants, and the like. Mulligan, who jokes that Angel Flight gives him "a socially acceptable excuse to fly all the time," has turned a passion for flying into service to others— and, in the process, has made his own life more fulfilling.

Then there's Rita Ungaro-Schiavone. She has found her niche not only by volunteering herself but also by recruiting others to the cause. Thirty years ago, Schiavone, now 70, founded Aid for Friends after resettling a disabled woman who had no heat, plumbing, or anyone else to help her. Today, on an annual budget of about $1 million, the organization's army of 16,500 volunteers delivers home-cooked meals during weekly visits to its homebound "friends," as clients are known. Schiavone has thousands of friends in and around Philadelphia.

The volunteers stay for at least an hour to provide "the hidden hungry," as Schiavone calls them, with friendship and such necessities as eyeglasses, smoke alarms, and walkers or canes. "One hour a week equals one life changed," she says. "It means all the difference in the world."

A new trend, and one that is increasingly popular among retirees, combines volunteer activities with vacations. An industry called voluntourism has sprung up to help tourists from all walks of life arrange volunteer vacations.

Lucille Sewell, a 68-year-old retired nurse from Mustang, Oklahoma, received a call from the director of the Baptist Medical Disaster Relief Team following the March 2005 earthquake in Indonesia. "He asked if I would be willing to go to Indonesia," Sewell said. "I just said yes." Ten days later, she was on her way to Simeulue Island. Sewell and her medical team spent a week there treating the injured.

When she returned from Indonesia, Lucille Sewell discovered she had a new perspective on life. "Before, I'd been mourning the loss of Leon, my husband [he died in 2002]. Now, I felt grateful for my family and friends. I felt ashamed of the little things I'd complained about. I was happy to have a house and a lawn to mow."

She was just beginning to settle down from her experience when the relief agency called again. "They needed an R.N.," she said. So she flew back to Indonesia, this time to Banda Aceh, one of the places hardest hit by the December 2004 tsunami.

By the time Hurricane Katrina hit the Gulf Coast in August 2005, Lucille Sewell was a veteran volunteer. This time, she didn't hesitate when the call came. Two days after the disaster struck, she was on a Greyhound bus headed for Louisiana.

Once volunteers act on their desire to help others, it often gets into their blood. Maybe they can't save the world, but they quickly learn that they can make a difference.

Michelle Nunn is out to make a *big* difference. She is the cofounder and CEO of Hands On Network, which encourages and supports thousands of volunteers from companies that are network members. Nunn's ambitious goal is to deliver 500,000 hours of service during what's called the Corporate Week of Service, double the network's active volunteers to 600,000 in just two years, and increase the number of Americans participating in volunteer service to 71 million from 64.5 million by the end of 2006.

THE JOYS OF GRANDPARENTING

> Grandparenting is about loving those grandchildren,
> teaching them, enjoying them, and supporting them.
> This is what grandparents do.
>
> —Dr. Arthur Kornhaber

Grandparenting provides significance in later life for millions of Americans. Their satisfaction comes from the knowledge that they are assuming important roles in the lives of both their children and grandchildren.

Grandparents today are generally healthier, busier, and more likely to still be working when the first grandchild arrives than grandparents of only a generation ago. In fact, the joy many people experience upon learning they are about to become grandparents is tempered by the feeling that they don't fit the traditional image portrayed in picture books and fairy tales. Nevertheless, grandparents generally agree that having grandchildren was "the best thing that ever happened" to them and made them feel "blessed," "satisfied," and "complete."

Grandparents are often the glue that holds a family together, the guardians of tradition. They help grandchildren understand that they are part of something greater than themselves. "My mother had three brothers," says Deidre, age 17, "and they used to do break dancing. My grandmother tells me about them and what they used to do. It's fun to hear about that." By telling stories about their children and their own early years, by sharing news about aunts, uncles, and cousins, and by providing a place to gather—usually their own homes—grandparents help preserve a family's heritage and keep its traditions alive.

Grandparents also have a lot to teach their grandchildren—in fact, just about anything and everything one can absorb from a lifetime of work and activities. A grandmother who came here from abroad tells me she enjoys sharing her native language and customs with her grandchildren. Grandchildren can also be enthusiastic students of history, gardening, cooking, sewing, hairstyling, fishing, ball playing, woodworking, or even whittling.

There's not much kids can't learn from grandparents, including strong moral values. Grandchildren will be the first to agree. They say their grandparents have taught them good manners, respect for others, and a strong work ethic. Grandparents also teach prayers to their grandchildren and take them to religious services.

Not all grandparents can tutor an algebra student or help a teenager prepare for a college entrance exam. But most are perfectly qualified to prepare a child for a lifetime of learning by introducing him or her to the joys of reading. Three-quarters of the grandparents we surveyed at AARP told us they read to their grandchildren. And older grandchildren told us that they also enjoy reading to their grandparents.

The teaching and learning goes both ways. Dave, a 61-year-old grandparent, says that "keeping up with my grandson, Robert, keeps me up to speed. Robert is only three, but he's already telling me that 'I need to check my e-mail.' I've figured out how to send him special e-mail messages. I've also started reading about kids his age so that I can get some new ideas about what might capture his attention."

One way grandparents and their grandkids share learning experiences and have fun together is through travel. Elderhostel, for example, has a wide range of travel experiences designed especially for grandparents and their grandchildren, ranging from sailing the coastal waters of Southern California—with participants helping to sail the ship and standing watch day and night—to discovering about space and space flight in a behind-the-scenes visit to NASA's space flight center in Houston, to a special class on circus skills at the Florida State University Flying High Circus.

Very few people inhabit picture-perfect families like those featured on television in the 1950s. For many grandchildren, their grandparents are also their primary caregivers. Well over 4.5 million children, or 6.3 percent of all those under age 18, live in grandparent-headed homes— and the number is going up. Many of these grandparents are responsible for the grandchildren's basic needs. Grandparents are also the largest providers of child care for preschoolers whose mothers are working; they care for 21 percent of such children.

Two such caregivers are Ila Schneibel, 58, and her husband, Sigmund, 57, of Stacy, Minnesota. The Schneibels have been caring for their 6-year-old granddaughter since her mother, the Schneibels' daughter, developed drug problems. The state granted the Schneibels legal custody last year.

"At first, we were totally overwhelmed," says Ila Schneibel. "It was a shock to the system." The couple pushed back the retirement they had planned to begin this year. "We can provide for [our granddaughter] financially better than her mom could," Ila says. "She is really thriving and has adjusted so well."

Opal Bufford, a retired South Bend, Indiana, nurse, thought she was through with child rearing at age 48. But when her daughter, Teana, a single parent, began "running around with a crowd we didn't approve of," Bufford and her husband stepped in and adopted their daughter's two young children, Megahn and Micah.

Then Bufford's husband died; finding little financial or social help, Opal Bufford and others in the same boat "started getting together just for the support." Bufford, now 60, says that "when you're raising grandkids, you tend to lose other friends. You don't go to the canasta club anymore." Soon the support group took up the battle for grandparents' rights, and in 2003 Bufford founded G.A.P. Limited, "Grandparents As Parents," to advocate for improved state child custody laws and to set up community-service programs for teens. Her goal is to have a G.A.P. chapter in every Indiana county.

Bufford also finds time to volunteer for causes ranging from Catholic Charities, to Kidsave International, to AARP. "No one would want to take on my schedule," she laughs. Yet she's proud that she is able to take care of her own grandchildren and still help other grandparents who, for whatever reason, have taken on the parenting role again.

ONCE A STUDENT, ALWAYS A STUDENT

> And gladly would he learn, and gladly teach.
> —*Geoffrey Chaucer*

Chaucer's description of the Clerk of Oxford, the one teacher in the motley assortment of pilgrims who make their way in his masterpiece, *Canterbury Tales,* could be applied to millions of people at or near retirement age. Today's 50+ Americans embrace lifelong learning as no other generation ever has. They are going back to school in record numbers, retiring near colleges and universities to take advantage of the course offerings and cultural activities, and turning educational travel into a booming business.

Take John Kossnar, a 55-year-old Chicagoan who recently retired from his job as a manager at the phone company. He and his wife,

Deb, who is also retired, have two children, Elizabeth, a senior in high school, and Nathan, an eighth-grader. Kossnar began contemplating and preparing for what he might do next even before he retired. He enrolled in the Great Books Program and then in a master's program at the University of Chicago, thinking he might teach part-time at a local college or community college after he left his job.

Now Kossnar does teach part-time, but not in the way he imagined: He is a substitute teacher in the local high-school district and enjoys it immensely. He also decided to learn the guitar at the age of 45, enrolling in Chicago's famed Old Town School of Folk Music. Since his son, Nathan, later started taking lessons, they have enjoyed playing together, though John freely admits that Nathan is the better guitarist. And when he is not substitute teaching or practicing his guitar, Kossnar may be found coaching Nathan's volleyball team or a team in the local "Senior League," which has players ranging in age from 55 to 79.

Just for the fun of it, Kossnar is also back at the University of Chicago, this time enrolled in alumni courses of the Great Books Program. "Last year," he says, "we read the complete Greek tragedies, and this year we're reading the complete *Norton Anthology of English Poetry*. I read some of these books in college, but reading them again now is like discovering them for the first time. I have a whole new perspective. Others I just never got around to reading." What makes the program really fun, though, says Kossnar, is the instructors and the other students. "There are people in there from eighteen to eighty-five. Some of our discussions get really interesting, and they're always thought-provoking.

"Maybe someday," Kossnar says, he will teach part-time at a local college. "But right now, I'm having too much fun. Deb and I are fortunate to be able to spend this time with our kids, and we just want to enjoy it."

John Kossnar and millions like him are defying the age-old notion that education is for the young, work is for adults, and leisure is for old people. Nothing could be further from the truth. The formal schooling we receive as youngsters is important, but it's only a small part of what is lifelong learning. It's no coincidence that graduation exercises are called commencements. And boomers, in particular, seem to be grabbing on to that word with gusto.

But boomers aren't the only ones who want to keep on learning as they age. At University Living, an assisted living residence in Ann Arbor, Michigan, Richard C. Adelman, the former head of the Institute of Gerontology at the University of Michigan, teaches a weekly class and holds discussion groups in which older people avidly comb through current events. "We bring our newspaper clippings and go at it," says Adelman.

Current events is one of two classes offered each year at University Living, a four-year-old facility that enables aging residents to continue to learn along with college students. The yearlong classes have included subjects ranging from the ethnic history of the United States to the novels of John Updike. Each year, university students are paired with residents for research projects, and they all take classes together.

"The main attraction for me was the fitness program and the classes and discussion groups," says 92-year-old Irene Skurski, a former legal secretary and Realtor. She helped organize Students and Seniors, a group that arranges faculty lectures on everything from Medicare to the music of Louis Armstrong. She has worked with several students in her three years at University Living, including one who made an oral history of Skurski's life. "We get to know them, go to lunch with them, enjoy knowing them," she says. "It's good for both of us."

Our remarkable innate ability to learn, make connections, and draw conclusions is one of the things that makes us human beings. Learning opens up possibilities and opportunities. We make discoveries, devise inventions, and master the use of them. When we learn, we take one kernel of information or knowledge and pile it on top of another, and another, and another until, eventually, we have taken a wheel and turned it into an automobile.

As they age, more and more Americans are pushing back their personal frontiers of knowledge by embracing the notion of active lifelong learning. This is not about brilliant new discoveries, such as solving Fermat's last theorem (someone finally did that about ten years ago), or writing *Moby-Dick* (there's only one Herman Melville). But what we learn enables us to develop opinions, shape ideas, express ourselves, earn our livings, be good citizens and neighbors, and generally live better lives. What we learn makes us fully human, with all the strengths and defects that entails. And being fully human and fully engaged is one rock-solid aspect of the 50+ generation's approach to retirement.

During World War II, Winston Churchill gave a speech at Harvard in which he declared, "The empires of the future are the empires of the mind." It's a wonderful phrase and an intriguing idea, the kind one might expect from one of the towering figures of the twentieth century. Yet forty or fifty years before this speech, few people would have expected it from Churchill. He had attended one of England's great public schools, Harrow, and then gone on to Sandhurst, England's version of West Point. He followed a mediocre academic career with an uninspiring military one. Yet Churchill came to be one of the finest writers in the English language, an effective government official, a statesman of incomparable ability, a pretty fair painter, and a first-class bricklayer. Winston Churchill never stopped learning.

OUR ROLE AS CAREGIVERS

> There are four kinds of people in the world: those who have been caregivers; those who currently are caregivers; those who will be caregivers; and those who will need caregivers.
>
> —*Rosalynn Carter*

At some point in our lives, nearly all of us will face caregiving responsibilities or will need care from a family member and/or friend. Today more and more members of the 50+ generation, especially those between the ages of 45 and 55, are facing the dual responsibilities of rearing children and caring for parents—and sometimes grandchildren and grandparents, too—and they feel squeezed.

Older people who need long-term care or ongoing assistance with daily activities prefer to remain in their homes, receiving the help they need from family and friends. Yet they do not want to feel as if they are becoming a burden if more intensive care is needed.

Their needs, preferences, and financial situations have given rise to an informal, unpaid caregiver force that numbers over 33 million and provides at least 75 percent of such care in the United States today. Caregivers help with the basic activities of daily living, such as bathing, dressing, and eating, and/or with peripheral needs for transportation, managing finances, and the like.

The typical caregiver is a 46-year-old woman who spends more than twenty hours a week caring for her mother; she has some college education, holds down a job, and has a median household income of $38,125. Most caregivers also contribute financially to the person they assist, spending an average of $200 a month. Almost 60 percent of caregivers try to balance work with their caregiver responsibilities, but over 60 percent have to make adjustments to their work life. Nearly four in ten men are caregivers as well, but women provide more hours and higher levels of care.

When caregivers list their own unmet needs, they most frequently cite: finding time for themselves; managing emotional and physical stress; balancing their work and family responsibilities. And when they get help, it usually comes from other family members or friends; the services of a paid helper are seldom used.

The needs of those faced with an elder-care crisis for the first time tend to differ from the needs of those regularly engaged in caregiving. Trying to find out what kind of help a person needs, what type of help is available, how to access it, and how to pay for it adds even more stress to the already traumatic crisis. And for the millions of people who are just beginning to worry about the ability of aging parents to remain independent these problems can be especially difficult to manage, particularly if they live far apart from one another. These potential caregivers know that the assistance they will be required to give will increase with the deteriorating conditions of older family members.

Given the difficulties of those receiving care and the needs of the caregivers, what we are left with is a complex, yet inadequate, system that is constantly in flux. The impact of coming demographic changes, coupled with the enormous demands we are already coping with, requires that we construct and maintain a much better long-term-care system that serves those in need and relieves the strain on caregiving families.

Not surprisingly, stress levels appear to be rising—and they will continue to do so until a better way is found. Greater longevity, the increased number of women in the labor force, and greater geographic dispersion of family members are putting severe strain on those who care for aging parents, spouses, siblings with developmental disabilities, other relatives, and friends. Adequate support systems to relieve the stress on caregivers are few and far between.

Karen Cain knows the problems firsthand. When her 82-year-old father was diagnosed with advanced lung cancer, she and her four siblings agreed to help manage his care. But they soon discovered that coordinating care for their father was more than they could handle, and they needed to act quickly to keep their dad alive as long and as comfortably as possible.

"Unfortunately, the health system is disjointed and uncoordinated," Cain says, "and you're thrust into it when you're irrational and emotional." She faced the difficulties of "dealing with an oncologist from one clinic, a pulmonologist from another, and local nursing agencies to monitor Dad at home. It was overwhelming."

But Cain was lucky. She was able to find Leslie, a care advocate from EverCare Connections.* "I immediately felt at ease," Cain remembers. "Not only did Leslie have years of nursing experience, but her background was oncology."

Cain's father underwent an in-home assessment to define his specific needs. The evaluation addressed medical concerns—pain management, nutrition, and medications—as well as mental status, mobility, home safety, transportation, support systems, and emotional stability. Working with EverCare's interdisciplinary team, Leslie compiled a

* EverCare is part of UnitedHealth Group, a partner of AARP.

report for the family that included recommendations for care, resources, and service providers. The report was shared in a family conference call so that everyone could discuss together the next steps in their father's care.

Leslie makes phone calls, sets up doctors' appointments, arranges for nurse visits at home, and coordinates communication among concerned family members. Cain describes Leslie as "an interpreter, translating the doctors' orders to our family, and then communicating Dad's needs to health-care professionals." Leslie is "calm and rational," Cain goes on, "a port in the storm. The pressure has been lifted. Now, instead of playing the role of caregiver and coordinating Dad's care, I spend precious time supporting Mom and Dad as a daughter."

Cain's situation is being replayed many times each day across America as all of us live longer and boomers grow older. The good news is that as people discover the nonsystem of long-term care in this country, they are taking steps to devise something that works.

Who can deny that the retirement experience is being enormously enriched by the passionate engagement of older Americans? Money is important, of course, but not nearly so critical to successful retirement as real enthusiasms and the freedom to pursue them. Still, we all need enough money to support whatever lifestyle we aspire to. Thus many of us face financial challenges ahead.

HOW WILL YOU PAY FOR IT?

I have enough money to last me the rest of my life,
unless I buy something.
—*Jackie Mason*

A classic cartoon in the *New Yorker* magazine shows a pair of disheveled characters eyeing a lottery poster. "Winning," says one, "is crucial to my retirement plans."

The joke, of course, is that it isn't a joke. For far too many people today, questions about retirement planning are met with a shrug of resig-
nation. The most obvious issue looming for current and future retirees
comes down to this: After they've determined the lifestyle they want to
live in their later years, how will they pay for it? On the whole, boomers,
in particular, aren't saving nearly enough. Meanwhile, many large employers such as IBM, Verizon, Motorola, Alcoa, and others (not to mention the troubled auto and airline industries) are switching from
traditional pensions to tax-deferred savings plans that shift the risk to
employees and make them responsible for their own financial futures.

Adding to the sense of urgency is the tug-of-war over the status of
Social Security. Our elected representatives missed an opportunity in
2005 to make Social Security solvent for the long term; now it looks
as if nothing will be done for a while, perhaps until after the next
presidential election in 2008. (For more on the Social Security policy
debate, see chapter 7.)

The point is that just as the nature of retirement is changing, so is
the way we will pay for it. Traditionally, retirement finances rested
on a three-legged stool that included Social Security, pensions, and
personal savings and investments. But in today's world, where generous corporate pensions and retiree health plans are becoming
relics of the past, a secure retirement must be built on four strong
pillars: Social Security, a combination of pensions and savings,
health insurance, and earnings from continued work. And making
sure that everyone has the opportunity and wherewithal to build a
secure retirement requires not just changes in public policy but also
changes in ourselves.

Let's look at the pillars in turn.

SOCIAL SECURITY

Social Security is the foundation of a secure retirement, the only
pillar of income that is guaranteed. Today nine out of ten older

Americans receive Social Security benefits and a quarter of all citizens over 65 rely on it for 90 percent or more of their total income. Social Security checks make up 40 percent of retirement income, on average, but fully 70 percent of retirees get more than half their income from it.

In addition, 18 million people under age 65 receive Social Security benefits, including disability and survivor benefits for people of all ages. In fact, 4 million people under the age of 19 now collect Social Security survivor benefits. If you know someone whose parent died or became disabled while he or she was growing up, you probably know someone who relied on Social Security benefits. My brother Jerry's wife died when my three nephews were very young. Social Security survivor benefits helped Jerry and his second wife, Donna, raise the boys and send them to college.

In short, our national pension system has been, and must continue to be, a significant income program for American society. Without Social Security, nearly half of all people 65 and older would be poor—just as they were as recently as 1960, before Social Security benefits were increased and indexed to wage growth. The fact that old age is no longer synonymous with poverty is reason enough to take great care in making any changes to the program.

Nonetheless, change is needed to assure that Social Security will remain 100 percent solvent. As nearly everyone knows, the system has a long-term financial shortfall. We must act soon to fix the problems; in 2008 the first boomers will become eligible for early retirement at age 62 and many will begin drawing benefits.

The system is neither broke nor broken. It does not need a radical overhaul. What it needs are reasonable, incremental adjustments to make it solvent and maintain guaranteed benefits for future generations. If Congress could achieve a bipartisan agreement and act soon, full funding could be achieved with an increase in revenues, an adjustment in benefits, or, most likely, some combination of the two (see chapter 7).

A COMBINATION OF PENSIONS AND SAVINGS

Social Security was designed as one leg of a three-legged stool, with the other two supports a worker's pension, earned through years of service to an employer, and the private savings the worker thriftily put aside and invested for retirement. No one could have foreseen how precarious the second and third legs would become.

Today half of all workers aren't covered by any kind of employer pension plan. What is more, many of them are living from paycheck to paycheck, leaving little, if anything, left over to set aside for the future. So, even as we talk about changes in the pension system, we have to remember that Social Security is the only pension half the workforce may receive.

As for those still fortunate enough to have traditional defined-benefit corporate pension plans, many of those plans are increasingly under attack as being too costly and no longer appropriate, either for the corporations themselves or for the new generation of mobile workers who often change jobs and can't take their pensions to a new employer.

Many companies are switching from defined-benefit plans to new cash-balance pension plans, which build pension values faster for younger workers and make pension funds more portable. However, transitions to the cash-balance model often discriminate against older employees. When IBM, for example, tried to switch to a cash-balance plan in the 1990s, some older employees, angered about reductions in accrued pension benefits under the new plan, sued. In 2003 a federal judge ruled against IBM, which negotiated a settlement that would cost the company $1.7 billion. This ruling was reversed in August 2006, but the plaintiffs were planning another appeal.

Negative publicity, followed by the *initial* IBM ruling, tainted the cash-balance pension model and hastened the movement toward tax-deferred savings plans such as the 401(k), named after the section of the bill that created it.

Tax-deferred plans rely mainly on the worker's own contributions and thus are roughly half as costly for employers as traditional plans, even if the companies match all or part of the worker's savings, as most do. The money is then invested by the worker in a range of investment options, with the worker assuming the investment risk.

The shift from defined-benefit plans to defined-contribution plans is in full swing. Some large companies are staying with their defined-benefit plans for now, but many others are not. Some companies have added savings plans to their list of options or offered them to younger workers instead of traditional pensions. After losing its court battle, IBM itself decided in December 2004 to close its traditional pension plan to new employees, offering them only a 401(k). And in January 2006 the company announced it was freezing its defined-benefit plan, a move the company says will save it $3 billion by 2010.

More and more of the companies establishing plans for the first time are opting for the defined-contribution savings model instead of the traditional defined-benefit pension plan. Whereas 29 million workers were covered by defined-benefit plans in 1985, only 23 million could say the same in 2002. Meanwhile, the number of workers covered by 401(k) savings plans quintupled to 50 million.

Why the wholesale switch? Well, for big companies with traditional pension plans, the costs have ballooned. Back in the 1950s and 1960s, when many of these plans were implemented, many retired workers drew benefits for only a few years before dying. But a worker reaching 65 today can expect to live for another eighteen years, creating an enormous, added cost.

General Motors, for example, which now has two retirees for every active worker, paid out $6.5 billion for pensions and $5.2 billion for retirees' health care in 2003, taking a huge bite out of its $150 billion in North American sales. Pension burdens at Ford (including retiree health care) and DaimlerChrysler, while lighter than GM's, still add about $1,000 to the cost of every car sold. The automakers' huge pension costs sharply curtail their ability to compete in a global market.

Adding to these costs was the bursting of the stock market bubble early this decade, which significantly reduced the value of pension assets. This has been compounded by the low interest rate environment, which increases projected costs. Together the cost and volatility now detract from the corporate bottom line.

When employers go bankrupt with underfunded defined-benefit plans, the Pension Benefit Guaranty Corporation (PBGC) steps in to make sure workers don't lose all their benefits. Since its creation in 1974, the PBGC, which covers 44 million workers and retirees, has taken over more than 3,200 failed pension plans. Financed by premiums from corporate pension funds and by the remaining funds in the failed plans it inherits, the PBGC itself has slid into financial difficulty. From a positive net balance of $10 billion in 2000, it now has a long-term shortfall between payouts and expected income; in 2004 alone, the deficit doubled to $23.3 billion. Recent legislation has increased the PBGC premiums by about 60 percent. With a cascade of underfunded pension plans hanging over the agency, led by the airline industry's $81 billion, the PBGC may be unable to fully meet its obligations as early as 2018.

All of these factors have served to move companies out of defined-benefit plans and into 401(k) plans. In fact, for companies looking to attract younger workers, the 401(k) is seen as desirable, since most new employees do not anticipate a long career with one company. But how have workers fared under this shift?

Because workers with 401(k)s tend to cut back on their traditional savings, the tax-deferred plans have essentially become the way people save. As such, the pension and savings legs of the old three-legged stool have merged into one. And with 401(k) plans come investment portfolios managed by largely inexperienced individual workers instead of traditional pensions under the wing of employers' more market-savvy financial advisers. So collapsing the two legs into one has left retirees and their portfolios on increasingly shaky ground.

One need look no further than the market meltdown of 2000–2002, when $7 trillion of wealth vanished (surpassing the percentage losses of the legendary 1929 crash), to understand the danger of relying on 401(k) plans for retirement. Three out of four stock owners, aged 50 to 70, surveyed by AARP in 2002 lost money on their investments when the bubble burst, and a third reported losses of 25 to 50 percent. Fifteen percent of retirees surveyed were contemplating going back to work, and among those still working, one in five were postponing retirement to try to recoup some of what had been lost. A year later, after a 29 percent gain in the Standard & Poor's 500 stock index, the portfolios of workers in their fifties were still down 9.3 percent, on average, from 1999 levels.

With or without stock market bubbles, workers who join 401(k) plans often make poor decisions. Investment advisers generally agree that younger workers, on the one hand, should allocate more to stocks than to bonds, because they have time to weather market slumps and reap the higher returns stocks generally provide. Older workers, on the other hand, should concentrate more on bonds, which provide guaranteed, albeit lower, returns, thus ensuring retirement income.

But far too many young employees opt for bonds or other low-rate, guaranteed contracts, while too many older workers load up on stock funds. Furthermore, most workers tend to ignore sound advice against buying too much of their own company's stock. To their sorrow, many Enron employees learned the danger of this strategy, losing all of their savings along with their jobs when the company collapsed.

Employees also tend to make poor decisions when they move from job to job. At least half the workers in one study took their money in a lump sum rather than rolling it over to their new company's plan. Only 35 percent rolled over the entire amount. Fourteen percent spent the whole sum on new cars, vacations, or other things.

The obvious hazards of savings plans have spawned a new effort in recent years to provide workers more strategic guidance on investments. Although companies are legally barred from offering direct investment advice, many are hiring professional advisers to help employees define and attain their investment goals. Others are tailoring their plans to encourage participation and minimize poor choices.

If, for example, enrollment in a 401(k) is automatic unless a new hire actively takes the steps to opt out, participation rises as high as 96 percent. Some plans have automatic increases in the percentage withheld for savings, rising by a point or so with every raise in pay. The additional bite from take-home pay is almost imperceptible, but the substantial gains at retirement time are both noticeable and welcome. Some plans automatically shift portfolio allocation over time, concentrating in stocks when workers are young and in bonds as they age. Others automatically roll over funds to a new employer's plan or to a retirement portfolio.

All these are good ideas, and, at last count, more than one in five corporate savings plans offered some measure of guidance for employees. But the fact remains that defined-contribution savings plans are here to stay and those who participate in them must do all they can to make wise investment choices and manage their accounts prudently. The first step, of course, is to participate in the plan if your company offers one and then invest as much as you can in it up to the legal limit. At last count, the pension funds of the average worker nearing retirement came to only $121,000, including money in traditional pension plans and 401(k)s. That figure was an average and included huge savings totals for a few and meager or nonexistent amounts for most. As of 2005, half of all workers reported that they had saved less than $25,000 for retirement. Even at the high end, that's nowhere near enough to finance the kind of lifestyle most people envision in retirement.

There are ways to manage your investment to get the most out of your 401(k) or other savings plan. Here are five important guiding principles:

1. Choose plans with low fees. Fees reduce returns on your investment over the long term, and even small fees can add up over time. For example, the difference in investing $100,000 over twenty years in a

low-cost fund—one with a 0.5 percent annual fee—versus a midcost fund (a 1.25 percent annual fee) is almost $50,000. The point is to maximize your retirement savings, so look for low-fee funds.

2. Choose from a limited selection of funds. Research shows that financial consumers are often confused by too many choices. Confusion leads to inertia, procrastination, or potentially costly mistakes. It helps, therefore, to find ways to choose among a smaller number of reasonable investments.

3. Consider buying index funds. An index fund builds its portfolio by buying all the stocks in a certain index, such as the Standard & Poor's 500. Index funds therefore mimic the price performance of the stock market as a whole or of a particular section of the market, and they typically outperform most actively managed funds. On top of that, they usually have low costs, thus helping investors to maximize their returns.

4. Diversify your investments. Putting all your eggs in one basket is especially risky when it comes to investing. A mix of stocks and bonds cushions market downturns while providing the opportunity for growth. A balanced index fund seeks to replicate the returns of both stock and bond indexes, combining the advantages of broad diversification with the concept of guaranteed benefits.

5. Rebalance your portfolio periodically. Over time, your desired mix of stocks, bonds, and cash can get out of whack, exposing you to more risk than is acceptable for your age and income level. Let's say that a couple of your stocks score big gains. That's a good thing, but now more of your total assets are in stocks than is prudent for your particular situation. Regular rebalancing maintains your desired allocations, preserves diversification, and controls risk, yet most investors rarely rebalance their holdings. Look for funds that offer automatic rebalancing, especially if you don't have the time, interest, or skill to rebalance your investments yourself.

By following these investment principles, you can make your savings plan into the solid pillar of retirement income you're counting on.

HEALTH INSURANCE

The third pillar of the new retirement system must be health insurance. The rapid growth of health-care costs (as discussed in chapter 2) and the growing need for long-term care posed by the aging population of boomers threaten the financial security of all Americans.

Out-of-pocket health-care costs now average 19 percent of income for persons 65 and over, and that's *after* Medicare and Medicaid have paid a major portion of the medical bills. The hit to low-income retirees is even greater. Indigent Medicare beneficiaries without Medicaid coverage spend 49 percent of their total income on health care.

When it comes to long-term care and how to pay for it, the issue has taken on added importance as the bulging population of boomers closes in on old age. The existing crazy quilt of public and private programs is nearly impossible for most people to fathom, let alone navigate. Insurance is available commercially, but at premiums that are affordable only by the relatively well-off.

In 2002, Americans spent $139 billion on long-term care for people of all ages, which amounted to 8.7 percent of our total health-care spending. The average annual cost of skilled care at a nursing home is $74,000. And an assisted-living facility can cost nearly $35,000 a year. Costs are even higher when special services and dementia care are added.

The high costs of long-term care and the preferences of the elderly mean that many of them are cared for in the homes of relatives or friends. Such caregiving, as discussed earlier, puts heavy stress on families, especially the women in the family and particularly low-income families. Women caregivers are often caught in a difficult spiral: They are forced to take time off from work, forgo promotions, and maybe even drop out of the workforce altogether to care for elderly relatives. Consequently, they work less and earn less, which reduces the Social Security and pension benefits they receive. But since women generally live about seven years longer than men, they have to stretch their meager resources much further.

The stark reality of today's America is that without insurance to protect against health-care expenses, virtually no one can feel economically secure.

EARNINGS FROM CONTINUED WORK

The fourth pillar of a modern-day retirement is income from work after traditional retirement age (see chapter 4 for a detailed discussion). More and more of today's generally healthier older Americans are continuing to work, and it's an idea heartily embraced by boomers seeking to redefine their retirements. A full 80 percent of boomers say they expect to keep working either full- or part-time after they hit so-called retirement age.

It's a strategy that could pay big dividends. A boomer who chooses early retirement at 62, for instance, would not only draw permanently reduced Social Security benefits but also start draining funds from his or her 401(k) account (if available), increasing the risk that private resources would be depleted before death. But a boomer who earns about $50,000 a year and continues to work until full benefits kick in at 66 can boost the size of his or her Social Security checks by more than 40 percent, from about $938 a month to $1,330 a month.

By the same token, postponing for four years the withdrawals from a 401(k) or an IRA account totaling $150,000 would fatten the nest egg by $32,000, even if the money were earning only a modest 5 percent. And if the worker could keep saving at the maximum tax-free rate of $6,000 a year, a rate that is scheduled to go into effect for those 50 and older starting in 2008, the savings would grow to nearly $210,000 by full retirement age. All told, the extra four years of employment would raise retirement income by at least $7,600 a year.

The same calculations apply after reaching age 66, since untapped savings keep growing and initial Social Security benefits keep rising by 6 percent to 8 percent for every year of delay in claiming them, up to the age of 70. And staying on the job doesn't have to mean toiling away forty or more hours a week. While many may intend to do just that, others are reducing the number of hours or days on the job or accepting a cut in pay for a new job with fewer responsibilities.

One interesting idea that may be gaining some traction is "phased retirement," in which employees phase down their career employment as they approach full retirement. Workers who retire in phases, or steps, are more likely to have a positive view of work and may stay in the workforce longer.

Some economists and policy makers suggest that the transition to longer working lives could be most easily made simply by legislating a further postponement of Social Security eligibility, perhaps up to age 68. This would relieve the pressure on the Social Security trust fund and help keep benefits fully funded for future generations. This idea is not very popular among the general public. Many wonder where they would find jobs at 68, and others point out that not everyone can work that long, especially manual laborers. Whatever the solution, the system should be flexible enough to take care of all workers, both those who are healthy enough to keep on working and those who aren't. People who need to retire at 62 should continue to have the option of doing so at a reduced level of benefits. People who choose to continue working can add to their savings, postpone benefits, and enjoy the reward of retiring with more income.

The four pillars are the best and most practical way to provide security for retirees in the post-2011 society. The combination of Social Security, pensions and savings, health insurance, and earnings from continued work can lessen the chances of poverty for older Americans and keep them healthy and independent, without placing an undue burden on their families and on society. But how will individual retirees manage such a system? How will it affect you, and what will you have to do and know in order to retire successfully?

Many books and articles are available to help you answer these questions, with formulas and philosophies for preparing to "retire."

The place to start is by calculating how much life in retirement will cost. It makes sense to figure out exactly how much you'll need before you decide how to accumulate it, but it's an exercise that only a third of Americans aged 40 to 59 have ever undertaken.

To determine what your financial needs will probably be, it is useful to draw up a realistic list of last year's expenses, making sure to include all the items in your checkbook and on your credit card bills. Sort them into categories—food, housing, car or other transportation, clothing, entertainment, travel, and so forth—and review each to consider how it might change in retirement.

On the one hand, the costs of such things as getting to work, dressing for the workplace, and dry cleaning will decline, as could housing costs if you plan to move to a smaller place in a less pricey community. On the other hand, you'll probably spend more for travel, particularly at the beginning, when you will be rewarding yourself for spending all those years in the daily grind. Health expenses will probably rise; they almost always do. And if you've taken early retirement, you may find yourself without employer-sponsored health insurance; only 29 percent of large employers extend insurance to retirees too young to qualify for Medicare at 65. Even if you avoid paying for health care from your own pocket, insurance premiums will inevitably rise.

Next, determine how much income you can count on. You can get a firm calculation of your Social Security benefits based on your personal-income history. You may also have a defined-benefit pension or a 401(k) plan and perhaps some money in a tax-deferred IRA account.

If you are among the lucky one in five workers who have a good old-fashioned defined-benefit pension plan, consult your employee benefits office to make sure you understand all the wrinkles. For instance, ask when you can start collecting and whether you will be better off taking a lump sum or a monthly check. The monthly check is almost always a better bet unless you have reason to believe you or the company isn't going to last more than a few years. If you're forced to take the lump sum, you should probably arrange to roll it over directly into an IRA account, where it can keep growing. Also find out if your monthly pension check will rise along with inflation. Very few companies index their pensions, but you need to know exactly where you stand.

Something else to think about is whether you should accept less monthly income now in order to provide a survivor's benefit for your spouse later. If you answer yes, should that benefit be half of your monthly payout or the full amount? If your spouse is in poor health or is covered by another pension, taking the full monthly amount you're entitled to now and dispensing with survivor benefits can add as much as 25 percent to each check.

Beware of pitfalls. Some pension plans, for instance, require you to work a minimum number of days during your last year on the job. So quitting a month early could mean a smaller pension—for only twenty-four years of service, let's say, instead of twenty-five. Worse yet, most companies base the pension on an employee's average salary over the last three to five years of service. If you lose credit for your last year at high pay and the calculation includes the year before your last big raise, your loss will be even bigger.

A major Catch-22 in the pension calculation resides under the unlikely label of "Social Security integration." In plain English, it refers to a formula that includes part of a worker's Social Security benefits in the calculation of the company pension. If your annual pension accounting statement says your pension will be $1,500 a month and Social Security tells you it will provide another $1,500, you might reasonably expect $3,000 a month. But you will be sorely disappointed if your company is among the approximately 50 percent of companies that use Social Security integration; it can reduce your pension pay by as much as half the Social Security benefit, leaving you with monthly income of only $2,250.

If your company has a cash-balance pension plan, calculating benefits can be almost impossible. What's worse, a recent Labor Department audit found that one-fifth of all companies with such plans shortchanged workers who retired early. To begin with, make sure all the information in your file (current age, length of employment, latest salary level, etc.) is correct and then try to calculate the benefits due to see if they match the company's figures. If you can't follow the calculations, it's probably worth hiring an expert to help protect yourself.

Your next step is to make sure you aren't leaving any pension money in a former employer's bank account. If you or your spouse ever worked at a company for, say, five years or more, it could have a pension waiting for you that you don't even know about. Sending a letter with your employment history to the Pension Benefit Guaranty Corporation in Washington could net a small windfall.

After you have determined your pension income, the next question is how much you can reasonably draw out of your savings each year without outliving your money. Assume that your combination of stocks, bonds, and cash will earn a conservative 5 percent a year. As a rule of thumb, that means you can withdraw 5 percent of the total balance each year without exhausting your funds. If your retirement accounts total $150,000, for example, that means you can add about $7,500 a year to your Social Security and pension income. But it's best to check your figures with a professional adviser who can help you determine the most realistic assumptions about your needs.

If the total monthly cash flow you come up with doesn't seem enough, it probably won't be. But you still have options—staying on your current job a few more years and postponing the benefits, for instance, or switching to a part-time job to supplement your retirement income. Or, if you're determined to quit the rat race altogether, scale down your expectations. Cut back on travel plans and discretionary expenses, for example, or find a cheaper retirement home, perhaps in a low-cost state. If you can sell your current home and buy a smaller, less expensive place, you can annuitize the profit: $150,000 in equity would bring a 62-year-old woman about $900 a month for the rest of her life.

Maybe you'll get lucky and come into a sum of money from an inheritance. As a group, the boomers are going to inherit some $10.4 trillion from their parents in what has been called the biggest intergenerational transfer in history. But it will be spread so unevenly that only a relative few will come out with big jackpots.

But let's assume you're one of them. The first thing to do is nothing at all. Put the windfall in the bank and consult a fee-only financial adviser to make a solid plan for the money. It would be unwise to blow it on a fancy new car or a trip around the world or to make the investment your best friend says is foolproof. Think it through. This may be the ticket to a more comfortable retirement, or financing for the education of your grandchildren, or part of the estate you leave your family. Take time to consider all the possibilities and get professional investment advice. If it takes a full year to decide what's best for you, so what? You haven't made much money at savings-bank or money-market rates, but you haven't lost a nickel, either. And count on your adviser to know the complex tax rules for handling lump sums without triggering big penalties.

Chances are, however, you won't have to deal with that happy problem, and you'll be depending on the retirement you made for yourself. So you'll live with it. But whatever you do, stay flexible, keep a cushion for emergencies, continue to save as much as you can, and maintain your job skills and keep in touch with your working friends—just in case you need or want to go back into the workforce. Try to adjust for changing circumstances, and, above all, prepare yourself.

The period we have traditionally called retirement can be a wonderful time of life. We all have a tremendous opportunity to reinvent it for ourselves, to make it whatever we want it to be. But we can't wait until that time is upon us to begin thinking about it. We have to plan and prepare, in terms of both what we want to do and how we will pay for it. If we do that, we will discover that these are years of tremendous change and self-discovery. Retirement really is a new phase of life, filled with opportunities to live and love, to learn and explore, to give back, to enjoy the life we have worked so hard to own, to seek significance, and to discover that personal fulfillment is the final piece of the new American dream.

four

The Opportunity to Revolutionize the Workplace

The world is full of willing people, some willing to work, the rest willing to let them. —*Anonymous*

Reinelde Poole "retired" twenty years ago from her teaching job in Marlborough, Massachusetts, but she has kept working ever since, for organizations such as the Chamber of Commerce and as secretary to three mayors. "I don't do this for money. I do it because I enjoy it," Poole, now 85, says. "I like proving to myself I can still do these things."

As boomers near the traditional retirement age, all indications are that more and more of them will follow in the footsteps of Reinelde Poole. As with every other phase of their lives, the boomers have re-defined work. More than 70 percent of people over 45 expect to keep working into their so-called retirement years, and nearly half of those who plan to work also plan to stay in jobs into their seventies. Work is becoming a normal part of the extended lives boomers count on—either because they want to work or because they need to. People turning 50 today have half their adult lives ahead of them, thirty or more years in which to be productive and earn money, keep fit and healthy, buy things and use services, teach and mentor and learn, and embark on new adventures. Simply stated, work is part of the vigorous lifestyle that more and more boomers expect to enjoy.

Kim Benz is one example. At 52, she took an early-retirement package from Procter & Gamble to spend more time with her son, who has special educational needs. With enough money to live comfortably, Kim says she was looking forward to spending time in her garden. "But when I left all that fast-paced work, my interest in gardening just disappeared," she says. It wasn't until Kim went back to P&G as a consultant for ten to twenty hours a week that her garden regained its charm.

Traditional retirement simply isn't a good fit for boomers like Kim. For others who are less financially secure, work is a necessity. Perhaps they didn't save enough for retirement or maybe their investments soured. The bursting of the dot-com stock market bubble, for example, definitely put a damper on some retirement plans. As stated earlier, an AARP study showed that of the investors aged 50 to 70 who lost money, more than one in five postponed retirement and 10 percent of those already retired felt compelled to return to work for monetary reasons.

Some people encounter a cascade of bad luck that leaves them no choice but to keep working. That's what happened to John Bartlett, a chemical and nuclear engineer and former assistant secretary at the Department of Energy. John never intended to retire; neither did his wife, Joan, a psychologist. But a few years ago, when he was 65 and she was 58, what the couple intended or wanted no longer mattered. Joan was in an auto accident that ended her career, and then the stock market plunge decimated the couple's investments. "It all came apart at about the same time," explains John. "This is draining the hell out of us." He now works in an Environmental Protection Agency office that supplies workers over 65 for environmental projects. He earns a modest $12.81 an hour but says he enjoys his work. The best part, though, is the health plan that covers most of Joan's continuing care. "I like to work," John offers, "but now I am impelled to work."

Stories like Reinelde Poole's, Kim Benz's, and John Bartlett's make me think about my own work life. I began full-time work forty-two years ago and have held seven jobs. I feel that I'm at the top of my game. Although I have no definite plans, I tend to see my next job as possibly affiliated with a university where I can teach and consult but also take some anthropology and archaeology courses and where my wife, Fran, and I can enjoy the cultural and sports activities of life on campus.

THE CHANGING NATURE OF WORK

> People who work sitting down get paid more
> than people who work standing up.
> —*Ogden Nash*

Long gone is the reality reflected in the sad refrain of an old folk song: "You worked so hard that you died standing up." Once upon a time, a boy might leave school at 16 and go to work in a field or factory where he could spend all his productive life. "Retirement" came when injury or sheer wear and tear left him unable to work anymore. At that point, if his family couldn't support him, he might earn a few dollars as a night watchman or in some other less demanding job.

But the nature of work has changed. I come from a family of steelworkers in Pittsburgh and Johnstown, Pennsylvania. My father worked in the scrap yard at the Universal Cyclops steel mill before moving up to work on electric furnaces, which paid a bit more per hour. I remember a mill strike when Dad and my uncle John dug graves to make ends meet. During another strike, two other uncles reopened an abandoned coal mine and dug out coal for home heating. When my uncle Andy retired, he simply came home one day, put down his lunch box, and said, "That's it. I'm retired." And he was. People got worn out from hard work.

But in today's workplace, brainwork has largely replaced brawn and few people are worn down by physically demanding and debilitating jobs. The overwhelming majority of Americans spend their working days not in agriculture (now less than 2 percent of the workforce) or manufacturing (13 percent) but in offices where they process information and provide an array of services. Even the dwindling proportion who do still labor in fields and on factory floors have less need for muscle. Farmers can sit in their air-conditioned tractor cabs, and factory workers monitor gauges and turn dials to control computers and robots; they rarely hammer steel or lift heavy weights.

Not all manual labor is gone from our economy, of course. Hotel maids, janitors, and landscapers still perform hands-on work, and such jobs still exist at factories, farms, and construction sites, too. Indeed, one reason people oppose raising the retirement age for Social Security is out of concern for the physical laborers who might not be able to extend their working lives.

But overall, the largest part of the U.S. workforce is made up of knowledge workers, and more than 4 million members of that workforce are between the ages of 65 and 74. By 2031, 49.9 million workers will be at or past the traditional retirement age of 65. Looking at the aging workforce from a slightly different vantage point, by 2020, 20 percent of America's workers will pass 55, and over the following seven years the 55-to-64-year-old segment will expand by 55 percent.

Why is this important? It's important because the United States is facing a shortage of younger employees. Close behind that bulging group of older workers is a relatively smaller group of 35-to-44-year-olds, a product of the lower birthrate that followed the baby boom. The group isn't big enough to replace potential retirees. Casual observation of various industries may mask the reality, but a shortage of workers is definitely on the way and in some sectors is already here.

The Economic Policy Foundation predicts the shortfall of workers needed to turn out the goods and services that keep our nation running will total 4.3 million people by 2011 and 35 million by 2031. Where will employers turn? One important source of qualified employees will be those boomers who want and/or need to keep working past the conventional retirement age of 65.

In some industries, the exodus of experienced employees is already approaching emergency proportions. The health-care sector, for example, faces a critical shortage of nurses. Joanne Disch, a professor of nursing at the University of Minnesota and an AARP board member, attributes the shortage to more than just retirements. Exacerbating the problem, she explains, is the insufficient number of educators needed to prepare young nurses to replace the retirees.

Elsewhere, veteran teachers are leaving our public schools (and younger ones are quitting, too); skilled blue-collar workers are walking away from factories and construction sites; and a severe brain drain is threatening the aerospace and defense industries. In the latter case, a looming threat was hastened by federal budget cutbacks a few years ago, which severely limited hiring and triggered layoffs among less-senior workers. The result: The average age of defense and aerospace workers has risen to 51, and half the workforce will be eligible to retire in the next six years.

Areas in which scientific knowledge is critical will feel the crunch more acutely because they are so dependent on seasoned employees. Gregs Thomopulos, president and chief executive officer of Stanley Consultants, an engineering, environmental, and construction services company headquartered in Muscatine, Iowa, explains that experience is crucial in the engineering industry: "In our profession, expertise combined with experience is more critical in our service to clients than most other factors. Our [employees] age fifty and over bring invaluable knowledge of our company and their areas of expertise to our client service—this gives us a competitive edge."

Stanley Consultants pays more than lip service to its older employees. Of its more than 900 professional, technical, and support staff, 34 percent are over 50, including 53 percent of managers and 77 percent of executives. Thomopulos says the mature workforce plays a critical role in developing the company's future leaders, both by acting as mentors and by sharing their knowledge as experts in the field. And the company works hard to retain its older workers, tailoring assignments and customizing retirement packages through its phased-retirement program, in which 75 percent of employees participate. Further proof of Stanley's attraction to older workers: In the past twelve months, 26 percent of the company's new hires were over the age of 50. AARP recognized Stanley's outstanding efforts by putting it at the top of our 2005 list of Best Employers for Workers over 50.

Also making changes is the nation's electric utility industry. The realization that half its 400,000-odd employees were due to retire in the next five years, taking with them a treasure of accumulated knowledge and judgment, set off alarm bells in time to prepare for the exodus, but only just: Apprenticeships in the industry typically take at least four years. "We've got to be moving right now," Dale Green, human resources manager for Colorado's Platte River Power Authority, argues. He has started a crash recruiting and training program. And as older utility workers prepare to leave, the industry is likely to offer them incentives to stay.

Some utility companies are already introducing programs that encourage retirees to remain connected. Atlanta's Southern Company, for example, has set up a "retiree reservists' pool" of several hundred former workers who can be brought in on a part-time basis to handle emergencies, train new employees, and staff short-term projects.

Despite the looming labor shortage, not every sector and every company is seeking older workers. Nor are all older unemployed people finding it easy to get back into the workforce. Not long ago, I received a letter from someone I had known in my Unilever days. He was having a very difficult time finding a new job and appealed to AARP to step up its efforts to wipe out age discrimination. We have been doing just that and also promoting older workers.

The whims and wishes of the aging boomers themselves will serve as an agent of change for older workers. Today's 50+ population wants products, services, and experiences that relate to them, that speak to their values and lifestyles, and that demonstrate an understanding of, and a genuine empathy for, their interests, wants, and needs. As chapter 6 describes in much greater detail, the demographic bulge is sparking a consumer revolution that, in turn, is opening up more opportunities for older workers.

Taken together, the changes in the nature of work and the makeup of the workforce are helping to push back the age of retirement. More or less arbitrarily pegged at 65 in the last century and with 62 having become the norm in practice, the retirement age has begun to creep upward over the last several years. Many people want to keep full-time jobs well into their seventies, a right guaranteed to most of us by the long-standing laws against age discrimination in this country. Yet many others still look forward to an early retirement or perhaps a phased departure from the workforce.

Eventually, though, by either choice or necessity, a majority of boomers will be working into their later years—and the nation's employers, many of which have traditionally looked for ways to show older workers the door, will accelerate the change in policies and practices aimed at retaining and recruiting mature workers. The graying of the workplace will affect more than just employers and their employees; our deficit-ridden national budget will get a much-needed infusion of tax dollars from older workers who continue to pay income taxes in support of a system that is paying them.

TODAY'S WORKERS, TOMORROW'S WORKPLACES

> The future is already here;
> it's just very unevenly distributed.
> —*William Gibson*

Back in the late 1990s, an executive at the Borders bookstore chain stumbled across two interesting facts: More than half of all books purchased in the United States were bought by people who had passed their forty-fifth birthday. Yet only 6 percent of the Borders sales force were older than 50. So the company devised a strategy to attract more mature employees, a change of direction that presages the future for the entire U.S. economy.

That future, as sketched by Borders, is a formal program for recruiting and keeping individuals who "could relate better to our customers," Dan Smith, the company's senior vice president of human resources, explains. He is referring to people over 50, who now account for 16 percent of the chain's thirty-two thousand employees; by 2010, Borders expects that share to grow to about 25 percent. Advises Smith: Scrap any notion that more mature employees are intractable, burnt out, and prone to sickness and absenteeism. That's all a myth. Rather, they are smart, energetic, dependable, and the kind of employees that every company wants and needs. What's more, he adds, they are easier to recruit and train, plus their turnover record is just one-tenth that of workers under 30.

These days, Borders goes to considerable lengths to sign up boomer-aged salespeople—in many cases hiring people who have retired from one career and are ready to start another. The company, which offers part-time or flexible work hours, recently added medical and dental benefits for part-timers. These include a vision plan, prescription drug coverage, disability payments, and a long-term-care option—all tailored to workers past 50. Borders is also considering adding an income annuity option to its 401(k) plan that would let employees set aside part of their pay for a guaranteed monthly income when they finally decide to call it quits. And it is already setting up a "corporate passport" system to make it easier for workers to move back and forth among stores in several regions. That way, someone could spend the winter months employed at a branch in Florida, say, and the summer working at a store in New Hampshire.

The "smart, energetic, dependable" employees Dan Smith describes above might well be named Ann Schecter, Bill Corporon, and Barbara Kinzer. Ann works part-time at a Borders in Union City, California, just to earn a little extra money. And when she's not working at Borders, she handles a full-time job at a home owners' association management company. Talk about energy. When she's tired from one job, Ann says, she still enjoys the other.

Bill Corporon, 58, is a part-time cashier at a Borders store in the Dallas area. When Bill decided to leave ExxonMobil after twenty-five years, he knew he wasn't ready to retire completely. "I retired once and missed the action of being in the workplace," he says. So he set out to find a job that would allow him to indulge his passion for reading and also accommodate freelance corporate writing assignments. Using our Featured Employers Web site, Bill connected with a Borders store manager who welcomed him as perhaps "overqualified" but still a highly desirable employee. Bill, who admits to being somewhat "technologically challenged," says the "young people help me out. It's a two-way street."

To say that Barbara Kinzer was "technologically challenged" when she started at Borders would be an understatement. Kinzer, 62, had been out of the workforce for twenty-five years. She had no idea how to even turn on a computer. But after receiving training herself, she spent eight years running the corporate training program at Borders' headquarters in Ann Arbor, Michigan.

Borders is not alone in its pursuit of more mature workers. Many employers are following the same path. In fact, AARP's workforce initiative includes more than twenty other companies, such as The Home Depot, Pitney Bowes, Walgreens, Kelly Services, Adecco, and Verizon. These companies are in the vanguard of the growing trend toward hiring and retaining people past 50.

One of my learning experiences about all this came as a result of a conversation in 2004 with Bob Nardelli, CEO of The Home Depot. At the time, Bob said The Home Depot had 1,800 stores (it has more than 1,900 today) and opens a new one about every forty-eight hours. These are huge stores that employ many people—some twenty thousand new employees are hired every year. Bob said the company especially values older workers.

Now Bob is a big advocate of community service, but he made it plain that hiring mature workers has nothing to do with good deeds. It's a business decision pure and simple, one that helps The Home Depot stay ahead of the competition. The company caters to both do-it-yourselfers and professionals in the home-improvement, construction, and building-maintenance industries. It wants experienced, knowledgeable employees who like to help customers and who are loyal and reliable. To my mind, that pretty well describes mature workers.

Like Borders and other big companies that are competing for mature workers, The Home Depot offers flexible schedules and health coverage even to part-timers. Benefits include medical, dental, and vision plans; short-term disability and life insurance; tuition reimbursement; a discounted stock-purchase plan; and the opportunity to participate in the company's growth through its Success Sharing program. The Home Depot also offers "snowbird" specials that let employees move to different parts of the country as the seasons change; for example, they can work in Florida in the winter and Maine in the summer.

Among those who've found a new life and livelihood at The Home Depot is Marcia Foster, age 60. Marcia, who lives with her blind mother and their dog, Buddy, in Chandler, Arizona, was devastated when she was let go by Motorola in 2002. Marcia had worked at the company for twenty-seven years. "Without a job, life can be boring and depressing," she says. "I needed to work. I really wanted to work." Marcia updated her computer skills and blanketed the area with her résumé but without success.

Then one morning, she read in the newspaper that The Home Depot had teamed up with AARP to recruit older workers. "I went online and applied on a Tuesday," Marcia recalls. "On Saturday, I got a call to schedule an interview." Only days later, she was working as a part-time cashier. I cherish the letter we received from Marcia: "Thank you for making my life new and exciting again. It has been too long since I have felt valuable."

Marcia Foster's experience exemplifies the power of work to change lives and the capacity of a committed partnership to make change happen.

Here are some other companies that are ahead of the curve in recruiting and retaining mature workers. All are partners with AARP in reshaping the workplace.

• New York Life Insurance Company has a wide range of services that benefit older workers. For instance, its New York City headquarters houses a backup child-care center that looks after employees' grandchildren. It also has a medical facility staffed by doctors and nurses that does screening tests for bone density, cholesterol levels, skin cancer, and other conditions whose incidence increases as workers age. And because "older workers have elder-care issues with their parents," says Fred Sievert, New York Life's president, "we provide counseling and support."

Such age-friendly initiatives earn positive reviews for the company and build loyalty from employees. Kathleen Lavin, a 50+ assistant vice president who gets regular checkups and screenings at the on-site health center and works out at the on-site fitness center, praises New York Life for "investing in my well-being to ensure that I am a healthy, energetic, and vital mature employee." It's a smart investment for a company in which 30 percent of its 8,000 employees are past 50. What's more, New York Life wants to up the ratio. "We put a premium on experience," notes Len Elmer, a senior vice president.

• The Principal Financial Group takes a unique approach to employee development. Instead of aiming its training programs mainly at new hires and younger workers, the Des Moines, Iowa, company has a "lifelong learning" program that holds all employees accountable for improving their knowledge and skills throughout their careers. Company personnel consultants will help schedule the courses each employee needs to achieve his or her individual development plan. By promoting the concept of lifelong learning Principal Financial is saying, in effect, that employees of all ages are valuable to the company. And employees find it valuable. Rachel Torres, manager of the Client Call Center for Principal's Annuity Services, has taken in-house leadership and industry classes as well as outside seminars to boost her continued learning and career development. "Continued learning, both in your profession and personal life, is a must at any age," she says. "Whether you take professional classes, read business books, or decide to learn yoga or another language, these are all rewarding experiences that keep you actively learning, stretching, and making life an adventure." And that message is being reinforced by a new "Happy Returns" program specifically designed for retired employees who want to come back. "Treating employees well is not just good sense," says J. Barry Griswell, chairman, president, and CEO, "it's good business sense, and we take it seriously."

• Loudoun Healthcare has encouraged dozens of nurses at its Leesburg, Virginia, facility to upgrade their technical and clinical skills in classes conducted on-site by instructors from nearby George Mason University. The partnership brings the classroom to the workplace and allows nurses to earn master's degrees at no cost. The program, which was started in 2001, is an effective recruiting and retention tool in a highly competitive field that furthers the careers of mature workers while meeting the hospital's need for highly trained nurses.

• Lincoln National Corporation formed a task force in 2004 to design flexible, age-friendly work arrangements for older employees wanting to take longer vacations or work part-time. Mature managers also mentor trainees at the Philadelphia financial services firm.

• St. Mary's Medical Center in Huntington, West Virginia, adjusts pension calculations so that workers can reduce their work schedules in the last few years before retirement without losing any benefits. Betty Napier, a 63-year-old registered nurse in St. Mary's Outpatient Clinic, took advantage of the part-time option to care for her mother from August 2003 to February 2005. Now back full-time, Betty will lose no pension dollars because St. Mary's uses an employee's top five salaried years, not the last five working years, to compute benefits.

St. Mary's also trains retired nurses who want to come back to work and offers them flexible and part-time schedules. Fifty-year-old Ruth McComas, an R.N. and mother of three whose last child was heading off to college, wondered what she would do with herself when the nest was empty. She was thrilled to hear about a new program at St. Mary's. "It sounded exactly like what I was looking for," she says, "a chance to get back into the field I chose twenty-five years ago because I love it." Ruth needed the training because she hadn't worked as an R.N. in twenty-five years. She also wanted to avoid full-time or shift work. "This progressive program allows me to work twenty hours a week," she explains, adding, "The best part is its flexibility. I can pick and choose the hours and the days I wish to work." Ruth sums up her experience with St. Mary's in three simple words: "I love it!"

● MetLife calculates that 30 percent of its workforce of 16,000 people are over 50. The large insurance company also says that one of its most productive agents is 84. All MetLife employees, both full- and part-time, have flexible work schedules and full health benefits, and retirees get health care, too.

● *Your*Encore is an Indianapolis-based agency with a Web site that proclaims: "People don't retire anymore, they just go on to do other things." The agency pairs retired scientists and engineers with temporary consulting jobs at such companies as Boeing and Eli Lilly. Executive Vice President Mike Kostrzewa says the agency has six hundred retirees on its list of available experts and their typical assignment lasts for twenty-one days. "They like to stay connected," he explains, "but on their own terms."

● Scripps Health makes flexibility the watchword for workers in its San Diego health-care network. Two employees in the same job category can share a single position, for example, allowing each to work fewer hours and still maintain skills. Other available options include compressed workweeks, telecommuting, and special accommodations that phase people into retirement. Rather than impose one-size-fits-all programs, Scripps wants its employees to be free to choose whatever works best for them and will go so far as to furnish home office equipment and train telecommuters to use it.

The flexibility has allowed Carolyn Jones, R.N., to take care of her family while putting in twenty-five years of work at Scripps Mercy Hospital Chula Vista. Now, Jones says, she's "considering a staged-retirement schedule so I can begin moving into retirement."

MORE TO BE DONE

The more I want to get something done,
the less I call it work.
—*Richard Bach*

All of these programs are excellent and on the front end of the curve. But they are only the beginning of what can and must be done. To prevent economic disruption, employers, employees (both current and prospective), and the government must move even faster to incorporate and expand on the positive developments that are already under way. Everyone I talk to—members of Congress, union and trade association officials, company executives, academic experts, interested nonprofit leaders, and employees—recognizes the opportunity. And virtually all of them understand the enormous benefit that older workers bring to the workplace and to the nation at large.

But there are still some people in this country who don't get it. They continue to harbor an attitude, a set of wrongheaded stereotypes, about aging. We see it in the entertainment industry, in advertising, in attempts at humor, and in everyday conversation. I believe these attitudes will change as the nation ages and as the 50+ generation dispels the myths and upends the stereotypes. But why wait? Let's rid our national conversation of the misleading characterizations now.

Consider the latest scientific evidence refuting the widespread assumption that aging impairs the brain. At most, studies show only modest declines in our working memory and speed of processing new information. And these limited effects of aging can be offset at little or no cost simply by redesigning training programs to slow the pace and add more discussion time, exercises, and feedback. Other studies have found that mature workers are eager to learn and, when properly trained, can actually outperform younger people. What's more, making training age-friendly doesn't make it less effective for younger workers; if anything, it becomes more effective.

A few years ago, in preparation for our initiative promoting older workers, we decided to find out what employers thought of workers over 50. We learned that employers see people over 50 as:

- *being committed to doing quality work;*
- *getting along well with others;*
- *having solid performance records;*
- *possessing basic skills in reading, writing, and math;*
- *being dependable in a crisis; and*
- *exhibiting loyalty and dedication to the company.*

The only desirable trait that employers thought workers past 50 lacked was a willingness to be flexible about taking on new technology and new tasks. But as we know from newer research cited earlier, mature workers are very willing to learn and certainly have the ability to do so. We see it every day in women such as Barbara Kinzer, who on her first day at Borders didn't even know how to turn on the computer and now manages the company's entire training program. Barbara and millions like her have obviously taken on new tasks and mastered new technology just fine.

If mature workers were ever balky about change and technology, they no longer are. Many boomers, having lived through the computer revolution, are comfortable (although perhaps not as adept as their kids) with cell phones, wi-fi, and all the other tools of fast-changing technology. Given time and exposure, and especially as the computer-savvy boomers age on the job, the technology myth, too, will fade away. When I watch older people zip through their BlackBerry messages while simultaneously talking business on a cell phone, I see the future of the mature workforce.

That future will arrive as competition, not legislation, brings about a complete transformation to an age-friendly economy. Employers, led by the companies mentioned in this chapter, are increasingly recognizing the competitive advantages of hiring, retaining, and retraining mature workers.

At the end of 2005, Towers Perrin, a human resources consulting firm, and AARP released a comprehensive study on the value of older workers. It showed that productivity often makes mature employees far more cost-effective than is generally believed. They are more engaged and more motivated than younger workers to exceed expectations on the job. In addition, the extra per-employee cost of retaining or attracting 50+ workers ranges from negligible to 3 percent in key industries.

Despite these findings, some companies, no doubt, will continue to dispute the value of older workers. However, the shrinking pool of younger workers may soon remove their options, notes Alicia Munnell, director of the Center for Retirement Research at Boston College. Pointing out that "increased employment of older workers seems like a natural solution," Munnell goes on to say that "employers will have to change their hiring and retention policies if they want to attract these highly productive older individuals."

Any list of creative corporate policies and programs should include adjustments in pension rules to put a stop to early-retirement incentives and increase benefits for employees who stay on the job longer. More enlightened government policies, such as incentives for employers to hire older workers and for individuals to continue working, could further an age-friendly vision of work. We also need changes in the tax structure and labor laws and strong enforcement of existing laws against age discrimination, which persists and is on the rise as the nation's workforce ages.

Corporations should also make sure that their younger managers and trainers learn more about dealing realistically and sensitively with older workers—for example, learning to assess productivity in terms of tasks completed rather than hours worked. Questions about whether older workers can report to younger managers are reminiscent of a much-debated issue from another era. Back then the question was whether men would be able to report to women managers. It's a nonissue today. Similarly, questions about whether older workers can report to younger managers are fading fast. The answer is, yes, they can.

Companies large and small should assess their own needs and determine how the aging workforce will affect them and what they can do to retain older workers. At AARP, for example, we have a number of older workers we don't want to lose. To that end, we instituted a phased-retirement program and more flexible work schedules. Other areas employers might consider include:

• Analyzing workforce demographics. How many employees by job description and work unit are nearing retirement, and how will this affect the organization? How hard will it be to replace these employees? What does the market look like in terms of competition for new workers and your best current employees?

• Tracking employee health issues and determining whether they are age-related. Research shows that older workers do cost a little more (even though this is largely offset by their value). Are there ways to address this cost issue, perhaps by helping older employees to head off costly treatments through age-related screening programs like the one at New York Life?

• Helping trainers develop age-friendly teaching methods, such as slower presentations with increased discussion; longer practice sessions; and interactive computer programs to aid learning. All of these methods can be based on a growing body of literature dealing with age-related training coming out of research programs in colleges and universities around the world.

• Conducting preretirement interviews when employees reach a specified age—58, say, or 60. Make it clear that this isn't an effort to push anyone out but rather to explain the options—including continuing to work—and to plan the succession for those who choose to leave. Besides making sure pension plans aren't skewed to encourage early retirement, companies should also consider offering other benefits to workers who delay taking a pension.

• Developing economically feasible and beneficial strategies and options for workers nearing retirement age, such as job sharing, flexible hours, and phased retirement.

Not every problem requires analysis. Sometimes an application of everyday common sense will do. When a utility in Omaha discovered, for example, that its older employees—and some younger ones, too—didn't like driving to work in harsh winter weather, the company set up a van service to transport people for a small fee. Absenteeism dropped dramatically. And when some older employees at an insurance company in Connecticut appeared to resist a company effort to hire disabled people, it wasn't because these workers were prejudiced. It turned out that the company was assigning the disabled individuals to workspaces near the exits and bathrooms of the sprawling building—locations older employees had claimed to meet their own changing needs. The problem was quickly resolved.

As the competition for older workers accelerates, companies will become more creative in devising entirely new approaches to problems. In the evolving workplace, ideas not yet imagined will help make extended work commonplace in the future. For instance, brainstorming sessions with mature workers may show the way to solving such difficult issues as how to help them care for their parents while staying productive on the job. I came to understand the gravity of this issue a few years ago, when AARP cosponsored a workshop on the topic with Fannie Mae. We attracted an overflow audience of human resource professionals from companies and other organizations who came to learn as much as possible about on-site assistance for employees with aging parents.

While employers are doing their best to compete and to create an age-friendly work environment, employees must also do their part by accepting responsibility and taking action to keep themselves employable. I was once invited to speak at a continuing education graduation ceremony at Georgetown University in Washington, D.C., and I was inspired to see so many middle-aged people alongside younger ones who were updating and expanding their knowledge of computers, human resources, management, and other areas. We all must be willing to learn new skills, take on new tasks, and keep up with the latest technology.

It is critical to acknowledge that there is no magic age at which people can no longer work, particularly in a time when brains trump brawn. Productivity, not age, should be the criterion by which our work performance is judged. Octogenarian Paul Rogers is a perfect example and someone I greatly admire. He served as a U.S. congressman from Florida for twenty-four years before leaving the House of Representatives in 1979. He was so instrumental in promoting health through legislation that he was nicknamed "Mr. Health." Since leaving Congress, Rogers has been practicing law and serving many worthy causes. At 85, he isn't slowing down.

As the world of work changes (and for the better), the economy we create, indeed the nation itself, will look very different. More and more people will be considering "retirement" at 72 instead of 62, and as discussed in chapter 3, the term itself is taking on new meaning. "Retired" may one day apply to people who have cut their workload by twenty hours a week and are collecting pensions as well as paychecks.

The payoff for all of us will extend beyond the economists' measure of increased productivity to include measures of quality of life and greater happiness. I'm not campaigning against the pleasures of the leisurely life, merely arguing that continued vitality demands activity, engagement, and the sense of fulfillment that comes from being productive. In his later years, the renowned journalist H. L. Mencken was asked why he stayed at his typewriter. "I go on working for the same reason that a hen goes on laying eggs," Mencken said. "There is in every living creature an obscure but powerful impulse to active functioning. Life demands to be lived."

Most people prefer to remain in their communities as they age, preferably in the homes and apartments where they feel most comfortable. And helping people to stay put is a real boon for the communities as well, because it allows them to benefit from the experience and wisdom their longtime residents can provide. In the next chapter, I discuss the age-friendly living arrangements and transportation options that can make the dream of "aging in place" a reality for most Americans.

five

The Opportunity to Build Livable Communities

For a community to be whole and healthy, it must be based on people's love and concern for each other.
                                                    —*Millard Fuller*

Most of us never think twice about living however we please, driving wherever we want to go, and engaging in whatever community activities interest us. That's par for mainstream living in America. But what happens when the largest group in that mainstream, the 78 million baby boomers, begins to feel the subtle (and not so subtle) currents of age pulling toward a new reality? For those already there, it's a lot to think about.

Most of us realize that life will change, but it need not be all that different—provided we work together to ensure that our needs for age-friendly housing, mobility, and community engagement are met in ways that will benefit not just us but society as a whole. Whatever we can do to make lives work better for people as they age will be of lasting benefit for ourselves and the generations to follow. We're all in this together. What's good for aging Americans will be good for all Americans.

To smooth the transition, however, we need to think ahead. This chapter does that by envisioning not only what our needs will be but also how we as individuals and the nation as a whole can find common cause in easing the aging of the largest population bulge in human history. And as the woman you will meet just ahead learned the hard way, it's much easier and less stressful to prepare before problems overwhelm us.

HOUSING FOR LIFE

Life's a voyage that's homeward bound.
—*Herman Melville*

At 57, Lizbeth Chapman had the rest of her life all figured out. She was a successful one-woman public relations firm, working from her home in Boston. She relied on e-mail to stay in touch with her clients, which meant she had the freedom to do business just about anywhere on earth. Now she'd found her future—a charming 55-year-old cottage in the seaside town of Wellfleet, Massachusetts. Lizbeth packed up her computer and moved to Cape Cod, planning to ease back on her workload gradually and stay in the cottage after she retired.

A wonderful plan—until, shortly after moving, she broke her ankle and had to be fitted with a nonwalking cast. For the next three months, the house, in her words, "became a prison."

Her wheelchair was too big for the doors and could barely squeeze through the halls. She couldn't get into the five-foot-square bathroom, much less turn around to get out. Outside, the wheelchair sank in the gravel driveway, making it impossible for her to navigate between her car and house. And even if she could somehow force the cursed thing to move, she would still encounter three steps up to the front door. Stuck in her chair and trapped inside her home, she had to hire help just to cook a meal—nearly everything in her kitchen was beyond her reach. Often lights were left burning all night because the switches were so hard to reach.

With a lot of help from friends, Lizbeth Chapman muddled along till her ankle healed. But the frustrating experience made her realize that her cottage might well be unlivable as she aged. What to do?

She was lucky. She had the time and money to make the place work for her. In 2005, five years after a broken bone fractured her sense of self-sufficiency, workers tore down the cottage and built a new Greek Revival–style house designed for easy living. The home owner and her architect focused on ways to ensure that Lizbeth could stay put no matter how her physical capabilities changed in succeeding years. "Decisions I made will allow me to live here for the rest of my life," she now says. The one-level house has extrawide halls and doors, an outsized walk-in bathtub, lever-action door handles, lots of open space, easily reachable kitchen appliances, and a paved path to her car.

Her only regret is that she didn't think of all this when she was planning her move to the cottage hideaway. She now knows that her fifties weren't too soon to visualize what her future needs might be.

But Lizbeth Chapman is hardly unique. Millions of us are failing to consider how our housing needs might change and suddenly finding ourselves in the wrong place at the wrong time. The solution is to plan ahead and, if necessary, make your housing physically friendly. Every year at our annual AARP member event, we have just such a house and a similarly designed mobile home on our convention floor. I really enjoy going through them and seeing how cleverly they fit anyone's needs.

And physically friendly housing does not have to mean retirement communities. That is what some people may want, but many others look for generational integration. This is certainly Fran's and my personal preference, rather than living in a community where people are separated into groups based on age. As a nation, we should strive to make homes and communities truly livable for people of all ages and all levels of physical ability. After all, we are dealing with a perfectly normal and inevitable transition from midlife to later stages. This transition need not bring separation.

Right now, though, America is a long way from that ideal. In a recent

AARP study, we examined how well suited the country's current housing stock is to our needs as we grow older. Here's what we found:

- *Only 24 percent of U.S. homes have lever-action door handles.*
- *Just 33 percent have bathroom aids, such as grab bars.*
- *A mere 34 percent of Americans can enter their homes without climbing steps.*
- *Only 37 percent have doors wide enough for wheelchair access.*

Let's consider what those numbers actually mean. For starters, two of every three of us can't get into our current houses without climbing steps. Even a relatively mild disability that affects breathing or walking might force us out of our homes and into some other setting in our later years. And since 76 percent of us live in houses where doors are opened by grasping a knob and turning, increasingly arthritic hands could make us virtual prisoners. Many of us have had a taste of this while recovering from an injury or illness. In my case, being on crutches for a while (including on the New York subway) and also going through hand surgery taught me how tough it can be just to open doors and walk up and down stairs.

As Lizbeth Chapman learned, it's not just rough-and-tumble kids who break bones. Accidents happen to all of us, including our parents and other older relatives. Just suppose your leg were in a cast. How would you navigate that too-high threshold at the entrance to your bathroom, which, at night, might seem like a low hurdle? How would you hobble down the cellar stairs on a broken leg to reset a tripped circuit breaker or shut off a water valve? Could you climb into the attic to check a roof leak? Could you lift a heavy garage door or wield a fire extinguisher? If you were in a wheelchair—and millions of Americans are, due to disability or old age or both—could you retrieve dropped door keys, change a ceiling light, or reach the top shelf in the refrigerator?

Imagine your town snowed in or hit by a hurricane. Would you be secure in a safe haven or trapped in a spiraling disaster? Hurricane Katrina taught us all a lesson about all this. Many of those who didn't make it to safety were older people living at home. Or suppose you lived alone and had a bad fall or suffered a stroke. Could you still get help if you couldn't reach the phone?

These are difficult questions, but increasingly, there are better and better answers. At the White House Conference on Aging last year, we helped sponsor a technology exhibit. It was full of new and improving devices to make older life more secure. Widely available electronic monitors, worn on your wrist or on a pendant around your neck, can summon help at the touch of a button should you or your spouse or parent take a fall. The AgeLab at MIT has developed a "personal smart adviser," a handheld gadget that scans bar codes in the grocery store and compares product ingredients with dietary recommendations from your doctor. They have already tested the prototype with diabetic boomers and their caregivers, and according to Dr. Joe Coughlin, director of the AgeLab, a consumer-products company and a grocery chain are considering putting the "smart adviser" on the market.

One of my favorite MIT projects is the Bio-Suit, for frail people who have trouble getting around. This is an outfit modeled after sleek Olympic track suits that will improve circulation, control body temperature, protect fragile areas such as the knees and hips during falls, and simulate the effects of muscles, actually helping people to stand and walk. As the suit's developer, Dava Newman, put it, "I think they'd certainly like it more than the standard aluminum walker, which is an insult to engineering."

And as for problem spots in our existing houses, many of the changes needed to keep them livable as we grow older are neither extensive nor expensive. Bathroom grab bars, for instance, and lever-action door handles don't require major renovations. Lots of people have already refitted their homes for the years ahead, providing ample experience for others to draw on.

The key is to plan ahead before circumstances put us at risk.

There's no need to move out of our homes, but if we want to and can afford it, smart, visionary builders are offering new homes designed specifically to meet the burgeoning needs of aging Americans.

Rose Gorospe, a 61-year-old nurse, was delighted to find just such a house—age-friendly and brand-new—in Murrieta, California. Constructed with wide doors, a wheelchair-usable kitchen and bathroom, and no steps to climb or thresholds to stumble over, the innovative design won praise from the National Association of Home Builders. Its long list of forward-looking features included drawers in the lower kitchen cabinets instead of shelves, and cabinets under the sink and stovetop that can be converted from storage space to knee space for someone wanting to cook and do dishes while seated.

What's more, the age-friendly features came at a wallet-friendly price: Because the builder started from scratch, the special amenities added only $5,000 to the total cost of construction.

Rose Gorospe hadn't been looking for such a house. "But when I came across this one," she notes, "I fell in love with all the features. I just knew it was ideal for a person my age." Best of all, she now has a home literally built for the ages—a house she can stay in comfortably for the rest of her life without ever feeling she has to move.

And these features aren't appealing only to older people. The disabled, the middle-aged, and young families alike find well-designed houses friendly and convenient.

Builders and home owners typically spend more on a home's public rooms and recreational spaces than they do on private spaces. "But when you get older," according to Susan Mack, an occupational therapist who helped design Rose Gorospe's house, "would you rather have that extra 12 inches in the bathroom or in the wet bar?" As savvy builders come to recognize the changing preferences of a boomer-driven housing market, the wet bar/bathroom trade-off will become a nonissue. Houses will simply be built with features that are particularly useful for people as they get older.

Not everyone wants or can afford a new home. Research over many years always turns up the same statistic: About 85 percent of

Americans don't even want new homes. They just want to stay where they are. Fortunately, there's plenty we can do to get the housing we want, when and where we want it. Building technology and techniques now offer lots of big and small ways to add more usable space and more comfortable configurations to our existing homes—many built for a time when few people gave much thought to age-related livability issues.

Are you one of those people who want to stay put? If so, let's take a moment to walk through your house and spot opportunities for making it more livable. Look at those old wooden double-hung windows: When did you last wrench them open? It's probably best to rip them out. New double-pane casement windows will be expensive up front, but the savings in heating bills will pay for most, if not all, of the extra cost within a relatively short time—and the ease of operation will take a load off your mind and your back. Look at the shower: You may still have separate hot and cold water taps. That wastes water while you may also have to struggle to get a good grip on the hot water knob, shivering while you wait for the right temperature mix. A single-lever mixing handle for the shower is simple, cheap, and efficient. What else? Some of your bookshelves may be nearly unreachable; your clothes closets (admit it) might look like crime scenes. And the attic. Our house, perhaps like yours, has an attic full of stuff we haven't used in years, if not decades. Clutter on or near the steps creates hazards. As for the garage, no one would venture in there without a road map. It's all easily fixable, though. First, toss everything you don't really need or want. For what's left, all sorts of new storage designs and devices are on the market. They can help bring order to chaos, putting things you actually use within safe and easy reach.

Now let's move on to the kitchen. That big pot of water boiling on the stove—you probably lugged it there from the sink. Way too heavy already—and it won't get any lighter a few years from now. For starters, let's get an extra-long faucet sprayer to fill pots while they're on the burner. And all the doorways—probably too narrow for a baby carriage, much less a wheelchair. The old kind of hinges prevent a door from opening as widely as the door frame itself. Newer offset hinges allow a door to swing open all the way, widening the doorway by almost three inches—ample space for a wheelchair or even a small piano. It's a minor fix with a major effect. You even use the old screw holes.

The reason to make such changes now, before you need them, is that you not only get your house ready for the years ahead, allowing you to stay put, but you also update the place for better living immediately. Whatever new features you install will almost certainly be technologically superior to what you've been living with (and maybe putting up with) for many years.

The Home Depot and AARP have partnered to provide information in all The Home Depot stores across the country on modifying homes for easier living. For boomers, it presents a good opportunity to improve the homes of their parents or other older relatives and friends. And of course, this is a good time to modify your own home. In short, fix now, enjoy now, and live happily thereafter.

Towns and cities full of updated houses mean better living for entire communities. We have the potential for a revolutionary breakthrough in all of this, a step toward a more livable America.

Most of these improvements require relatively modest outlays of time and money. And even major alterations that call for a contractor can be affordable with advance planning. In Houston, for instance, it costs about $5,000 to $6,000 to convert a bathtub to an accessible shower, $875 to fit the shower with an antiscald valve, $1,000 to widen a door and move the light switch, and $5,000 to install a stair glide on staircase treads to carry a seated passenger up or down a flight.

I grew up in a house with basement stairs and bedrooms on the second floor. When my parents got older, they had a lot of trouble with stairs. Our family decided to try the stair glide and see if it worked. Not only did it get my parents up and down stairs they otherwise could not have climbed, but it also let them enjoy a number of additional years in their home.

It's smarter for 40- and 50-somethings to anticipate any possibilities and make gradual changes than to wait to be hit by a large expense all at once. Most of us can find some resources for remodeling. At last count, 80 percent of Americans over 50 owned their own homes and 67 percent of this group were free of mortgage debt. If we act, we will be rewarded for our foresight—with better living now and a higher selling price later should we choose to move. For the most part, house values often rise with such improvements.

Some state governments are willing to lend a hand for home improvements. For example, Georgia and Virginia both offer state tax credits to disabled people who make changes in their houses that let them go on living there. And since 1999, when the U.S. Supreme Court mandated that states help disabled people stay in their communities and out of institutions, at least four more states—Indiana, New Hampshire, North Dakota, and Washington—have started funding home modifications. The court decision also prompted the U.S. Department of Housing and Urban Development to offer home-improvement grants. This makes sense from a government standpoint, since it is a lot less expensive to help people stay at home than to provide institutional care.

Safe, affordable, livable housing in our country tends to be a personal and family issue. However, government has a role to play as well. For example, many older people, and even some boomers, have equity in their homes but not much in the way of income or other assets. Rising real estate taxes can present a big problem. Some government relief can help people stay in their homes when they otherwise might have to sell them. This is an important issue that comes up time and time again in public opinion polls.

There are lots of other housing issues for which citizen advocacy is needed. Although they tend to know it, we must remind our elected representatives and support them in acting, so that quality of life is sustained by keeping people in their own homes, where they can stay connected to family, friends of all ages, and familiar surroundings.

At the state and local level, we can advocate for building and zoning regulations that promote both age-friendly new housing and older-home renovations. In Georgia, for example, a coalition of home builders and advocates developed an EasyLiving Home™ program that includes features to provide easy access to the home and easy passage and use within the home. These features include a step-free entrance with a threshold no more than one-half inch high, a minimum of thirty-two inches of clear passage space for every interior door on the main floor, and no less than one bedroom, a kitchen, some entertainment area, and at least one full bathroom, all on the main floor.

To make houses friendly to disabled visitors, Florida has long required a minimum twenty-nine-inch door opening for at least one residential bathroom in every new home to assure basic accessibility. The most extensive laws of this type are in Pima County, Arizona, and Bolingbrook, Illinois. They require a zero-step entrance, wide interior doors, and several other access features in all new single-family homes. Together, the two communities provide more than 10,000 "visitable" homes.

Another approach is to subsidize the visitability requirement for housing through state or local funds. Georgia does this by offering a tax credit to persons with disabilities for including certain features (such as a no-step entrance and reinforced bathroom walls) in a new home or in retrofitting an existing home. Virginia offers a tax credit to anyone, regardless of disability, for similar features that are added to an older home. Another idea is to revoke rules that discourage shared housing units or "mother-in-law" apartments. In addition, we can promote innovations such as community information banks, which help people who want to renovate find financing or funding as well as qualified builders.

At the federal level, we can work with Congress to provide tax breaks or low-interest loans to help low-income home owners renovate. We also need to mandate more aging-in-place features in subsidized housing units; to back federal incentives to encourage builders, both public and private, to develop innovative designs; and to provide adequate government funding for a range of affordable housing options.

State and federal budgets are tight, and this is not a call for a massive new government housing program. Nor is it a big spending plan to "solve" the problems presented by the boomer population bulge. Quite the contrary: To keep our nation healthy and strong, and to afford the aging of America, we must advocate commonsense, cost-effective ideas for helping Americans stay right where they are as they age—living as independently as possible in the homes and communities they know best.

MOBILITY FOR LIFE

> Our community is the place where we as older
> individuals can be most effective. In no other
> place can we gain so much cooperation and
> win so many champions and supporters.
> —*Dr. Ethel Percy Andrus*

Let's imagine that we have all found a way to buy and/or modify our homes and those of our parents for age-friendly living. We are now set for life, right? Well, not quite. Living the good life as we age means more than having a smartly designed and constructed roof over our heads. We also need mobility outside our homes. We have to be able to get out and around and to stay connected to our communities. And that is one of the toughest obstacles to aging in place.

So much of personal independence derives from our ability to move freely around our communities. America has often been called an automobile society, and it's largely true. To find yourself, for whatever reason, cut off from mainstream mobility, no longer part of America's freewheeling ease, is especially frustrating—and age-ifying—because, in the United States, there's usually no getting from here to there without a car. If we can't get to our jobs or volunteer activities . . . if we can't visit friends, go walking or go to church, or run down to the hardware store for screws to fix the screen door . . . if we can't get to the dentist, the hospital, or the supermarket on our own, our lives become hostage to the convenience of those we must rely on to transport us. Our cherished quality of life is diminished along with a vital piece of our independence.

One of our AARP board members, Dr. Byron Thames, tells of a nurse who retired at 62. She and her 65-year-old husband moved to what they thought was their ideal retirement home in an idyllic little town with just one traffic light. It was charming, quiet, and—unbeknownst to them—a threat to their mobility. The woman had a touch of arthritis, nothing serious, and her husband had some macular degeneration but could still drive—a necessity for reaching the closest commercial center, and doctor, eight miles away.

Within two years, though, ideal and idyllic were trumped by isolation. He had to stop driving, and she was having a hard time getting in and out of the car. Far away from family and friends, they had no recreation, no social life, and no way even to get to the food store. Byron and his wife, Judy, visited their friends on weekends and brought groceries, but the shut-ins had to make do without any extras between visits. The nurse began to put on weight, worsening her arthritis. Her husband went from having a couple of drinks before dinner to frequent cocktails throughout the day. The couple ended up having to sell their house and move to a town with buses, taxis, and easy access to physicians, stores, and other necessities.

The Bill of Rights says nothing specific about mobility, but in a culture founded by adventurous immigrants and dominated by car-driving commuters, the right to move about at will verges on the sacred. We identify with our cars, valuing them as quasi-relatives in the most automotive culture on earth. And we take it to extremes.

Outside our cities and even inside some urban areas, public transportation is often an afterthought. In many areas, existing public transit is geared to rush-hour commuters, not off-hour travelers. For many without cars, or without the ability or interest to drive, catching a local bus is a time-consuming, even hit-or-miss proposition. In rural areas, public transportation may simply not exist. And for the millions who have to depend on friends, relatives, or volunteers to drive them where they need to go, it can be very difficult.

As people age, they often find it harder to drive, especially at night. I'm not just talking about the elderly but about today's boomers as well. People want their cars and aren't going to give them up easily. Those with driving impediments try to compensate in many ways, such as driving only at certain hours or avoiding high-traffic areas. But this only takes us so far. What can be done? The first step, which is starting to happen but needs a push, is an enlightened conversation about public transportation and mobility. Urban sprawl and traffic congestion is getting so bad in so many American cities that this alone is bringing about debate, never mind the issue of older drivers. At its most fundamental level, we need better, more decent options for getting from here to there. Boomers have considerable clout as voters and consumers to push for useful, affordable alternatives.

Eventually, though, we won't be able to ignore the noncar transportation problem. The numbers won't let us: By 2020, a projected 6 million Americans aged 75 and over will not be able to drive. That's slightly more than the populations of Chicago and Houston combined. And that doesn't count those who will have restricted their driving to some degree. We need to keep these people in social contact and prevent the isolation that can come from being stuck at home.

Figuring out how to move so many people, day in and day out, is a huge task. Volunteer drivers already play an important role, and this will grow. For instance, Faith in Action—an interfaith volunteer initiative with local coalitions that help people with long-term care needs remain independent—does a lot of this (AARP recruits volunteers for them). This is also a big business opportunity for entrepreneurs who are innovative enough to come up with profitable alternatives to driving, especially in rural, suburban, and exurban areas where mass transit is now considered impractical. Too few customers over too big distances, the experts say. And yet local trains existed and even thrived in those same areas fifty or sixty years ago. And what about the thousands of school buses that sit empty and idle for hours every day? We have lots of room for creative collaboration, serving older and younger passengers to the benefit of all, but we need to get moving on these big issues.

There are assorted ideas worth discussing in any local or national debate. In outlying areas, for example, care providers often maintain fleets of vans to transport clients, usually for limited uses and to single destinations—a visit to the adult day-care center, say, or the physical therapy clinic. Perhaps such organizations can pool their vans, creating a network that clients could call to take them to a range of destinations. Sure, there are cost, rules, priorities, and liability issues. But if more people weigh in, creative thinkers and activists will find a way around these roadblocks and others. The Atlanta Regional Commission, for example, is experimenting with driving pools. The commission sells discounted vouchers to people who are at least 60 and can't drive. These vouchers allow them to hire someone they know to drive them around rather than depending on a formal government program. Both the people using the vouchers and the commission find that the $16.79 average cost to users is well worth it. MIT AgeLab director Dr. Joe Coughlin foresees another solution—the emergence of "car clubs." As he describes the idea, people who no longer drive may pool their resources to buy a car, then share it with a younger driver who serves as the chauffeur. This could be especially attractive in college towns filled with graduate students who can't afford their own cars.

Some urban and suburban communities have set up fleets of small, low-rise buses that travel on flexible schedules between residential areas and commercial centers. In some rural and exurban areas, widely scattered residents can telephone "dial-a-ride" to be picked up by a small bus or van that arrives at a prearranged time. In places such as Country Meadows, a retirement community near Pittsburgh, where my father lived for a while, there always seems to be van service to get around. These solutions to the mobility issue are good ones, but we need much more. And to make this work, citizens and politicians must work together.

We might take a cue from European planners. Urban communities in both Britain and Denmark, for example, have found that the simplest and least expensive solution to transporting older or disabled people is simply to subsidize their use of commercial taxis. Europe is also ahead of the United States in the use of Flexcars or Zipcars as a way of providing support for those who do drive or who have friends willing to drive them. In this system, vehicles are available in city and suburban neighborhoods for short-term rental by customers who have signed up for the service. People of all ages can call the central office, be directed to a car parked in their neighborhood, and use their service-provided electronic ignition cards to take off for an hour or two to shop, dine with friends, or pick up someone at the airport.

We also have another big window of opportunity in the area of mobility—making cars easier to operate for all who are still able to drive and at the same time making us better drivers so that we can continue to do it safely as we age. There are refresher courses in safe-driving techniques that are both inexpensive and effective. Lots of organizations offer them, including the AARP volunteer program, Driver Safety, which puts about 700,000 people through the course every year. Bentley Lipscomb, our AARP Florida state director, aims to enroll the millions of older drivers on Florida highways. Helping them improve their driving skills, and to know when to be tested and when to put down the car keys, is critical for everyone involved.

Physical fitness is an essential part of leading an independent and healthy life for people of all ages. The lack of physical fitness can slow the impairment of reflexes, flexibility, vision, and hearing—all critical to safe driving. In addition, certified driving rehabilitation specialists (CDRSs) could help people recover from acute episodes that impair their driving. One key issue is testing drivers to be sure they have adequate, unimpaired abilities. This is a controversial issue among many older people, who fear losing their licenses. We need to help people retain their driving competencies to the maximum extent possible, and competent drivers should retain their driving privileges regardless of whether they are 18 or 88. But when driving is no longer feasible, other options for getting around should be available.

When it comes to making cars easier to drive, automakers have huge opportunities to compete for boomers and older customers— who together are the overwhelming majority of Americans. The fact is that most cars are physically designed for people under 30, who have great eyes, quick reflexes, and well-oiled joints. When you hit 35 or so, it typically gets harder to leap nimbly aboard a high-riding SUV or extract yourself from a low-lying sedan, much less a sports car. It always interests me to see the car ads in our magazine. These manufacturers know that the 50+ crowd has the money to buy and also must be catered to in style, comfort, and safety.

Our U.S. highways also need improvement. Poor highway lighting befuddles drivers of all ages; better lighting would benefit everyone by cutting down on accidents. And have you noticed how bewildering traffic signs have become? There is a no-left-turn sign right outside our office that may or may not be operating at different times of the day. It's impossible to tell. At too many intersections and on too many high-speed expressways, there is a mind-boggling profusion of signs. It's scary to see someone trying to back up along a highway shoulder, but it's easy to miss a desired exit. The size, lettering, and location of traffic signs ought to be rethought. More left-turn lanes with protected turn signals would reduce risk on busy streets, as would traffic-calming techniques such as narrowed streets, medians, and nonprogressive traffic signals. Improved highway safety for everyone is clearly needed for individual drivers as we age, helping to keep us mobile longer and connected to life.

As the population ages, the absence of comprehensive solutions in this country for both drivers and nondrivers is a frustrating fact of life. We can all weigh in because so much of this is local and regional, and citizen activism can make a big difference. But it is also a national problem, so that we need to work at all levels to create needed change.

Of course, the mobility gap, while widespread, is not a universal irritant. Big-city dwellers with access to mass transit systems (Chicagoans, Bostonians, New Yorkers, and Washingtonians, for example) have less personal stake in this issue. What their urban areas offer is an incentive to stay put and age in place, enjoying the cultural riches and variety of a great city. And more and more city people are deciding to do just that. They want to stay near friends and relatives and in familiar surroundings. They decide that there is no better place to be as they get on with life. Fran and I raised our kids in Washington, D.C., with the easy subway system and the riches of the Smithsonian, but we have also lived in New York (and nearby, in Hoboken) and Atlanta. Big-city life definitely has its attractions.

Indeed, as some of us age and seek greater mobility, we are making what once seemed an unlikely return trip from the suburbs back to the central city. Since the mid-1990s, this backflow has grown from a trickle to a stream in cities such as Los Angeles, Chicago, and Austin. "Cities aren't going to replace the Sun Belt," according to Mark Muro, a senior policy analyst at the Brookings Institution, who is studying urban migration. But especially for people with above-average incomes, "city life is an increasingly popular option," he says.

Take George Keller, 66, a retired Army physicist, and his wife, Alice. They were "just flat tired of getting in the car to go anywhere," he confesses. So they sold their home in suburban Maryland and moved to a condominium in downtown Asheville, North Carolina, an increasingly popular small city with public transit and a vibrant urban life within easy walking range. They are putting far fewer miles on their car, Keller notes, and it would be even less "if we didn't have grandchildren in Maryland." For many years I have been making annual baseball bets with an old friend, Dick Murray, who also chose Asheville for his "retirement." I can certainly see the advantages of life in a smaller city.

The lure is even more tempting when the small city is part of an older person's roots. I remember a high school reunion Fran attended a few years ago in Missoula, Montana. Most of her classmates who had moved away (many to California) declared that they wanted to come home to Missoula at some point. And why not? It's a wonderful town.

Still others are moving to age-friendly planned communities where they can walk from their new homes to centralized communal facilities and be driven in community vans to more distant stores and entertainment. My brother, Jerry, and his wife, Donna, live in one—Sun City Hilton Head, near Bluffton, South Carolina. These are very nice, relaxing communities, but just as with city life, they aren't for everyone.

Another idea is slowly gaining momentum: Developers in some areas are creating walkable new communities specifically designed to avoid urban sprawl and foster easy mobility. Residents of all ages are welcomed, and the surroundings make it easy to meet others and form neighborhood bonds. Unlike conventional suburbs, the King Farm Community in Rockville, Maryland, for instance, has small house lots that serve to shorten walking distances and streets that are bordered by wide sidewalks. Parks and common areas are scattered throughout the community, and a free shuttle bus takes people from their homes to the Washington subway, to the commercial area, and to extensive recreation facilities. In this livable place for all, King Farm's residents remain part of a mixed community while also retaining their mobility as they age.

The transformation to many or all of the age-friendly solutions described in this chapter won't happen overnight and won't be easy. Assuring mobility will be even harder than redesigning housing, because the first is a public issue, the second more of a personal choice.

Difficult as they may be, however, these changes are going to happen, for two reasons. The first is dollars, and the second is demography. First, money drives entrepreneurship and business change, and the boomer segment—though not all boomers, of course—has the financial clout to alter the marketplace and attract new products and services. (I discuss this in more detail in the next chapter.) Second, demographics—the size of the boomer population, as consumers, citizens, voters, and activists—make it necessary and create social and political pressures across the entire country that these challenges be met.

Mobility is the ticket that will enable 78 million boomers to avoid isolation and remain connected to their communities as they age. The ability to move about with relative ease and stay in touch with people and places will help maintain mental and physical well-being. For that reason, mobility is likely to be a big inducement for aging in place. Why leave a community where you are a part of its life?

But that question supposes that you still feel welcome and engaged, and you may not. So the case for aging in place must move beyond better housing and mobility to confront community attitudes. They can be either the biggest hurdle or the biggest breakthrough in the effort to integrate the generations. In the next segment, I make suggestions for turning all American communities, large and small, into places where people of every age can be engaged and productive.

ENGAGEMENT FOR LIFE

Only connect.
—*E. M. Forster*

Humans are social creatures who crave contact with others. Isolation can make us physically and mentally ill. Interaction with parents, children, pals, pets, neighbors, churches, jobs, teammates, and clubs forms the bonds that keep us alive and healthy. We don't even have to live near one another, with today's communications. I stay in touch with two old friends by e-mail and phone, and we see one another about twice a year, at college sports events.

AARP chapters provide good examples of bonds that improve lives. A while ago I was participating in a community event in Buffalo, New York, and chapters were sending members by bus from all over upstate

New York. It was a cold winter day (seventeen degrees in Buffalo) and the chapter participants coming from Binghamton had a problem; their bus windshield defroster stopped operating. As ice formed on the windshield, a decision had to be made. The folks on the bus voted to press on to Buffalo, while the bus driver wanted to turn back. (Of course the driver won.) That's community spirit and true (though cold) grit. Engagements and activities like this summon our best instincts, pump up our self-esteem when we succeed in helping others, and give structure and purpose to our days.

When we are isolated and disengaged, we lose sight of our better selves and fail to become all that we can be. We've all probably worried about a relative or neighbor who, for whatever reason, pulled back from companionship and society. Engagement is the Miracle-Gro of human existence. When our hearts are nourished, we nourish in return. We cherish loved ones, remember birthdays, and perform other kindnesses for no other reason than love and friendship. We keep old friends and cultivate new ones. We give to charities and volunteer our time for good causes. We dash off letters to editors and legislators and get involved in local politics. We feel obliged to serve on school boards and community planning committees. We care, and it shows: Our activism strengthens the civic vitality of our communities, and the positive emotion our involvement engenders fortifies our own immune systems. We feel healthy; therefore we are. And this makes a great difference in American society.

Of course, life never stops changing, and no one escapes hard times. In midlife or later, children leave, parents die, friends move, couples divorce, businesses fail, or illness intervenes.

But we offset these difficulties with the emotional energy that flows from interacting with others. That is precisely why engagement isn't just a good thing; it's the main thing. All of us need to cultivate it throughout our lives.

Some people seem to be born with a gift for friendship and a life-long habit of staying in touch, no matter the changes brought on by passing years. Friends they met in strollers may now be in wheelchairs, but they keep exchanging letters and proudly reporting their children's and grandchildren's achievements.

These people have drawers full of family photos, more memories than they'll ever have time to slip into albums. They own huge address books stuffed with old names they will never erase. They constantly add new items to large calendars already crammed with coming events, visits, and trips to anticipate. They read new books, see new movies, and are quite likely to have descended on their congressperson's local or Washington office at least once. Some, like my mother-in-law, left vivid stories of visits to foreign places and people they met.

I remember my very first alumni event, when I saw the oldest of Penn's gray-haired alumni marching at the front of the reunion parade. They were proud and fully engaged.

Such alumni even attend minireunions whenever the opportunity arises. I have, too. A few years ago my college football coach, John Stiegman, had an informal reunion for his players. My buddy Don Challis and I went, along with a number of other players, some coaches, and a sportswriter who had covered the team for *The Philadelphia Inquirer*. We looked at one another—a cardiologist, an actor, several financial types, lots of businesspeople—and we all thought, So this is how it turns out. It turned out pretty well. The idea, of course, is not to disengage, never to lose contact with one another.

In a nation of people largely accustomed to relocating throughout our lives and careers, long-lasting engagement is a great joy, providing a wonderful zest for life.

There is a paradox here. As we grow older, we can be at the same time engaged and yet somewhat disconnected. We are more likely to be firmly attached to our communities by virtue of home ownership, marriage, and a kind of informal seniority. (My father, for instance, lived in the same town for eighty-eight years.) Our children and perhaps grandchildren are locally involved. We've managed community events and served on town boards. We are engaged; we are known.

Yet despite these community ties, some connections can begin to fray as we age. Our kids suddenly live and work half a continent away, or even farther. We may begin scaling back our own work schedules, taking us out of the company loop. Close friends move to warmer places. Others pass away. Health problems arise, perhaps nibbling away at our savings. It's time for a change. But what should it be?

Some people opt for retirement communities, like those being organized by many colleges. They can be real estate ventures, to be sure, but they also have the purpose of keeping retired alumni engaged and active. College towns are lively places, offering sports and cultural events, as well as the opportunity to learn new things. Most college-linked communities offer residents discounted tuition or the chance to attend classes at no cost. I met a man at a college event who had moved from Boston to Philadelphia just to audit courses, free of charge. There are plenty of opportunities to serve as volunteers, museum docents, and the like. School spirit is usually ageless; just look at Helen Bastian. At The Village at Penn State, a mile north of the campus in State College, Pennsylvania, the 84-year-old alumna shows her spirit by regularly wearing Penn State blue and Nittany Lion paw-print earrings. My mother-in-law rooted for the women's basketball team at the University of Montana (the "Lady Griz") virtually her entire life.

For most aging Americans, though, the preferred option is not a planned community—on a college campus or anywhere else. What most of us want, as I noted earlier, is to stay put in our own homes. And at least one group of Boston neighbors has found a way to do that while still enjoying the benefits of a "retirement" community. They have banded together to form a virtual retirement community called Beacon Hill Village.

It all started when a dozen longtime residents of Beacon Hill, in their fifties and sixties, got together and agreed that they would prefer their charming urban neighborhood to any independent-living or continuing-care community in the suburbs. But they knew they would need help as they aged. Beacon Hill is an area of leafy streets, steep hillsides, uneven brick sidewalks, and narrow stairways. Its gracious old homes have been mostly converted to apartments, but only a few have elevators. It isn't an easy place to live as residents grow older.

The founders of Beacon Hill Village envisioned a kind of cooperative in which members could remain at home but still get the assistance they needed or wanted, from grocery delivery and handyman service to cultural outings, exercise classes, and home health care. They pooled their resources and put up $95,000 to start, and two years later Beacon Hill Village launched its first membership drive.

The virtual community now has some 300 members who each pay $550 a year ($750 for a household) to cover the services they use. Thanks to donors, including the Boston Foundation, people with incomes of less than $45,000 can get subsidized memberships at $100 a year ($150 per household). The Village staff, led by executive director Judy Willett, negotiates discounts for housekeeping and concierge services, electricians and plumbers, catered meals, and home health services (from the Senior Health Practice at famed Massachusetts General Hospital). The staff also organizes events ranging from a moonlight sail on the Charles River to seminars, concerts, and lectures by Boston authors and academicians. "We're providing them the support to live fully and with quality of life," Willett explains.

One member, Miriam Huggard, has lived on Beacon Hill since 1931. Now 92, she relies on the Village to take her to the supermarket and carry her groceries back to her second-floor apartment. "It's a security blanket for me," says Huggard, a retired nurse. "Otherwise, I'd have to move. I couldn't possibly do all the things they provide." When Ms. Huggard took a bad fall, for example, the staff arranged for an aide to sleep over after she returned from the hospital. The volunteer neighbor-to-neighbor program sent her regular visitors, and the Village-approved caterer provided meals at a discount. "I never feel stranded," she says.

Beacon Hill Village is a model experiment in helping people remain in their homes and engaged with their communities. Observers from as far away as Japan have expressed interest in replicating it. But even without setting up nonprofit membership organizations, we can find ways to achieve similar goals. One variation on Beacon Hill is a phenomenon known as NORCs (naturally occurring retirement communities), which develop by default as residents gradually age in ordinary mixed neighborhoods and younger people move elsewhere. These places can evolve in tandem with the changing needs and growing political clout of the older residents who stay put.

Engaged independent living probably begins for most people with good neighbors—special people entrusted to keep an eye on us and our homes, to check when something odd or worrisome occurs, to take in the mail, receive packages, and monitor the furnace when we're away. Poet Robert Frost famously wrote that good fences make good neighbors, but he was not old at the time. As we age, many of us don' t want any barriers to keep our neighbors from dropping by. We understand that neighboring is basic to keeping communities safe and people engaged. Our neighbors for the past twenty-eight years, the Lazorchicks, keep an eye out for us, and we for them. And in a wonderful stroke of good fortune, my son, daughter-in-law, and two grandsons live on the other side of us. Talk about good neighbors.

Besides neighbors, most people have a social network of friends of varying ages who can be relied on for informal contact, emotional support, recommendations for service providers, and practical help, such as when newspapers need to be taken in or a prescription picked up. As people grow older, their social circle may shrink but may also become more intimate; the help provided stays constant or even increases. And for the helpers and the helped alike, the circle's relationships and companionship are crucial to feeling connected, secure, and in control.

A second level of engagement involves membership in one of the many organizations—religious, professional, civic, or political—that enrich American life and mediate between citizens and their leaders. It has been argued that boomers are not joiners (Harvard professor Robert D. Putnam wrote a book with this thesis, called *Bowling Alone: The Collapse and Revival of American Community*). But nearly 80 percent of people over 50 belong to at least one organization, and one out of four belong to more than one. Organizations give their members an identity, a sense of purpose, goals to accomplish, and continuing social contacts and influence that keep them engaged and connected with the world around them.

In his classic work, *Democracy in America,* French historian Alexis de Tocqueville observed back in 1835 that our country's liberty derived largely from the vitality of its voluntary organizations. It is hard to imagine today's America without millions of joiners—people who gain fulfillment at some level as part-time advocates, fund-raisers, veterans, trustees, political campaigners, lay ministers, kids' coaches and mentors, and volunteer firefighters.

But intense engagement tends to plateau at middle age and fall off beyond 65 or so. Older Americans have enormous political impact, because some two-thirds of those over 65 tend to follow political events and vote on a regular basis. But fewer of them remain active campaigners as they age, turning over their organizing lists to younger citizens. Even so, communities are considerably more livable for everyone when people of all ages are publicly involved in community affairs. The experience and wisdom gained from decades of living and doing helps communities avoid repeating old mistakes and making new ones. I recall being asked to speak to a group of professionals at a foundation. "What shall I talk about?" I asked the person who invited me. "Just talk about yourself," he said. "You've made lots of mistakes in your career. It should be interesting and amusing." It's true; mistakes can be good teachers.

So how can community and organization leaders make sure that these important voices of experience are not lost to them? That requires creative thinking. I think about it all the time at AARP. At the community level, it can certainly include enhancing livability by promoting inclusiveness, safety, and the amenities that make engagement possible. Walking trails and sidewalks with benches are good examples. We were promoting physical activity among older people in Richmond, Virginia, and a group of our volunteers mapped out a 150-square-block section of the east end of the city for improved walking and biking. Many of the retired residents who studied the maps quickly identified poor walking patterns between two elementary schools and many missing sidewalks near the area's hospital. They also identified two five-point intersections that were challenging to both young and elderly pedestrians. These improvement goals were presented to community residents and separately to community organizations and city committees. The results were incorporated into the city's redevelopment plans for that district of the city, and new signs were put up to identify walking routes to a neighborhood park. In addition, the councilwoman for this district requested and was given $50,000 from the City Council for a "walkability" audit of her entire district. And the schools are using the maps to look into "Safe Routes to School."

In 2003, I was honored to receive the Porter Prize from the University of Pittsburgh Graduate School of Public Health. It included a very nice award—$10,000. We put that money to work by donating it to the Allegheny Trail Alliance, with half of the fund set aside for Friends of the Riverfront. They use volunteers to landscape and maintain the walking and bike trails within the city. And to add a contribution of our own, AARP in Pennsylvania recruited its members as volunteers to help with the landscaping and maintenance. They love it because it keeps them active and engaged and out in the fresh air. Older urban communities might follow New York City's lead by razing abandoned buildings and creating vest-pocket parks and community gardens. Gardens, in particular, trigger creative talent, attract volunteers, and can become informal social centers for all ages.

The best mixed-use development puts parks, entertainment, healthcare facilities, senior centers, and clusters of shops and professional offices in close proximity to residential areas. But no matter how well placed the facilities and amenities, people of any age are reluctant to leave their homes if they don't feel safe and secure. So communities have to work with law enforcement and neighborhood groups to improve security for everyone, enlisting as many people as possible in community service.

To keep all age-groups engaged in community activities, officials should make it easy for citizens to meet at community events and social activities, to volunteer for causes, and to take part in discussing community issues and decision making. In Montgomery County, Maryland, where I live, there is a lively and important community debate under way about housing density. Oftentimes the devil is in the details. For instance, the settings where people gather—libraries, community and recreation centers, parks, and public spaces in town offices—must be well designed and comfortable, so they are places where people like to go and where casual conversations are possible.

Beyond making settings inviting, something worthwhile must happen in them if social contacts are to be fostered. Communities can and do sponsor any number of activities ranging from special-interest clubs to farmers' markets, cultural events, and walking groups. The list is limited only by community interests and imagination and by the willingness of volunteers to be involved. Schools and nonprofit organizations provide plenty of opportunities for community service and volunteer activity, often publicized through local newspapers and broadcast media. People often relate to a specific issue or local problem, especially busy boomers who want to take something on, get it done, and move on. Leaders have to make it easy for organizations to recruit new members, hold meetings in the community, and engage their members in active service.

I talked earlier about the need to keep people from becoming socially isolated. Since everyone isn't mobile and many people are confined to their homes, we need to focus on the range of home programs and services that are available. When possible, it is important to get people out the door and down the street. Within the Meals On Wheels program, there is debate about whether delivering certain kinds of meals actually keeps people at home when otherwise they would go out.

As in every other facet of modern life, the Internet is an essential part of social contact and engagement. Its vast resources of information, chat rooms, blogs, and communication by e-mail with distant friends and relatives can wonderfully extend and reinforce efforts to keep people engaged. Many baby boomers are computer-literate, and the coming years will surely see an explosion of online activities and services directed their way. People older than the boomers are the fastest-growing segment of Internet users, many presumably getting their start by e-mailing grandchildren. Both at home and in care and community centers, computers and technology of all sorts will keep us engaged not just in our own communities but also in the wide world beyond. Navigating the complex tangles of health care, long-term care, and other intricacies of American life is not easy, for any-one of any age. This is an opportunity as well as a problem. Now is the time to develop friendly systems on the Net—perhaps using volunteers as well as information technology to help people find their way through these complexities.

Age-friendly housing, mobility, and increased social engagement will require time, energy, and money, as well as a continuing commitment from all of us to make America a more livable place. There will also be enormous cost savings in keeping people independent and living at home whenever possible.

To make these good things happen, we truly need to embrace a new American ideal of livable communities. Only then will we be able to rouse citizen and political support for creating the necessary change. It won't happen overnight; rather, it will take years of patient, determined effort. That's why we need to start now.

The case for livability will be made, and won, by the growing ranks of Americans who are discovering that aging isn't someone else's issue. It's everyone's. And boomers and their older fellow citizens have the weight, both in the marketplace and in the voting booth, to persuade the rest of the country that livability is an issue that should concern all of us. In the end, livable communities will make our national community a far better place for everyone.

six

The Opportunity to Change the Marketplace

The greatest obstacle to discovery is not ignorance,
but the illusion of knowledge.

—*Daniel Boorstin*

Stereotypes usually contain at least a kernel of truth. And once a stereotype takes root and gets applied to a whole group of people, it is very hard to reverse.

Take aging, for instance. Seventy-five or even fifty years ago, people aged more rapidly than they do today. Pick up an Agatha Christie mystery, many of which were written in the 1930s and 1940s, and invariably you will encounter a doddering "old" soul in his or her sixties. Poor, frail, and powerless was how older people were often seen back then—and many Americans did fit the bill. And it wasn't all that long ago that a study of children's attitudes elicited the words "sad, tired, and mean" from a young girl asked to describe how she would feel when she got old. Of course, she was only mimicking the stereotypical attitude passed on by her elders.

Today, however, such images, and the realities that underlie them, are changing fast in many, but not all, sectors of our society. Leading the way is the American marketplace, where there is money to be made (and lost) based on how companies portray and market to a vast population of healthy, active, fun-loving people with enough disposable income to enjoy a meal out, not to mention a vacation or the latest electronic gadget. A few savvy marketers of goods and services are way ahead in the race to appeal to the 50+ market, some are just hitting their stride, while still others are barely out of the starting blocks. But the race is definitely on, simply because no preceding generation has matched today's 50+ crowd for its ability to contribute to society, *including as consumers.*

Indeed, long-held negative notions like the old-fogy stereotype are crumbling under the combined weight of demographics and dollars. Products and services designed specifically to attract the 50-and-over crowd, which has never been shy about demanding what it wants, are multiplying—all to the good of society at large.

Take Sam Farber and his successful Copco Housewares company, for example. Farber abandoned retirement in 1990, when he realized that a mild case of arthritis was making kitchen chores difficult for his wife, Betsey. After consulting with consumers, chefs, retailers, gerontologists, and designers, Farber came up with Good Grips, a line of tools that ease household tasks and boast a smart, ageless design.

Opportunities like this are everywhere, and new products and services aimed at meeting the wants and needs of people 50+ are being introduced every day. Other offerings are being adapted or tweaked to appeal to this fast-growing market. All this works to everyone's advantage. We have more choices, more companies seeking our business, and more competitive prices.

Sure, there will always be a youth market and a yearning for youth, but recent trends are proving that that market is a dwindling one. Peter Drucker, the late, great management thinker, aptly sized up the American marketplace when he reminded his audience of the "old rule that the population group that is both the biggest and growing fastest determines the mindset and the mood . . . the fastest-growing age-group is 55-plus." The changing demographic and the lifestyles of older Americans are convincing marketers that consumer demands are shifting and that age is just a number. And this is not the first time the marketplace and other elements of society have had to scurry to catch up with shifting demographics.

> At heart the boomers were consumers,
> not revolutionaries.
>
> —*Steve Gillon*

When Kathleen Casey Kirschling was born one second after midnight on January 1, 1946, at St. Agnes Hospital in South Philadelphia, who knew that she would be the first of 78 million babies classified as the boomers? Or that her brand-new life would one day read like a synopsis of her generation's optimism, activism, and ability to reinvent itself? Kirschling was profoundly affected by the assassination of President John F. Kennedy and by the Vietnam War. She married early, got divorced, and then remarried—happily so the second time. A health-education professional who "perceived health as an area that was good for you because it was more holistic," Kirschling went back to school to get a master's degree and then became a teacher in the health field.

Now, at 60, Kathleen Casey Kirschling isn't retiring; she is shifting from full-time teaching to part-time consulting, so that she can indulge her desire to spend more time volunteering as a Red Cross disaster-relief instructor. "Baby boomers have been labeled as self-absorbed," says Kirschling, "but lots of us have learned that it's best to be productive and to give back." Her own glass, she says, "is always half-full." Among her blessings: two daughters who live nearby (one attended the same college as Kirschling when she was pursuing her master's), "five grandchildren under the age of seven," and a forty-six-foot Grand Banks trawler emblazoned *First Boomer.* She is a worker, a volunteer, a wife, a mother, a grandmother, and a consumer.

Boomers like Kirschling have long since changed the face of the United States, and now, as that face shows some wrinkles, they are changing the world of marketing. "What's next?" has shoved aside thoughts of "I'm slowing down." And given that the boomers and their elders control the bulk of the country's wealth (70 percent), they have the wherewithal to follow wherever their thoughts may lead.

Collectively, they pull in more than $2 trillion in annual income, account for 50 percent of all discretionary income, and are house-rich: More than 75 percent of people over 50 own their homes—free and clear in nearly 70 percent of those cases. The median net worth of households headed by an individual between 55 and 64 was $165,000 in the year 2001, $97,000 for households headed by an individual between 45 and 54, but only a little over $12,000 for households headed by someone under 35.

This isn't to say that all older consumers are wealthy, far from it. Fortunes have improved over the years, but one-quarter of them make $25,000 a year or less and have little savings. But as a group, the boomers are the wealthiest generation, although 70 percent came from low-income, working-class, or small-business households.

Credit isn't a problem for many in the 50+ group. They comprise 40 million credit-card users holding nearly half of the nation's credit cards. By and large, they are in solid financial health.

These folks not only make plenty; they spend it, too. Spending is often spurred by life transition events (more frequent for people in their fifties than at any other age), such as divorce, remarriage, a birth or death in the family, kids leaving home, adult children moving back in, or the acceptance of caregiving responsibilities for elderly parents. For most people, these are also their peak earning years. People 50 and older are the new consumer-spending majority. They account for at least half the sales of women's apparel, appliances, housing, groceries, take-out food, entertainment, health insurance, and new cars and trucks. They buy three-fourths of all prescription drugs and about half of over-the-counter medications. They also purchase 25 percent of all toys and account for a 21 percent increase over the past three years in the rate at which people join health clubs. And new markets are emerging for senior housing and senior care, all linked to new living, working, and retirement patterns.

The market for home-office supplies and furniture is also growing rapidly, as is the market for new and affordable technology. Why? Because since 1995 the 50+ age-group has been the fastest-growing segment of the population with home-based businesses, in which people put their experience and talents to work for themselves. This exciting trend toward entrepreneurship is lucrative for the marketers of laptop computers, wireless Internet service, e-mail, fax machines, copiers, scanners, cell phones, pagers, BlackBerries, phone-company-based voice mail, and the like.

Yet all work and no play is hardly the anthem for these vital, active, and involved people. They want to experience life to the fullest. Pop singer Cyndi Lauper proclaimed that "girls just want to have fun," and people 50 and over like to have fun, too, especially when it revolves around new experiences.

Not surprisingly, travel ranks high on the list; this age-group travels more than any other. They account for 70 percent of all cruise passengers and 72 percent of all recreational vehicle trips. The Travel Industry Association of America predicts fivefold growth in the global travel industry's income over the next two decades. People 50+ are also willing to dig deep into their pockets to make the most of the travel experience. On a typical vacation, they spend 74 percent more than younger travelers, and when they can afford it, they go first class: 80 percent of all high-end travel and 65 percent of cruises are by those 50 and older.

Changing social roles at different stages of life also influence consumer behavior. For example, there are 60 million grandparents in the United States—72 percent of Americans aged 50 and over are grandparents. The average age of a first-time grandparent in the United States is only 48. But whatever their age, grandparents tend to dote on their grandkids. They spend time and money—over $30 billion annually—on them. More than ever before, grandparents are taking their grandchildren along to restaurants and other outings. So-called grand travel, in which grandparents take the grandchildren but not the kids' parents on vacation, is also gaining in popularity. Disney certainly knows and cares about this phenomenon. Other marketers do, too. I'm planning just such a trip right now.

For marketers, the message is obvious: Disregard at your own peril the expanding 50-and-over group that buys boatloads of products and services, frequently eats in restaurants, goes to movies, stays in hotels, works out at the gym, travels, builds new homes (or renovates existing ones), rents cars, goes back to school, and is eager for new adventures. Yet outdated impressions and misguided assumptions are keeping many marketers from discovering the treasure trove under their noses.

> The farther back you look, the further ahead you can see.
> —*Winston Churchill*

Demographers were wholly in the dark when the baby boom began. They had predicted a decline in the birthrate in the 1950s; instead, it rose to 3.8 children per woman from 2.1 in the Depression-plagued 1930s. What the prognosticators had overlooked was the euphoric effect of winning World War II on people accustomed to instability since the Great Depression. Now renewed hope and dreams for a brighter future were in the air.

Society responded to overflowing maternity wards, a housing shortage, and elementary-level classrooms crammed with students by building new schools, inventing the suburbs, training pediatricians, and investing in research that would lead to vaccines and cures for devastating diseases such as smallpox and polio, measles, and mumps.

A long period of national prosperity followed in the 1960s, making the boomers the country's most affluent and best-educated generation. As young adults, they used newly reliable birth control to advance the sexual revolution and women's massive march into the workforce, changing forever the face of American business and creating a whole new service industry in child care. At the same time, many of them— joined by their older brothers and sisters—strongly influenced public policy by protesting the war in Vietnam and embracing the War on Poverty.

Time magazine cemented the impact of the boomer generation by collectively naming it "Man of the Year" in 1966. Despite the under-25 set's vast numbers and "myriad subspecies," wrote *Time*'s editors, this is a "new kind" of generation, "cushioned by affluence," marked by a distinct distrust of authority, and (even then) the most "intensely discussed and dissected" in history.

The marketplace danced to the boomer tune as well. The traditional diaper industry expanded to fill the needs of infant and toddling boomers, and Pampers disposables were invented when Victor Mills, a Procter & Gamble employee, began looking for an easier way to diaper his boomer grandson. Gerber, which could barely keep those little jars of strained fruits and vegetables on the shelves, introduced a new line of baby-care products in the early 1960s. A few years later, it segued into life insurance, primarily juvenile life policies.

Toy companies reaped a bonanza as sales of tricycles and bicycles, hula hoops and yo-yos, baby dolls and Barbies took off. Electronics makers had their heyday with transistor radios and television sets. Levi Strauss, which had been around since 1853, saw its revenues (and net profits) grow fivefold when blue jeans became the teenage uniform between the early 1960s and early 1970s. Not so lucky was Playtex, which had been the first to advertise bras and girdles on television in the 1950s. Its sales went bust when liberated young women burned their bras along with a few other articles of lingerie.

McDonald's fed boomer teens' craving for convenience food and turned a small, one-store California business into a fast-food behemoth. Soft-drink makers such as Coca-Cola and Pepsi got in on the windfall by washing down all those burgers and fries; sales of soft drinks skyrocketed, led by boomer youths who consumed more than half of all soft drinks sold.

Entertainment venues also boosted their fortunes by responding to the tastes of the boomers. The blockbuster rock 'n' roll concert was born when 60,000 screaming Beatles fans filled New York's Shea Stadium in 1965. Moviemakers and distributors and record companies also cashed in as boomers bought more than half of all movie tickets and records sold in 1968.

Much of this commerce was fueled by television advertising, which was designed as a mass medium to attract the massive audience.

Simply put, the boomers and television grew up together. In the late 1940s, there were about 400,000 television sets in the country; by 1953, there were nearly 20 million. Schoolchildren, captivated by *The Mickey Mouse Club* and *Captain Kangaroo,* inspired the term "media generation"—and when they emerged from their trance they begged their mothers for the products they had seen advertised.

Television became the perfect medium to propel sales of Chatty Cathy and Tony the Tiger's Frosted Flakes. The success of television advertising is reflected in the budget numbers. In 1950, when Kathleen Casey Kirschling was four years old, companies spent only 3 percent of their annual media budgets on television; five years later, the number was an astonishing 80 percent. By 1960, when the oldest boomers had reached their midteens, television advertising generated a staggering $1.5 billion in sales annually.

Meanwhile, researchers were tracking and measuring every boomer move. Marketers pitched to them relentlessly, an obsession that continued through the radical 1970s and the so-called greed decade of the 1980s and on into the early 1990s, when boomers were raising children of their own and ads were directed to boomer families.

But suddenly, in the late 1990s, as boomers headed into their fifties, they went from being the darlings of Madison Avenue to advertising has-beens. Marketers continued their infatuation with young audiences as the boomers slipped into middle age. They had lost their cache, or so marketers thought. Storied ad executive Jerry Della Femina considered himself, at 50, a "dead man walking" to marketers. To the advertising world, youth is "excitement and pizzazz," he wrote, while people over 50 are "gray cardigans and flowery housedresses." Della Femina, now 69, believes that advertisers feared that ads targeted toward older consumers would alienate the young. "People over 50 are seen as consumers who sit home at night in their underwear, buying jewelry and autographed baseballs from the Home Shopping Network," he wrote in the late 1990s.

In Hollywood, people over 50 are hardly seen at all, compared to younger actors. Many of even the most popular actresses start to fade away as they get older. The great screen actresses over 40 have been put on "Hollywood's Gray List." Even the iconic Meryl Streep has to settle for plum supporting roles, as in *Prime* and *The Manchurian Candidate*.

But the 50+ crowd in Hollywood is starting to fight back. Ray Wise, who starred as Don Hollenbeck in *Good Night and Good Luck* and has been a working actor for years, told *AARP The Magazine* deputy editor Nancy Graham at our Movies for Grownups gala that his best work has come after age 50. And actor Jeff Daniels strongly believes that we need better movies for grown-ups: "Movies for grown-ups or movies that challenge, movies that are smart and take chances can find an audience . . . I think Hollywood can do a better job." Actress Goldie Hawn is out to prove him right. She is now struggling to finance a comedy called *Ashes to Ashes,* which she has written and wants to direct and star in with Kurt Russell. Moviegoers in the 50+ demographic, she says, "need to stand up and say, 'We're not being served and I'm mad as hell and I'm not taking it anymore.'" Ed Marinaro, who starred in *Hill Street Blues,* is also frustrated with the lack of work for "older actors" and is looking to produce his own films using the talented men and women who are considered too old by the moviemaking crowd.

The AARP publications' advertising sales team experienced the same frustration. To shake Madison Avenue out of its lethargic approach to older consumers, they tried running a campaign several years ago in trade magazines like *Advertising Age*. The ads showed older people in various death poses. The message was that these are vibrant consumers who haven't kicked the bucket yet. Some of the ad headlines were:

- *"To most marketers, consumers die the minute they turn 50."*
- *"According to most marketers, 10,000 people die every day."*
- *"These days, doctors don't pronounce you dead, marketers do."*

Now, though, more and more companies are coming back to the market they once avoided. Overall, programming for and about teens and 20-somethings still dominates television, with only a relatively low percentage of contemporary advertising messages targeting the 50+ market segment. But the pace is picking up because the 50+ market is booming while the much-celebrated youth segment has leveled off. In this decade alone, the 25-to-44 age bracket will shrink by more than 4 million customers and lose more than $100 billion in purchasing power. By contrast, the 45-to-64 group will expand by about 16 million consumers and $360 billion in spending power.

No wonder marketers are awakening to the folly of ignoring the rapidly expanding 50+ group. Richard Hobbs, of the American Institute of Architects, made the case when he said, "The impact of the aging population on markets, employers, and culture cannot be overstated. Just as the baby boom flooded maternity wards, ignited school construction, and made 'youth' the cultural icon of the 1950s, 1960s, and 1970s, the 'senior boom' of this century will shape the 2010s, 2020s, and 2030s."

But marketers must recognize today's older consumers are engaged and independent. For most boomers, the years after 50 are no longer about empty nests and slowing down; they view this life stage far more positively. Marketers who want to capture this audience had better be smart enough to abandon the old stereotypes.

Management consultant and author Tom Peters remarked on the tendency of marketers to jump all over "left-handed seventeen-year-olds who do this, that, or the other," while generally missing "the truly giant trends like the . . . 80 million boomers who are loaded with bucks." Peters is right. I recall in my early days in marketing, women 18 to 34 were the target audience for just about every consumer product we sold. Once, in a burst of creativity, we targeted younger female heads of cat-owning households for a new pet food.

And today numerous businesses and industries have not yet grasped the full import of the population shift. Like the hapless Charlie Brown and his baseball team, many companies seem bent on snatching defeat from the jaws of victory. They imitate Lucy, who, having missed so many fly balls before, explains away yet another lost opportunity by saying, "I let the past get in my eyes." Marketers do the same thing when they focus on youth and ignore older markets.

If they are experts in consumer research, how can so many marketers let themselves get bogged down in myth and misperception when it comes to the 50+ population? For one thing, many young ad agency executives (average age: 29) have yet to comprehend the older consumer realistically. "When a twenty-nine-year-old says fifty, they envision ninety and polyester and a park bench," says Candace Corlett, principal partner at New York–based WSL Strategic Retail. Companies and their ad agencies that want to compete need to hire creative boomers who understand, relate to, and can target their peers.

Marketers must also recognize that older consumers are not all the same. They reflect the diversity of our nation. The melting pot has become a mosaic. In a nation where Polish kids eat empanadas, Hispanic kids mimic Yiddish, and kids from Yemen twirl on ice skates, their parents and grandparents are just as varied. Hispanic Americans are the fastest-growing minority group in the country, and more Asians, Africans, and people from the Caribbean are coming to the United States as well. The 50+ market consists of more than just boomers. Marketers, social scientists, and commentators often speak of three large segments:

• The GI generation. Born in the first quarter of the twentieth century and dubbed "the greatest generation" by former NBC television news anchor Tom Brokaw, this segment is known for its civic responsibility and social cooperation.

• The silent generation. Born in the second quarter of the century, this group is said to be typically more risk-averse and conformist than the younger crowd.

• The boomer generation. Born from 1946 to 1964, boomers are characterized by ambition, skepticism, and activism. Its members' expectations and behaviors tend to differ from those of their elders.

The boomer generation itself is divided into so-called leading-edge and trailing-edge segments. The galvanizing experiences for the leading-edge boomers, born between 1946 and 1955, were the Vietnam War and the cultural revolution—modern feminism, civil rights, and environmentalism (not to mention the Woodstock music festival). Trailing-edge boomers, born between 1956 and 1964, entered college and started careers after the Vietnam War ended in 1975. They began their adult lives with high expectations, only to confront sky-high interest rates, political malaise, and intense economic competition spurred by their huge numbers. The two segments' interests are allied but not identical.

To successfully reach the 50+ crowd, marketers must discard the following four myths.

MYTH NO. 1
Older consumers are reluctant to part with their money.

The belief that older consumers are tightfisted, if not downright stingy, has been grossly overstated (if it were ever true at all). In fact, nearly 55 percent of boomers are eager to spend their money on themselves and their families. They see their so-called retirement years as a time to focus on family, but they also plan to pursue their own hobbies and interests, socialize, travel, and simply relax.

And with fewer people retiring outright and more retiring later (see chapter 3), the 50+ group will continue to earn longer and have more to spend. The old rule of thumb that retirees should expect to spend at 70 percent of their preretirement level no longer applies. While many will change their lifestyles to require less, many more will spend everything they've got.

MYTH NO. 2
Older consumers already have everything they need, so they limit their purchases to replacement items.

Consumers 45 and older may have everything they need, but they don't have everything they want. They buy 50 percent of the tickets sold for concerts, plays, and movies, and, as previously noted, they account for 50 percent of spending on dining out and take-out food. They also spend on big-ticket items: The average American household buys thirteen new cars in a lifetime, seven of them after the head of the household turns 50. They buy one of every five new cars and one of six new trucks.

Homes represent another huge expenditure. Consumers 45 to 64 already spend more than any other age-group on items ranging from furnishings and equipment to upkeep and supplies. This trend shows no signs of stopping, with many boomers saying they plan to spend the extra disposable income they will have after the kids move out on improving their empty nests. In addition, of the more than 1 million vacation homes sold from 2003 to 2004, almost all were bought by boomers. All told, they account for 52 percent of total U.S. consumer spending.

MYTH NO. 3
Older consumers resist switching brands more than younger consumers do.

Marketers who let the past get in their eyes tend to think that the expanding population of older people will just buy more of the same things they've always bought. But if marketers think that hardening of the consumer arteries sets in and older people automatically buy all the same products and brands they've always bought, the marketers are badly mistaken.

A large majority of people over 45—87 percent—say they are brand loyal for some items, but they aren't loyal at all to other products or services. It just doesn't pay in today's marketplace.

Brand loyalty seems more a function of the product or service than the age of the consumer. For instance:

- *Loyalty to banks is around 60 percent for all age-groups.*
- *Loyalty to airlines and athletic wear is under 25 percent for all age-groups.*
- *People of all ages tend to be reasonably loyal to health and beauty products like soap and cosmetics.*

Clearly, marketers can't afford to be complacent. There are still plenty of opportunities to win (and lose) customers. About 58 percent of all consumers 45 and over say they would switch to a competitor's product if it somehow met their needs in a better way and they would even spend a little more for it. That holds true in electronics and computers, financial services, insurance, and travel services, among other product categories.

What might cause consumers to switch brands? Usually it's a reputation for better quality, familiarity with other products from the company offering the new brand, or a believable product claim about a proven advantage over the previous brand. And more than half of these consumers said they would switch to a similar product that was priced a lot lower or, sometimes, even a little lower.

Does this last reason sound like a contradiction from people who would also spend more to get something they want? Perhaps. But what it says to me is the boomers, not surprisingly, are savvy and adventurous consumers. They look for quality and value, and they have no problem buying a product they've never purchased before—regardless of the price—if they think it will please them in some way or another.

When it comes to shopping for cars and trucks, for instance, about 46 percent of older consumers claim to be loyal to a specific manufacturer, and their loyalty tends to increase slightly with age. But an innovation or some new piece of technology, in addition to the quality and familiarity factors, can still entice 50+ consumers to switch brands.

Those interested in SUVs, minivans, and pickup trucks have little compunction about making a switch. For this group, loyalty actually declines with age. Changing needs play a part—once the kids are grown, many people are ready to trade in the minivan for the car they've always wanted. Moreover, the boomers came of age in the 1960s era of experimentation and unlimited possibilities, which makes them rather unpredictable. Look at Honda.

Honda thought its minivans were just for under-50 soccer moms and once the kids were grown these boomers would move up to fancier Acura models. Instead, Honda discovered that 40 percent of its minivan buyers were empty nesters, mostly boomers, who wanted roomy vehicles to carry grandchildren, elderly parents, and all those home-repair materials from The Home Depot. Honda responded by introducing an upgraded Odyssey minivan outfitted with leather seats and featuring zoned climate control and other pricey features that appeal to wealthier, older buyers.

MYTH NO. 4
Older consumers are technophobic.

Not only are many older consumers unfazed by technology, but the 50+ group buys computers at twice the rate of younger consumers. The majority have a computer in their homes, 42 million (and growing) use the Internet, and online purchases have increased almost tenfold among people aged 45 to 59.

Gateway is a company that understands the market. Its primary target is the 50-to-64-year-old consumer. "They are responsive to technology and willing to learn," says Gena Fried, a Gateway marketing manager. Fried is "impressed by how much technology they own—from MP3 players to digital cameras"—and by how much this group buys. "We realize that people fifty and older are highly influential in many purchases," she says, "not only for themselves, but for their children, grandchildren, and their own parents." In fact, they spend about three times more for online holiday shopping than the national average for all age-groups.

People 50 and older are avid users of the Internet not only for buying merchandise but also for services. "They like to go online to change their [insurance] policies or order new policies at times that are convenient," says George Thacker, senior vice president of marketing at The Hartford,* the Connecticut-based financial services group.

Combine buying power with a willingness to try new products and services and to embrace technology, and the true image of the older American consumer begins to emerge. These consumers are not all that different from younger consumers, except that they usually have more money and more leisure time, which adds up to the potential to change the marketplace.

So the question is: How do companies persuade those 78 million Americans aged 50 and over, whose pockets and bank accounts hold two-thirds of the nation's wealth, to buy their products and services? What does it take to reach what Sony calls zoomers? A little romance, that's what.

People fall in love with brands. They develop an affinity that leads to loyalty. And, interestingly enough, the primary qualities they say attract them resemble the qualities that bring people together in personal relationships. In describing the products they choose, consumers use words like "their type," "a winner," "integrity," "smart," and "feels right." They also say the product must help them "express their individuality and style" and "be good with money."

---

* The Hartford is a business partner with AARP.

Sounds like the response to a questionnaire from a dating service, doesn't it? And just as in human encounters, the "date" doesn't always work out. The affinity may not be there. The brand may turn out, upon closer inspection, to be something the 50+ consumer neither wants to own or use. Perhaps it doesn't meet his or her needs—not the right fit for "someone like me"—or maybe the company or the brand doesn't come across as trustworthy. For whatever reason, the consumer and the brand part ways before they enter into a marriage.

Sometimes advertising aimed specifically at older people can itself be a turnoff, souring the chance for a significant relationship before the meeting ever takes place. Half of consumers asked about age-specific advertising found it insulting or condescending, while the other half thought just the opposite—that it was sensitive to their needs and the feelings of their age-group. Which industries' ads seemed to have the right touch? Among the most successful were automobile, home electronics, and computer and tech companies. Less appealing were ads by insurance companies, financial services firms, and women's apparel makers.

Increasingly, more marketers are understanding that not all consumers 50 and older are alike, and they are developing messages, products, and services that address specific wants and needs. It can be tricky, though. The head of a leading cosmetics company told me, for instance, that he markets to older women but doesn't "want them to know that I know they're older." So he advertises in magazines that skew toward older readers but try not to say so.

> As for the future, your task is not to foresee, but to enable it.
> —*Antoine de Saint-Exupéry*

Certain companies are leading the charge when it comes to targeting the needs and interests of older consumers. "The issue snuck up on packaged-goods firms," admits Elva Lewis, associate director for corporate marketing at Procter & Gamble. "We had no prior expectation or particular focus on the fifty-five-plus consumer." But P&G sprang into action after a segmentation study of its North American consumers showed that empty nesters and people 55 and over were a huge market for the company, second only to households with children. Not to mention, adds Lewis, that this group was underserved and "feeling neglected."

P&G is now reaching out to what Lewis calls the *carpe diem* (seize-the-day) segment. "They are always in motion," she says. "They travel to Vegas and Disney World. They have vacation homes. They are very upbeat, very demanding. They soak up information like sponges. They are determined to make the most of this phase of their lives—and we are determined to develop a relationship with them."

P&G has even changed its approach to cosmetics marketing, which, more than any other category, has equated beauty with youth. After discovering that women over 55 accounted for 20 percent of its Cover Girl brand sales, P&G launched its first-ever line of makeup targeted to older women. To sell its new Advanced Radiance Age-Defying Makeup, the company turned to 51-year-old former supermodel Christie Brinkley. Why Brinkley? "She represents the new fifty-year-old," says Anne Martin, the head of marketing for Cover Girl. Martin is betting that Brinkley's active, energetic lifestyle will help Cover Girl recapture the boomer women who bought the brand's products in the 1970s and 1980s.

It took twenty-three months of losses to persuade Gap to target a more mature clothing market instead of the teenagers it had long coveted. The retailer regained profitability after launching its For All Generations program, featuring 60-somethings in ads and in-store posters. Gap is now taking the idea a step further with a whole new chain, Forth & Towne, which targets mature women and follows in the footsteps of superstar women's retailer Chico's. Chico's single-handedly invented (and has since dominated) the older-woman's clothing market.

Sony discovered that a commercial featuring a gray-haired astronaut taking pictures with a Sony camcorder appealed to older consumers; the company's camcorder sales posted double-digit growth.

By doing its homework, Sony found out how to capture the imaginations of older people. The so-called zoomers, 50-to-64-year-olds, were active and wanted to try new things—in this case, camcorders. By jettisoning the stereotypical view that only younger people buy camcorders, Sony expanded its market. Or, in essence, it created a new market: Many of the zoomers had never bought a Sony product before.

Capturing the older market requires some subtlety. Even people in their seventies and eighties don't necessarily see themselves as old. By and large, people see themselves as younger than their chronological years, in what might be called extended middle age. As the Anheuser-Busch marketing people discovered, customers 50 and over want advertisers to talk lifestyle, not age. A 65-year-old doesn't necessarily need a 65-year-old actor to tempt him to try a low-carb Michelob Ultra or a titanium driver or a stationary bike. If the product is his type, it can do the tempting.

Recognizing that the older market has special needs prompted General Mills's Pillsbury brand to come up with smaller packages that accommodate empty nesters and singles. The key ingredient to what now seems an obvious idea was fresh thinking—and a fresh attitude about the lifestyles, health, and disposable income of people 50 and over.

Special needs can also extend to topics and products that, at first glance, might strike marketers as being off-limits. But few things are. Advertising for Viagra and Depends proves the point. Boomers and older people want products and services that enable them to live better lives.

As with any market, companies have to ferret out the various subgroups within broad demographic groups and then figure out what appeals to them. It requires a great deal of research and a lot of listening—in other words, Marketing 101:

• Men are not necessarily better prospects than women. The gap between their spending is narrowing, not to mention that women typically marry older men and outlive them. As a result, there is a large population of older single or widowed women who wield enormous financial power and want to remain engaged with life and the culture around them. Opportunities abound for marketers of products and services that address women's various life-stage needs and opportunities.

• Female longevity has many facets, especially for boomers. Parents and grandparents are living longer, too, making caregiving a critical and time-consuming issue for boomer women. The business community has come to realize that the 50-something woman is often juggling a full-time job while dealing with members of the older generations' living arrangements, finances, medical needs, and more. Companies are thinking about products to help women shoulder the burden and also to find some respite.

• Older people do not automatically cut back on purchases because of rising prices. Core inflation has been fairly benign in recent years, though housing and health-care costs have outpaced general inflation. But in contrast to 1981, when about 90 percent of older people said that price was the primary consideration for both luxuries and necessities, only 56 percent said the same twenty years later. Attitudes and wherewithal have obviously changed. Sure, aging Americans may pay close attention to everyday expenses, but oftentimes they're saving in order to splurge on a vacation, a new car, or other big-ticket items. One prediction is that many will spend a great deal on cosmetic surgery, but they'll do it with subtlety. "I didn't want to get rid of every last wrinkle," one woman told me, "just enough so that when I look in the mirror, I see what I thought I should look like at this age."

What really appears to attract 50+ consumers—and sells them— is quality and relevance, with price a distant third. Effective marketing appeals are often aspirational, with marketers asking: What do my older customers want? What do they aspire to do and be? How do they see themselves?

Of course this is easier said than done. For example, not everyone aspires to be a big shopper or big spender. My brother, Jerry, and I like to think of ourselves as minimalists—reducing rather than adding to our goods and possessions. Yet the facts are that Fran and I have taken numerous trips, bought a minivan to have room for the grandkids, and added a couple of bedrooms to the house to accommodate family visitors. In other words, we don't necessarily aspire to be consumers, but nonetheless, we are.

Marketers need to put themselves in their customers' shoes—and to involve some older marketing executives to make sure the shoes fit. They can take a page out of the book of Catco, a company that was wildly successful in the 1990s marketing toys and gimmicks like its inflatable Balzac to teenagers. Part of the company's success could be attributed to its clever choice of marketing executives, particularly 14-year-old Mary Rodas.

People 50+ benefit from a competitive marketplace, with companies vying for their attention, and from the products and services coming our way. However, there is a dark side to consumerism. As more and more marketers seek ways to tap into the unprecedented buying power of people 50 and over, we must be constantly on the lookout and be able to discern the good deals from the bad, the legitimate marketers from the illegitimate.

CAVEAT EMPTOR—BUYER BEWARE

Without question, the marketplace is much more complex and fragmented than it was a generation ago. The pace of change has quickened, and consumers face a demanding set of challenges—not just for ourselves but also for parents and other aging relatives and friends who may look to us for guidance.

To navigate the marketplace successfully, we need to be able to discriminate among an ever-expanding choice of products, services, and providers. By and large, there are more decisions to make and less time in which to make them. Despite the Internet, in many ways comparison shopping is becoming much more difficult. Consumers also encounter nearly incomprehensible language "explaining" contract terms and conditions, pricing mechanisms, product options, rebates, risks, and fees. The array of choices and decisions would be difficult for anyone to comprehend, but the challenge is especially daunting for the elderly and for those with minimal financial and consumer literacy.

Worse yet, there are many unscrupulous marketers who target older people as lucrative pigeons for their scams and phony offers. The telephone is one of the shysters' favorite tools. The U.S. Department of Justice estimates that telemarketing crooks cheat one out of six consumers every year, costing Americans more than $40 billion annually. And every year, national, state, and local law enforcement officials report numerous cases of older people losing their life savings to crooked telemarketers. I heard one story about an elderly woman who was persuaded by a telemarketer to regularly leave checks for him under her front door mat. Of course, dishonest telemarketers call people of all ages, backgrounds, and incomes, but 80 percent of their calls typically target older consumers, whom federal agents describe as the "cornerstone of illegal telemarketing."

Don't think that rogue telemarketers limit themselves just to the easy marks among the elderly. They also prey upon older people who are well educated, have above-average incomes, and are socially active in their communities. The sales pitches are sophisticated and include phony prizes, illegal sweepstakes, sham investments, and fictional charities. And in what they call recovery rooms dishonest telemarketers sometimes scam victims all over again by promising to help them recover money lost—for a fee, of course.

How can you avoid becoming a victim of telemarketing fraud? One important step is to be willing to report suspicious telemarketing activity and repeated, unwanted mail advertisements to your state attorney general, your local police, and your local postal inspector. You can also use the Federal Trade Commission's consumer complaint form to report suspicious calls, mail, or advertising appeals. And if you haven't already done so, be sure to put your name and number, and those of your parents and other family members, on the FTC's Do Not Call Registry. It's illegal to call someone who has registered, and telemarketers who continue to call are subject to penalties. Contact the FTC's registry complaint line if your wishes are ignored.

One of the very best ways to stymie a telemarketer is simply to hang up the phone when a stranger calls trying to sell you something you don't want. Unfortunately, because many elderly people consider it rude to respond in such a fashion, they frequently end up in long conversations with shysters. Here are some other steps you can take to avoid scams:

- *Ask telemarketers for their company's name and address, plus a phone number where you can call back at a time of your choosing.*
- *Ask a caller to send written material to study before you make a purchase, and ask about a company's refund policies.*
- *Call the local consumer protection service in your area and in the state or city where an offending company is located; ask if any complaints have been made against the firm.*
- *Talk to family and friends or call your lawyer, accountant, or banker to get advice before making any purchase or investment over the phone with a stranger.*

In Colorado, AARP and the attorney general's office operate Colorado ElderWatch, a phone-in program involving sheriff's departments and Better Business Bureaus around the state, which lets people check on everything from roof- and driveway-repair offers to lottery winnings. West Virginia has a similar program.

One of the fastest-growing crimes against consumers is identity theft, and because people 50 and over have accumulated some wealth, they are often prime targets. Identity theft occurs when someone pretending to be you uses your Social Security, credit card, and bank account numbers to borrow money, open new credit card accounts, or charge thousands of dollars' worth of cars, clothes, vacations, and the like.

As with telemarketing fraud, identity theft is big business. According to the FTC, 27 million Americans have had their identities stolen over the last five years, with losses to businesses totaling $50 billion annually. For the victims, the aftermath of identity theft is aggravation, confusion, and hours of time spent trying to clear their names and straighten out their financial accounts.

The actual case of someone we will call John Doe is a good example. Doe first suspected something was wrong when he applied for a new-car loan. Though his credit had always been excellent, his loan request was denied. When he asked why, the dealer told him he had too much debt to take on any more. Shocked, Doe checked his credit report. It showed that, in the previous month, he had supposedly charged 29,000 dollars' worth of new appliances and furniture and 4,000 dollars' worth of clothes to his credit card, applied for and received a home-equity line of credit, and then charged an expensive trip to the new credit line.

Five years later, Doe is still fighting the fallout from identity theft. He has spent more than 100 hours trying to clear his name and retrieve his excellent credit rating. "Although I didn't lose a penny," he said, "it cost me hours of frustration and anxiety. And even today, companies still turn me down when I apply for a new credit card. It's a nightmare."

The identity thief gets personal information in many inventive ways. Rings of thieves often go to city dumps or apartment Dumpsters to comb through trash for receipts with names and financial information. E-mail fishing expeditions are another ploy. Pretending to be an eBay user or a representative of an online business you have previously used, a crook will e-mail you claiming there is a question about your account. The thief's inquiry is allegedly designed to make sure all your information is correct.

Identity thieves may also steal your purse or wallet; pilfer information such as bank statements and preapproved credit card applications from your mailbox; pose as your employer, loan officer, or landlord to get your credit report; and surreptitiously watch your transactions at automated teller machines and phone booths to capture the personal identification number (PIN) needed to activate your ATM card.

How can you protect yourself against the increasing epidemic of identity theft?

- *Check your credit report at least once a year and correct any errors.*
- *Don't give out your Social Security number unless it's absolutely required by reputable parties—for example, agents of the federal or state government.*
- *Don't have your Social Security number printed on your checks.*
- *Get a new driver's license that doesn't include your Social Security number.*
- *Resist requests from businesses seeking your Social Security number (some businesses routinely include the number on their application forms, for example). Ask why a business needs your number; when customers balk, managers will usually waive the requirement.*
- *Carefully dispose of papers containing personal information; for instance, tear up or shred charge receipts, bank statements, expired credit cards, and credit offers. (I used to kid my wife about shredding our discarded financial papers; now I thank her.)*
- *Carry only the minimum number of credit cards and leave your Social Security card, your birth certificate, and your passport at home unless specifically required to bring them along.*
- *Be aware of others nearby when you're using your PIN, and don't throw your ATM receipt in a nearby wastebasket.*

- *Don't give out your credit card or bank account number over the phone, through the mail, or on the Internet unless you can confirm that you are dealing with an actual representative of a legitimate business.*
- *Secure personal information in your home, especially if you employ outside help or are having work done.*

Consumers should also be cautious about vacations and other trips. With the desire to travel on the increase among older Americans, more people are looking for cheap vacations. It's fine to hunt for bargains, but don't turn your dream into a travel nightmare by accepting offers at face value. If a deal sounds too good to be true, it probably is. It's important to look closely at all offers and read the fine print.

To avoid becoming a travel victim, be an aware traveler. Here are some of the most common scams:

- Instant travel agent offers. You are told that you can qualify for all the wonderful discounts and upgrades available to travel agents just by sending money for some training material and a travel-agent ID. The problem is, the travel industry won't accept the ID. Another twist involves selling travel packages to other "instant agents," for which you get a share of their earnings. This type of multilevel marketing is illegal. Of the nearly 50,000 people drawn into just one of these schemes in 2000, the FTC says that 43,000 made nothing or lost money, 4,000 made less than $50, and only 6 made $100,000.
- Vacation certificates. Here the promise is a bargain-priced vacation, but the certificates don't mention the add-ons. When you add up all the fees and extras, you wind up paying more for this "bargain" than for a conventional travel package. Your airfare may be free, but your anticipated cheap hotel room may cost you $350 or more.
- Free, but at what price? You get a free or low-cost trip but then find that your room is cramped and grimy and the food is terrible or nonexistent. The promoter then magically finds an upgrade but at an outrageous price. A variation on this scam requires you to stop over in

Florida or some other state before going on to your chosen destination. When you try to pick up the vouchers for the rest of your trip, you're trapped into a lengthy, hard-sell presentation to get you to buy a time-share. If you don't listen, no vouchers.

• Down payment downer. You receive a notice saying you've won a super travel bargain. All you have to do is make a deposit with your credit card and select your preferred travel dates. But once you make the deposit, the promoter strings you along, claiming various problems in selecting dates until the deal expires or the phone number is disconnected. Getting a refund is next to impossible.

• Flimflam at the fair. You register for a free trip at a booth at the state fair, shopping mall, or sporting event. But what you have actually won is a high-pressured telephone pitch and a deal for off-season or weekday travel to some remote location.

Using common sense and researching your trip can help protect against travel fraud. Be wary of "great" deals, resist high-pressured sales pitches, and ask detailed questions about promotions. Get all the details, including the total cost and the refund policy, in writing before you pay, and never allow yourself to be rushed into sending money by overnight express. Finally, buy travel services only from a business you know.

Scams and fraud exist in almost every field imaginable. But if we educate ourselves to be smart consumers and use common sense, we can avoid being victimized and help shut down fraudulent operations. And the marketplace, and society, will be the better for it.

seven

The Opportunity to Advocate for a Cause

There is little hope for democracy if the hearts of men and women in democratic societies cannot be touched by a call to do something greater than themselves.

—*Margaret Thatcher*

I have always been attracted to organizations that have a strong social mission. That's what led me to CARE, to the Campaign for Tobacco-Free Kids, and certainly to AARP. Dr. Ethel Percy Andrus founded AARP forty-eight years ago on the principles of collective purpose, collective voice, and collective purchasing power. She saw AARP members as an army of useful citizens who had the ability, the experience, and the desire to promote and enhance the public good. And she believed there is strength in numbers.

But no matter how great your numbers, real strength starts with the individual—or with those individuals who want to get where they're going. AARP became a reality because one retired school-teacher from California couldn't buy a health insurance policy. Dr. Andrus knew where she wanted to go—and she got AARP headed in the right direction.

Today AARP has over 36 million members. We do not have a political action committee (PAC). We don't give money to political parties or candidates. We don't endorse or oppose candidates for office. We are strictly nonpartisan, and we call the issues as we see 'em. So our power to advocate and bring about change is not in our checkbook; it's in our members. To them, and to millions of other Americans, it is important to stay informed, to care, to express their opinions—and to vote.

Good citizenship means more than voting on Election Day. It means being active participants in our democracy. The more people are informed about issues that concern them, communicate their ideas and opinions to their elected officials, and engage in public dialogue, the better our nation will be.

Because we are a representative democracy, we elect officials to exercise our power—to make decisions that affect all of us. No one has ever described this better than Abraham Lincoln in his Gettysburg Address when he defined our government as being "of the people, by the people, for the people."

And that's where power always has and always will lie, with the people . . . with us. No one knows this better than people 50 and over. In their younger years, they defined citizen activism and advocacy. Their youth was a time of great movements on behalf of great causes—civil rights, antiwar, feminism, education, and the environment. And while advocates on the left were taking their case to the streets, advocates on the right were uniting behind the ideas of Senator Barry Goldwater of Arizona and launching the conservative movement in America. Regardless of the cause, people found that through collective engagement behind a collective purpose and speaking with a collective voice they gained the power to change society. Changes brought about by the involvement of citizens in all of these causes have shaped the America we know today.

Associations like AARP and many others play an integral role in our democracy and are an important element of citizen advocacy. De Tocqueville wrote about this unique role in *Democracy in America*:

> If [Americans] want to proclaim a truth or propagate some feeling by the encouragement of a great example, they form an association. In every case, at the head of any new undertaking, where in France you would find the government or in England some territorial magnate, in the United States you are sure to find an association. I have come across

several types of associations in America, of which, I confess, I had not previously the slightest conception, and I have often admired the extreme skill they show in proposing a common object for the exertions of very many and in inducing them voluntarily to pursue it.

There are many ways to reach a "common object" in our democratic society, such as education, helping neighbors and others who need lifting up, legal action, and volunteering for a worthy cause. But the most powerful, and perhaps fastest, road to broad-scale change is to advocate in the political arena for policy reform.

In this chapter, I present three case studies in advocacy in which I have been involved—the battle over tobacco control legislation, the fight for prescription drugs in Medicare, and the debate over Social Security reform—as well as two other examples of citizen action. Advocating for policy change is hard work, and you win some and lose some. But even when you lose, things generally move forward, and eventually you try again. The movement for women's rights, for example, didn't start in the 1950s, when many of us remember how things began to change. It was built on a much earlier foundation that went back far into American history. So sometimes policy and social change is fairly fast, and sometimes it is slow. In each of these stories, citizen involvement in the cause was essential. In our own system of local, state, and national government—legislative, regulatory, and judicial—there are many opportunities to advocate for a change, and by doing so each of us can do something to make America better.

ADVOCATING FOR THE CONTROL OF TOBACCO

> Democracy is cumbersome, slow and inefficient,
> but in due time, the voice of the people will be heard
> and their latent wisdom will prevail.
> —*attributed to Thomas Jefferson*

The tobacco wars in the United States had ebbed and flowed for years, and although the hazards of tobacco use were well known, smoking and chewing tobacco were addictive and tough to quit, and the tobacco companies were highly effective at marketing, lobbying, and staying in the mainstream of corporate America. They had many law firms, lobbying shops, and public relations and advertising agencies on retainer, they gave large amounts of money to political parties and candidates, and they were formidable in every way.

But by the mid-1990s, there was change in the air. The industry was almost too successful, and youth smoking was going up. The Joe Camel character was everywhere, and so was the Marlboro Man. In fact, Joe Camel was as familiar to kids as Mickey Mouse, and public concern was rising. More reports of the health hazards of smoking were coming out, including the dangers of secondhand smoke. Confidential industry documents, which became available as the result of lawsuits, showed that tobacco companies deceived Congress and the public about what they knew about the health hazards of their products and carefully controlled nicotine levels to maintain or increase levels of addiction and that marketing to children was an industry strategy.

State attorneys general, led by Mississippi's Mike Moore, were suing the tobacco companies using novel legal strategies. In Washington, the Food and Drug Administration (FDA) commissioner, Dr. David Kessler, began an aggressive effort to assert FDA jurisdiction over tobacco by calling nicotine a drug and cigarettes a drug delivery device. President Clinton became the first sitting president willing to take on the tobacco industry and announced in August of 1995 that the FDA would propose a rule to regulate tobacco and that the goal was to cut underage tobacco use by 50 percent over a seven-year period.

Dr. Steve Schroeder, the president of the Robert Wood Johnson Foundation, recognized the need for new actions against the tobacco industry and led his organization and its board into vigorous support for a comprehensive approach to reduce tobacco use. The foundation's assessment revealed that more muscle was needed in public health advocacy to support the promising new actions against the industry and against tobacco use, especially among youth. Immediately after the Clinton announcement, the foundation announced a grant to begin the Campaign for Tobacco-Free Kids. I was appointed head of the fledgling group, and we started out in a back room of the Advocacy Institute, hosted there by Mike Pertschuk, a codirector of the institute and a longtime advocate for tobacco regulation and control.

This was my first start-up operation since the early days at Porter Novelli, and it was exciting. Matt Myers, a private attorney with a long history of fighting tobacco, joined us as our general counsel and my good partner. We began by borrowing staff from the American Heart Association, the American Cancer Society, and the Advocacy Institute and then hired our own people. With our initial grant from Robert Wood Johnson, we started fast, but we needed much more funding. The opportunity came when John Seffrin, the CEO of the American Cancer Society, and Dudley Hafner of the American Heart Association committed funding if the Robert Wood Johnson Foundation's board would provide the bulk of the money, which they did, and it all came together. Now there was an organization that was well funded, well staffed, focused entirely on tobacco, and aggressively doing battle with the industry. This was the first time a group could bring a real counterweight to Big Tobacco, by lobbying on Capitol Hill and in state capitals, utilizing the media and supporting state and local campaigns. We took the issue to the public and we framed it in terms of youth tobacco use, the one place where we felt, and research showed, the public draws the line. Besides public support, another reason for a youth focus was that the vast majority of adult smokers began as kids.

Although we kicked things off immediately, with advertising and media stories and advocacy in support of the FDA rule and against tobacco and the corrosive impact of tobacco political contributions, it took several months to put the organization into place for the work ahead. In April 1996, we had a public event to celebrate that we were battle ready. As part of that event, we established a program to identify youth around the country who were making a real difference in their community, and we honored a young tobacco control advocate from Illinois, Anna Santiago, as our first Youth Advocate of the Year. This began a long-term effort to tap a powerful force in the fight against tobacco—youth advocacy. To this day, young leaders around the country constitute a growing, energetic citizen army, educating their peers, lobbying policy makers, working on smoke-free ordinances and other changes in their communities, and taking on the tobacco industry.

With mounting pressure against the tobacco companies because of the lawsuits by the states, the FDA rule, the release of previously secret tobacco industry documents, and widely publicized congressional hearings, the tobacco industry approached the White House and the lead state attorneys general in private and informed them that they were prepared to make genuine public health concessions. With the support of the White House, Attorney General Mike Moore, along with his counterparts from other states—both Republicans and Democrats, including Christine Gregoire, now the governor of Washington State—began secret negotiations with tobacco executives in the spring of 1997. The attorneys general saw these discussions as an opportunity to make unprecedented progress in the effort to curb tobacco use and lessen the ability of the industry to market to children. They also wanted payment for the millions of dollars the states were spending on disease and death (largely through Medicaid) resulting from tobacco use. The industry wanted a settlement to bring more predictability on Wall Street and among investors, and they wanted legal liability protection. Both sides therefore had good reason to find compromise.

The state attorneys general wanted help in their negotiations on the public health issues, so they and the White House asked us to participate, under the condition that we maintain confidentiality, and Matt Myers was our representative in the talks. During this series of discussions, we kept our allies, especially the American Cancer Society, the American Medical Association, the American Academy of Pediatrics, and the American Heart Association, updated and sought their advice. Of course, secrecy and confidentiality don't last long in major negotiations like this, and a few weeks later *The Wall Street Journal* broke the story. An uproar began.

There were daily media accounts of the negotiations, based on information that had been leaked to the media, plus plenty of speculation. The White House played an active behind-the-scenes role from the beginning. And the public health community, especially many longtime antitobacco stalwarts, were divided and highly vocal about whether talking to the enemy was a good thing or capitulation. We had warned the White House against a weak or premature compromise with the tobacco industry, but our position was that the time was ripe for creating change. The industry was under pressure, tobacco was on the public's agenda, various class-action lawsuits and other legal actions against tobacco companies and the FDA-proposed rule were issues that could go for or against either side—since victory in court is always uncertain—and kid smoking was at a very high level and growing. If there was a time to fundamentally change the tobacco landscape in America, this was it.

Two months later, on June 20, 1997, in the midst of daily news accounts and much public discussion, the attorneys general and the industry announced an agreement, according to which the industry would pay $368.5 billion to the states in compensation and would accept FDA regulation of nicotine and stronger health warnings on cigarette packs, fund tobacco prevention and smoking cessation programs, impose dramatic marketing restrictions, and add monetary penalties if youth smoking did not go down. In return, the industry was to receive some immunity from class-action lawsuits and punitive damages for past misconduct and an annual cap on damages they might have to pay in any single year. At a press conference later that day that was called by the attorneys general, we did not endorse the agreement but said that "the agreement goes well beyond the provisions of the FDA rule in terms of reducing youth access to tobacco products and curbing tobacco marketing. It also provides for getting secondhand smoke out of the workplace and other public places, improving health warnings on cigarette packs, funding a sustained public education and counter advertising campaign, funding state and local tobacco control activity, setting up programs to help the fifty million adult smokers to quit, and monitoring the tobacco industry's corporate behavior."

Then came the real battle. Because of the proposed FDA oversight, the marketing restrictions, and the legal protections for the industry, Congress would have to pass legislation approving the settlement. This set the stage for one of the most intense and acrimonious periods in the history of the tobacco wars.

Throughout the summer of 1997, there was continuous media coverage of the contentious debate over the merits of the settlement among the Clinton administration, the public health community, the Congress, and the public. The tobacco companies stayed low-key, except to say essentially that they considered the agreement fair to all sides, that they wanted it to pass, and that they would be good corporate citizens as a result. We and the attorneys general expected President Clinton and his officials, who had been kept apprised of the negotiations, to perhaps call for refinements in the settlement but to support it and its passage by Congress. Instead, the administration spent the summer studying the deal and commenting through the media. Then, in September, the president brought us together in the Oval Office and declared that he would build on and improve the agreement and that Vice President Gore would be the point man for this. The president said little or nothing about any of the specifics of the agreement, including the industry liability protection issue.

Now policy makers in the administration and Congress, columnists, and various other opinion leaders began second-guessing the attorneys general and the industry regarding the agreement they had reached. There was intense pressure, and media headlines to be had, in calling for more costs and penalties to be borne by the tobacco companies. We listened carefully and whenever a commentator identified a serious flaw in the agreement, we agreed to correct it during the legislative process. We and our public health partners formed a coalition, which included our allies the Cancer Society and Heart

Association plus the American Academy of Family Physicians, American Academy of Pediatrics, American College of Chest Physicians, American College of Preventive Medicine, American Medical Association, the Association of State and Territorial Health Officials, the National Association of County and City Health Officials, Partnership for Prevention, and others.

We said that we would work hard to improve the settlement and get it passed by Congress. Among the improvements we proposed were a strengthening of the FDA's oversight over tobacco, tougher industry penalties if tobacco use among children did not decline, and higher prices of cigarettes to deter kids from smoking.

That fall, as congressional hearings got under way, the piling on of the tobacco industry continued. To make things even more complicated, longtime allies Dr. Kessler, the FDA chief, and former surgeon general C. Everett Koop declared the settlement inadequate, called for much tougher provisions, and formed their own coalition to support their position. They said that no legal protections for the industry were acceptable under any circumstances.

As 1998 began, tobacco was a top legislative issue. *The Washington Post* called it "a matter of life and death" and said "the demands on the President and the Congress were not just political, but moral. The question, in fact, is whether they can set aside normal politics long enough to pass decent, comprehensive tobacco legislation." Our champion for tobacco control legislation was Republican senator John McCain, chairman of the Senate Commerce Committee. In March, he announced that he was going to introduce his own legislation building on the June 1997 agreement, correcting its weaknesses, and addressing the concerns its public health opponents had raised. He involved Drs. Kessler and Koop in his discussions and on March 31 introduced a bill that he believed was far tougher and met all of the concerns that the public health community had raised. The bill passed out of the Commerce Committee on April 1, 1998, by a vote of 19–1. It was much more costly to the tobacco companies, but it still contained industry liability protections.

We and our coalition partners were in good spirits, even though we realized that legislative passage was going to be difficult. One faction of the Congress didn't like what they considered clamping down on an industry that was producing a legal product, and they believed that smokers had personal responsibility for their actions. I recall a debate at the Cato Institute in which Dennis Vacco, then attorney general of New York State, and I squared off against an ardent libertarian from Cato and his debating partner, then attorney general William Pryor of Alabama, on this issue. But on the other side of the political spectrum there was still a strong view that the industry was getting too much and should have no liability protection whatsoever. Their view was that the industry needed to be put out of business as the only answer to smoking in America.

State coalitions were active, generating grassroots support on all sides. Youth advocates were out in force, and public opinion was polled and reported on in the media almost daily. But in the midst of all this frenetic action, the unexpected happened—the tobacco companies, angry about the changes in the agreement and distrustful of the Clinton administration and of Congress, backed out of the deal. In a speech at the National Press Club less than two weeks after the Senate Commerce Committee bill emerged, Steven Goldstone, the chairman of RJ Reynolds and a key architect of the settlement, spoke disparagingly of the constant barrage of attacks on the industry, the backtracking on the agreement, the inability of policy makers to perform fairly, and the harm that the new legislation would do to his industry. Goldstone declared that not only were his company and others going to walk away from the now-changed proposal, but they were going to defeat the legislation.

Matt and I were at the Press Club for the speech, and as I listened to Goldstone, I had a strong feeling that I expressed to the media afterward: "The tobacco industry can't win this, because the American public won't let them." I was proved wrong. We declared that "the tobacco industry is only willing to play along if it controls all the terms of debate. By walking away from the democratic process of developing comprehensive legislation, the tobacco companies have returned to a strategy of trench warfare and deception—the same hard-line strategy they used for decades to get their way in Congress and to conceal the truth about their addictive products and youth marketing efforts."

We went all out to pass the McCain legislation. "Total crunch time" is how our communications director, Kay Kahler Vose, described it. But the tobacco industry went all out, too. And the Koop/Kessler opponents of tobacco liability protection spoke out in opposition as well. The result was a welter of messages aimed at the public, legislators, and opinion leaders. And the industry had more money and therefore a bigger voice. A head-to-head battle between us and the tobacco industry was a David versus Goliath confrontation. They spent an estimated $60 million in a lobbying and advertising blitz to scuttle the legislation. Their well-researched message was that big government was out to raise people's taxes again. They also had research that they presented to their allies in Congress saying that tobacco was an issue that was not going to hurt them at the ballot box in the November midterm elections. In addition, the tobacco companies garnered the support of much of corporate America, based on other companies' concerns of a "slippery slope"—if the government came down on tobacco, who would be next: fast foods? While this ignored the fact that tobacco is a lethal product and hamburgers aren't, it did resonate with many business leaders at the time.

Our message to our allies around the country was to engage their grassroots supporters to contact their senators and urge them to stand up against the tobacco companies and for America's children. We asked them to support amendments to strengthen the McCain bill and to oppose amendments that would weaken the legislation, especially efforts to water down FDA authority over tobacco. We e-mailed citizen advocates throughout the nation, provided updates on legislative events and talking points on the key issues. The Heart Association, Cancer Society, and other organizations with strong grassroots operations and lots of volunteers held rallies at senators' home state offices and generated calls and letters to Congress. Patricia Sosa, our person in charge of this, often ended her e-mails with: "This is our moment. Thanks for your help!"

A scheduled one-week debate in the Senate, beginning May 18, stretched into four. The Campaign and our allies set up a "war room" in the ballroom of the Holiday Inn on Capitol Hill. Computers lined the room, and coalition members went in and out all day, visiting members of Congress, providing news, and having frequent briefings throughout the Senate debate. We held a big rally at the White House with over 1,000 youth advocates and several young spokespersons, including 1998 Olympic gold medal figure skater Tara Lipinski. Both President Clinton and Vice President Gore spoke, and the kids waved their signs and sported T-shirts calling for "Tobacco Legislation Now." Then the youth advocates went to Capitol Hill, where Senator McCain and other senators came out to thank the kids and give them support. And youth advocates were active around the country with their T-shirts and their call for legislation. They staged rallies at their senators' offices.

At one point a coalition teammate walked into the war room and related a comment she had heard came from a member of Congress: "Who are these public health people? They can't help us, and they can't hurt us," meaning that we didn't have the political contributions and clout the industry had. This energized us all the more. We would let them know who we were. Most of the members of Congress already did, as they got our message. We pulled out all the stops. We testified on the Hill, spent several million dollars (although far less than the tobacco industry) on advertising, lobbied members of Congress, provided information to congressional staffs, drafted letters to the editor and op-ed pieces for grassroots supporters in the states, held press conferences, and at one point put on events in ten states in less than twenty-four hours. We also continued our work with tobacco grower organizations, because they and we supported provisions in the bill to help them out and they had become wary of the cigarette companies.

As the battle raged on and we kept up the pace, I had a bad feeling one afternoon when a cabdriver, not knowing who I was, commented on the issue, saying that he didn't like having the government tell business what to do and he didn't like the idea of huge tax increases on cigarettes. It was an omen. While we continued to enjoy the support of a majority of senators, things were not looking good for beating back the filibuster that was occurring on the Senate floor. In early June, *The Washington Post* reported that the bill was stalled, and the tobacco industry's heavy media campaign was gaining traction outside Washington.

Two weeks later, the Senate had a vote, not on the bill itself, which appeared to have majority support, but a procedural vote called cloture, to end debate. Cloture requires sixty votes to pass, not just the fifty-one that would normally constitute a majority. The McCain cloture vote received fifty-seven votes and thus fell short by three. After four weeks of Senate debate, it was over. The bill was pulled from the floor. We had lost the battle for comprehensive tobacco control legislation.

It was a bitter defeat. A few days later, RJ Reynolds's Goldstone appeared on the cover of *The New York Times Magazine,* and in the article he was quoted as saying, "What have these public health people achieved in forty years? They think they'll end smoking by bankrupting us, but believe me, that's not going to happen." We held a press conference to say that "the Senate vote was a defeat for America's health . . . but the public still wants to . . . protect kids from tobacco." We went on to say that "the high prevalence of youth smoking has not changed or gone away. This was a major battle, but by no means the end of the war."

In the aftermath of that bruising fight, the attorneys general decided to negotiate a new agreement with the tobacco companies to settle their cases that would bypass Congress, and they did in the fall of the year. This new Master Settlement Agreement (MSA) resulted in $206 billion for the states over its first twenty-five years. While it did have some restrictions on tobacco marketing, the vast majority of public health provisions in the 1997 agreement were omitted, and even the marketing restrictions fell far short of the original agreement. Two years later, the Supreme Court ruled that the FDA did not have regulatory oversight over tobacco, and so the McCain legislation that failed took on even greater significance and would have been necessary to achieve this jurisdiction.

The split in the public health community was slow to heal. And Senator John McCain was a leader whose cause had gone down, not the first or last time a senator would champion, and lose, a key piece of legislation. Some six years later he, Mike Moore, and others were interviewed on a television program by Peter Jennings, who later died of lung cancer. Senator McCain expressed his disappointment at what had happened and said that he had been told by both Dr. Kessler and Dr. Koop that they would support his legislation and that he was deeply disappointed in both of them for not doing so.

For his part, former attorney general Mike Moore directed his disappointment at the White House, for not embracing the original settlement after Moore had come to believe they told him they would. And he was upset with Koop, Kessler, and the elements of the public health community that opposed the legislation. As Moore put it, "They kept telling us, 'We don't need this settlement. We'll get incremental improvements in the public health. Y'all just go back to Mississippi and whatever else and settle your little lawsuits. And we'll take care of this big picture up here in Washington.'" To add to the story, Jennings pointed out that many of the states that had received money in the second settlement—the MSA—between the attorneys general and the tobacco industry had promised to use much of the money to combat smoking. But many of them did not keep that promise. As Jennings said, "Virginia used some of the tobacco money to pay for new seats at a speedway. New York bought sprinklers and golf carts for [this] golf course near Buffalo. Georgia used tobacco money to renovate a hotel. Alabama helped fund a boot camp for teenagers, nothing to do with smoking. And North Carolina actually spent some of its tobacco settlement money on a tobacco warehouse." Florida, however, had used a good deal of its settlement money to fund a very successful youth antismoking campaign and reduced smoking among middle-school students by nearly 50 percent. But then, in the middle of its success, the state cut the program down to a tiny fraction of what it had been, and the momentum was lost.

Sometimes you can learn more from defeat than from victory. At the Campaign for Tobacco-Free Kids, we didn't stop—we reviewed and revised our strategies and kept going. We increased attention and support to the states to help them fight for money from the MSA and to work for other state-level policies, like increased tobacco taxes and smoke-free public places. We improved our grassroots coordination and strength, reaffirming that social change is, in large part, generated by people at local levels. We built new partnerships, including expanded alliances with the tobacco growers. We redoubled our congressional lobbying and moved to support international tobacco control. Above all, we didn't change our aggressive, hard-charging style. Although I have left the Campaign to go on to AARP, I am proud to serve as its board chairman, and Matt and his team are better and stronger than ever.

Where are we today in fighting tobacco use and tobacco-caused disease, and where might we have been if the McCain legislation had passed? Since 2002, tobacco taxes have been raised in forty-one states, and the tobacco companies raised prices about 45 cents a pack to pay for the Master Settlement Agreement. These price increases are critical because they are the biggest single reason that youth smoking declines. If the McCain bill had passed, there would have been a much bigger increase, perhaps twice as much, by the industry that would have driven smoking rates down even faster and possibly further.

The nation has made enormous progress on clean indoor air. This is where local activists have made a huge difference. Major cities, including New York, Chicago, and Washington, D.C., as well as counties and towns across the country, have gone smoke free. As people speak out and step up, more and more municipalities will follow. The industry lobbies against each one of these, but the tide has turned. The 1998 legislation would have made this mandatory, but citizen action is doing the job, albeit more slowly.

Today, because the MSA did not require the states to spend any of their settlement money to reduce tobacco use, only about $500 to $600 million is being spent annually for smoking prevention and cessation. This compares to more than a billion dollars a year for prevention and more than $1.5 billion a year for cessation under the McCain legislation. These expenditures are crucial, since evidence demonstrates conclusively that these public health programs are effective. The original 1997 agreement and subsequent McCain legislation would have also curtailed tobacco marketing far beyond what the MSA achieved. And perhaps most important, there is still no FDA regulation of nicotine, tobacco products, or industry marketing. Companies today can still introduce a tobacco product into the marketplace with virtually no oversight. This is a major loss; as someone said during the legislative battle, "Whoever controls nicotine wins."

Tobacco still kills well over 400,000 Americans each year (which costs the nation some $92 billion annually in lost productivity), but the good news is that *adult* smoking is down about 10 percent since the days of the 1998 legislative battle. That's a lot of men and women who aren't lighting up, but there are still between 45 and 50 million adult smokers who need encouragement and help in quitting. Unfortunately, more than one in five high school students still smoke.

So despite the legislative defeat, step-by-step progress is being made. The area that is perhaps most promising is the youth movement. The Campaign continues to recognize Youth Advocates of the Year from all over the country, and kids are working as hard as ever to bring about change. We realized from the very beginning of the Campaign that these young advocates aren't just ground troops; they are generals—strategists—in their own right. So a few years ago we appointed our top Youth Advocate of the Year to serve on the Campaign board. They bring brains, energy, and courage to the cause. They now organize and run Kick Butts Day, an annual event in thousands of schools across the country, conduct youth advocacy workshops and symposia, do media appearances and community events, and lobby city, state, and national legislators. The kids have now developed their own coalition, Ignite, an independent, youth-led organization founded by Campaign youth advocates for high school and college students. Katherine Klem, a Campaign award winner as a high-school student, took a semester off from the University of Virginia to organize Ignite chapters at the college level, as well as state chapters across the country. In addition to the University of Virginia chapter, Ignite chapters are active at Wellesley, the University of Florida, Dartmouth, and other schools. Katherine says that beyond their tobacco work, she hopes that Ignite members will run for public office as they grow older and in that way make an even bigger difference in America. Citizen activists do make a difference, and these kids are helping lead the way.

MEDICARE: THE BATTLE FOR PRESCRIPTION DRUGS

When I came to AARP in 2000, the association already had a long history of fighting for prescription drugs in Medicare. This was an important concern for our members and their families. It can best be described in a letter I received from an AARP member in Carrollton, Kentucky. She wrote: "Medicare will not help seniors with any cost on medicine. My husband's a diabetic, has had two heart surgeries and has had asthma since childhood . . . He is 68 years old. I am 65 and have congestive heart failure and a lung disease . . . We have to spend so much on medicine, we barely live—can't go anywhere except to the doctors and grocery. Please help people like us."

This is only one letter, but our research showed that the sentiment was widespread. For many people, and certainly for older Americans, lack of access to and nonaffordability of prescription drugs are difficult and frustrating problems. On one hand, they need and value the drugs their doctors prescribe. On the other hand, many people simply can't afford them.

Without the pharmaceutical research and the products that follow, Americans' lives would be more painful and, in many cases, shorter. We have a lot to be grateful for—and a lot to look forward to, as medical research into Alzheimer's, Parkinson's, and other diseases progresses. But we faced a major problem: Our members and their families couldn't afford or sustain rising drug costs—and still can't in many cases. The marketplace is out of balance, and spending on these wonderful drugs that combat disease and ease suffering is too high. As we approached what was to become the debate over the Medicare Modernization Act in 2003, here's what we were facing:

- *Spending on prescription drugs rose on average about 13 percent a year between 1993 and 2001. For the next decade it was expected to rise about 12 percent a year.*
- *Prices of brand-name prescription drugs had been rising at nearly four times the rate of general inflation.*
- *Nearly one American woman in five between the ages of 50 and 64 reported she did not fill a prescription because it was too expensive.*
- *Millions of older Americans were skipping doses or splitting pills to save money.*
- *Prescription drugs were also the fastest-growing item in many state health-care budgets, not just because the prices were higher but also because more people were using the drugs and often they were demanding the most expensive brand-name drugs when a lower-priced version would work just as well.*

A study by Harris Interactive found that higher out-of-pocket drug costs were causing massive noncompliance in the use of prescription drugs. Millions of Americans were not asking doctors for the prescriptions they needed, did not fill the prescriptions they were given, didn't take their full doses, and took their drugs less often than they should. Moreover, the higher people's out-of-pocket costs for drugs, the more likely they were to be noncompliant.

We were hearing from our members—like the woman in Kentucky—every day on this. We realized it was a huge and persistent problem that wouldn't go away by itself. It was affecting not just low-income seniors but middle-class people on fixed incomes as well. Helping our members, and all older Americans and their families, to cope with this was one of our highest priorities. We believed that the best way was to support affordable drug coverage in Medicare, with cost containment so that a Medicare benefit could be sustained.

We were also concerned about Medicaid and the states' abilities to sustain these programs. Forty states were facing Medicaid shortfalls caused largely by unsustainable drug costs. High drug costs were also continuing to drive the increase in Medigap premiums. And businesses large and small were feeling the squeeze of high drug costs. Many were either dropping drug coverage or requiring employees and retirees to pay significantly more. This was fueling even more public demand to do something about the problem.

Efforts to provide relief through pharmaceutical industry discount cards and other means were laudable but were simply not enough. The problem was much bigger than that, and it had to be solved systemically, by achieving affordable and sustainable drug coverage in Medicare.

THE BATTLE INSIDE THE BELTWAY

When the Medicare Modernization Act (MMA) was conceived, debated, voted on, and made law in 2003, it was extremely contentious and partisan. There were essentially three battles comprising this war over Medicare reform. The battlegrounds were policy, process, and politics. In all three, it was clear that citizen advocacy would play a critical role in determining the outcome.

The first battle was over the *policy* itself. In just about any large-scale social legislation, which this was, policy discussions are fierce and compromises are eventually reached when possible . . . or rejected. In the MMA, there were a variety of policy issues, including whether all Medicare beneficiaries would be eligible for the drug benefit and whether traditional fee-for-service Medicare would be preserved or everyone would be propelled into managed-care plans, whether or not they wanted to enroll in them. Also there was the proposed gap in coverage that came to be derided as the "doughnut hole."

A short description of the benefit helps to answer some of the tough questions and harsh criticisms of the new law, especially about the "doughnut hole." First, for most beneficiaries, the legislation requires both a deductible and monthly premiums. Medicare pays 75 percent of drug costs between $250 and $2,250. A gap in coverage (the doughnut hole) follows with no further Medicare payments up to $3,600 of total out-of-pocket costs. From that point on Medicare picks up 95 percent of all costs.

Second, coverage for the poor and near poor is far more generous. They don't pay a deductible or premiums, and there is no doughnut hole—only modest co-pays of one to five dollars. (There is an asset test for those in the upper ranges of low-income people.)

The administration and Congress had set aside $400 billion over ten years to pay for drug coverage in Medicare. This wasn't enough to cover all beneficiaries completely, so most congressional supporters of the legislation and AARP recognized that these funding limits meant that dollars had to be targeted to those most in need—the poor and those with catastrophically high costs. There were also financial incentives built in to persuade companies with retiree coverage not to drop this coverage. To spread the available money to cover these objectives there had to be some gaps; hence the doughnut hole.

As the policy issues were being worked out and debated, some people told me that since they didn't have a lot of prescriptions now, they did not plan to enroll immediately. We explained that such reasoning was a gamble they might lose if they required much more expensive prescription drugs later. Part D (as the prescription drug benefit in Medicare was called) is insurance against later needs. Our analogy was that you can't wait until your house is on fire before you take out a home owner's policy. Those who postponed enrollment would pay a financial penalty for each month they delay. Congress added this provision to attract everybody, so there was a much larger pool of those insured.

Other policy arguments centered on the possibility of a higher premium for wealthier beneficiaries, the level of co-payments, premiums, and deductibles, and providing incentives for corporations not to drop their retiree drug coverage as the new Medicare benefit came into effect. A particularly incendiary issue was whether the federal government should be able to negotiate directly with drug manufacturers to obtain the lowest prices for Medicare beneficiaries. The MMA instead relied on competition among the various insurance plans that would provide the benefit to negotiate cost savings. This idea was supported by the Congressional Budget Office (a nonpartisan arm of Congress), which issued an opinion that the difference between the government negotiating drug prices and the insurance plans doing so would be negligible.

The second battleground of the MMA war was over the *process* of creating and passing the legislation. For the most part, the majority Republicans kept Democrats out of the negotiations. In the conference committee (where the bill was hashed out for a final vote after both the Senate and the House passed their versions), no Democratic House members were invited in and only Democratic Senators Max Baucus of Montana and John Breaux of Louisiana represented their party's interest. The dispute over process also extended to the final House vote, which was kept open far longer than the twenty-minute period—actually, for three hours—while Republican leaders pressed their rank and file to vote for the bill. So the normally fierce party partisanship was even more intense over the MMA.

Finally *politics* confounded the debate. Democrats had always "owned" Medicare and did not want to see President Bush get credit for reform. It was said that a Democratic nightmare was watching the president sign a Medicare bill in the Rose Garden of the White House. On the other side of the aisle, Republicans were determined to use their majority to pass and claim credit for the new benefit, the most important since Medicare's inception in 1965. And they wanted to do it their way or no way at all.

Many pundits, politicians and others—both those friendly and hostile to the bill—have said that the MMA would not have passed without AARP's support. I think they're right. We fought and negotiated hard to get all the improvements we possibly could in the legislation, and then we not only endorsed it, but we went to our members and the public and promoted its passage as strongly as we could. Our board of directors and management made this strategic decision after a lot of thought and discussion, and we did so because we fully believed that it would help our members and the country in the years and decades to come. We also realized that with the Democrats essentially locked out of negotiations, someone else had to stand against some of the more negative aspects of the proposed legislation. After tough negotiations and fierce debate in both houses of Congress, the MMA passed. While we didn't get everything we wanted, Medicare is now stronger and better for older Americans and their families . . . and for the boomers to follow, when they reach beneficiary age.

The run-up to this legislative victory was a long time in coming. We had worked on getting a prescription drug benefit into Medicare for years, and in 2003 it was do-or-die. The budget deficit was growing fast and money for social programs was becoming increasingly scarce, the war in Iraq was becoming a greater fiscal demand for Congress, and a presidential election year was ahead in 2004, in which little or no major legislation could be expected.

We said throughout the debate that the MMA was not perfect, and it certainly is not. But the good substantially outweighs the problems with the program.

I have learned over a long time in dealing with social programs and legislation that "perfect" doesn't happen on Capitol Hill. It only happens in the movies. When you hold out for perfect legislation, what you often achieve is nothing at all.

We have lots of work to do over the coming years to make improvements in the Medicare law, but overall, the program is a net gain. Finally, after years of coming up short, older Americans and their families won major assistance in the struggle against the high cost of prescription drugs. Now there will be far less chance of older people having to split pills (and reduce effectiveness) to make them last longer, skip doses, or even throw prescriptions away because they simply couldn't afford to fill them at the pharmacy.

Not having prescription drugs covered in Medicare was a false economy. In the end, Medicare often wound up paying far more than the needed drugs would have cost when patients landed in the hospital because their illnesses had gone untreated and spun out of control. The example President Bush used in a number of his speeches leading up to the legislative change was high blood pressure. Medicare wouldn't pay for the pills to control it but would end up paying for the surgery or other care if a stroke was the result.

The Medicare drug benefit doesn't solve the whole problem, of course. Shortly after the bill was passed, it was estimated that the benefit would pay only about 25 percent of Medicare beneficiaries' drug costs, and it doesn't help younger Americans with high costs of medication. But the federal budget can only be stretched so far. Even the "doughnut hole" has some reason behind it, because Congress took the money available for the drug benefit and allocated it where it would do the most good—helping poor people and those with very high pharmaceutical costs.

The returns aren't in yet on how effectively Medicare Part D will address the cost of pharmaceuticals for older Americans. But our long-term goal has to be to make prescription drugs more accessible and more affordable, not only for people on Medicare but for everyone, including the large numbers of uninsured and underinsured. It would be a huge step forward for health care and better health overall in America.

THE BATTLE OUTSIDE THE BELTWAY:
MOBILIZING THE GRASS ROOTS

What I have explained so far may give you the impression that the 2003 prescription drug debate and legislation played out entirely in Washington. That is by no means the case. AARP and other organizations had for years been working at the grass roots to raise the issue among Medicare beneficiaries and also among younger Americans.

In 1999, we began pushing hard for a prescription drug benefit in Medicare. We made little headway in Congress, but we did firmly plant the idea in the minds of both legislators and citizens. We did so by holding grassroots events all across the country. We did even better at the state level, where our volunteers and staff were able to persuade several states to begin their own pharmacy programs to provide financial assistance to older people who needed to buy drugs. This was an important base to build on, leading up to the big showdown in 2003.

The pharmaceutical companies began their own campaign in 2000—and spent $30 million on it—to protect their own interests in the face of rising public demand for some Medicare drug benefit.

In the same year, we distributed copies of a pledge to our members, their families and friends. The pledge said: "I want an affordable prescription drug benefit in Medicare. I'm one of millions of Americans who believe Medicare should offer prescription drug coverage. Even better, I'm one of millions of Americans who can use my voting power to make sure that happens."

The idea was to get the point across that there is strength in numbers. We felt that by mobilizing in force, promoting one big idea, we would cause good things to happen, even if incrementally. We knew it would be a long campaign.

To capitalize on this beginning momentum, we launched a drive to collect hundreds of thousands of signatures on petitions demanding the drug benefit. We collected them at county fairs, mall events, baseball games, voter vans, and AARP chapters and Retired Teachers Association units.

In 2002, with still no action on Capitol Hill, we went back to the grass roots. AARP members generated 200,000 contacts with Congress, by letter, e-mail, and phone calls. To drive home the idea that the high cost of drugs was having an adverse effect on families, we held "kitchen table" events in Pennsylvania, Illinois, California, Iowa, and New Hampshire during the Presidents' Day holiday. A kitchen table event is one where people, as if sitting at their kitchen tables, figure out what their drugs costs are and how to go about meeting their needs. On Memorial Day, we held similar events in Tennessee and Florida. And then in August, when Congress was in recess, we sponsored meetings and rallies in Nebraska, Maine, Arkansas, Louisiana, Pennsylvania, and Illinois.

The purpose of these events was twofold. First, it was to raise consciousness among people that a drug benefit was truly possible. The second was to focus on states that had members of Congress who would be especially involved in any Rx legislation.

If you're fighting for something, you have to know what you are fighting for. So, later in 2002, we did additional polling to find out what our members needed and expected in terms of a Medicare drug benefit and found that: (1) the premium should be no greater than $35 a month, since one higher than that would drive too many people away from a voluntary drug benefit in Medicare; (2) a $250 deductible appeared to be the maximum most people would accept; (3) 50 percent co-pays were too high; (4) everybody hated the doughnut hole, not exactly surprising us; and (5) protection against catastrophic costs was essential.

From the grass roots we got our direction. We knew we could not get everything everybody wanted, but we got a very handy guidebook.

In 2003, with still no action in Congress, we kept our community activities going. For example, at our national event in Chicago (attended by more than 17,000 people), we held an event called Pillstock, evoking Woodstock for the boomers. Marie Smith, then our volunteer president-elect, fired up the crowd and enlisted them in the fight. She said, "With the power vested in me, I am now going to deputize all of you to become AARP's drug ambassadors and block captains. Will everyone please stand and repeat after me: 'I promise to call Congress and get my friends and neighbors to call, too.'"

We held simultaneous rallies in California and in Washington, D.C., to keep enthusiasm alive for the long-overdue debate on a drug benefit in Medicare. Over 100,000 people contacted their members of Congress during one AARP National Call-In Day. Marie, other members of the board, and many other volunteers and staff were pushing the same idea to fix the early legislation and get it passed—we called it "fix it and finish it"—at town hall meetings in places such as Palm Harbor, Florida; Morgan City, Louisiana; Waterloo, Iowa; and Amherst, New York. They delivered the same message: We wanted Congress to get off the dime and get down to business.

At the time of these grassroots events, a lot of us thought the drug benefit might be going nowhere. Congress just didn't seem interested. That's when the Washington drama, with which I began this section, kicked in. But it was all the citizen support and the grassroots efforts that caused the resulting drama on Capitol Hill. Enough lawmakers had heard from constituents, and the message was getting through. In the end, they simply had to face the facts and get down to the work of drafting legislation. They did, and the result was the Medicare Modernization Act.

The drug coverage in the MMA is going to help millions of people, especially those with low incomes and those with high drug costs. But the law contains more important benefits as well—a first-time physical examination for those newly eligible for Medicare, early detection and screening for chronic disease, electronic prescribing to improve efficiency and cut down on medical errors, and chronic-disease management.

But the policies, the process, and the politics—especially the politics—remain contentious. Opponents of the MMA continue to attack it. Its early implementation got off to a rocky start, and improvements in the law are still needed.

It would be a step forward to close the doughnut hole so there was no gap in drug coverage. But with the budget deficits as big as they are, that doesn't seem likely any time soon. Some of the private plans, however, have reduced the size of the doughnut hole for those who enroll in their Part D programs.

There are parts of the law that we can improve, and should. First, the asset test for some low-income people is inhibiting their enrollment. These people are being penalized for doing just what they should be doing—saving what they can for retirement. We should eliminate the asset test and find ways to make up the cost elsewhere.

Second is the prohibition against having the government negotiate drug prices. As I pointed out earlier, the Congressional Budget Office didn't think it would make much of a difference as compared to having the big insurance plans do the negotiating. But what if CBO is wrong? The Veterans Administration—a government agency—has been successfully negotiating its own prices for many years. We ought to give the government Medicare drug price negotiation authority. If nothing else, it could be used if the big plans don't achieve expected discounts, and it will keep downward pressure on pharmaceutical prices.

These are two more battles that I think are worth fighting. As I said, the MMA is far from perfect and no one ever gets exactly what he wants. When he was president, Ronald Reagan once said, "If I can get seventy percent of what I want right now, then over time I can pick up a little more here and a little more there." That's a good example to follow. We may never get "perfect," but we can get better. That's worth the battle. And the only way we can do it is through citizen advocacy, in the state houses and the Congress and at the grass roots.

SAVING SOCIAL SECURITY

As discussed in chapter 3, Social Security is critical to the retirement of most people. It accounts for an average of 40 percent of people's retirement income and far more than that at the low end of the scale. Fully 70 percent of retirees get more than half their income from Social Security, and a quarter of everyone over 65 has almost no other source of funds, relying on Social Security for 90 percent or more of total income.

In sum, this national pension system has been an enormous benefit for American society. Because of Social Security, only one out of ten older Americans live in poverty. Without it, nearly half of all seniors would be poor—just as they were as recently as 1960, before Social Security benefits were increased and indexed to wage growth. That old age is no longer synonymous with misery and hopelessness is reason enough to strengthen the system, but to move cautiously in making any changes.

Nonetheless, change of some sort is inevitable. As nearly everyone knows, the Social Security system faces a long-term funding shortfall. The key to the system's solvency is the Social Security Trust Fund, which collects payroll taxes from current workers and uses the money to pay benefits to current retirees. As long as enough money comes in from workers and the money is there when needed, this pay-as-you-go system poses no problem. In fact, since 1983 Social Security has been much more than pay-as-you-go, running big annual surpluses that are invested in federal Treasury bonds and notes, which will earn interest until they are redeemed to pay benefits in future years.

But the sheer number of baby boomers about to burst out of the office cubicle and off the factory floor and into retirement will put a strain on the system. Each year, more and more pensioners will be drawing benefits and fewer and fewer workers will be making contributions. In addition, added longevity means that the retirees will be collecting benefits for more years.

The first boomers will reach age 62 and begin taking early retirement, at reduced-benefit levels, in 2008. The next year, if the funding mechanism hasn't been repaired by then, the annual cash flow surplus will start to shrink as benefits paid outrun income from payroll taxes. In 2017, the surplus will disappear and the trust fund will have to begin drawing down the interest owed it by the Treasury—the interest accumulated on all those bonds and notes purchased with the previous years' surpluses. Ten years after that, it will have to begin redeeming the bonds themselves, thus draining away its capital just to pay the benefits promised to current retirees. By 2040, the trust fund will have run through its "stored-up" assets and will depend entirely on the incoming payroll taxes from the smaller pool of workers at that time.

The problem is made even worse because the trust fund assets aren't actually "stored up." The Treasury bonds are there all right, backed by the full faith and promise of the U.S. government. But the actual money itself is borrowed and spent each year as part of the general budget. If instead, the money were used to pay down national debt, it would make government borrowing cheaper when the time comes to pay out interest and principal on the Social Security bonds.

Alarmists picture this scenario as bankruptcy for Social Security. It isn't. To begin with, the threat, as I have said, is not immediate. The system has enough money to pay benefits at current rates until 2040 (for perspective, in 2040 the oldest surviving baby boomers will be 94 years old and the youngest will be 76). After that, even if no changes were made, current payroll taxes would still bring in enough to pay benefits at 74 percent of the current scale. And if our elected officials act reasonably soon, full funding could be restored with a relatively small increase in the payroll tax, a reduction in benefits, or some mixture of both. In the last such adjustment, in the 1980s, Congress raised the payroll tax and decreed a gradual postponement of benefits. Under current law, most boomers will qualify for full retirement benefits at 66, but workers born after 1960 won't get full benefits until they are 67.

PUTTING SOCIAL SECURITY REFORM
ON THE NATIONAL AGENDA

Following his reelection in November 2004, President Bush announced his intent to tackle Social Security reform. He said that all ideas for reform were on the table, but his proposal was to change Social Security from a social insurance system with guaranteed benefits to a system of voluntary private accounts created by taking money out of Social Security payroll taxes. We viewed this "carve out" approach, as it was known, as a bad idea that would not only make the solvency problem worse but would also do away with the guaranteed benefit that makes Social Security the foundation of retirement security.

As 2004 came to a close, we began a campaign to protect Social Security's guaranteed benefit while making it solvent for the long term. We were opposed to creating private accounts by taking money out of Social Security. The concept of private accounts *in addition* to Social Security was one we had long supported. This would be a way to add to people's savings without unraveling the Social Security safety net. We decided that we would have to engage our members as never before. In addition, we needed to involve *future* Social Security beneficiaries, many of whom worried that the program wouldn't be there for them when they retired.

We began to gear up in 2004, so in early 2005 we were ready for a full debate on Social Security. On Monday, January 3, our staff began making appropriate contacts in both the House and Senate to inform them about the national advertising campaign we were beginning the following morning. The next day, the Capitol Hill publications, *The New York Times*, the *Los Angeles Times, USA Today, The Washington Post*, and selected newspapers in more than forty key media markets began carrying our full-page ads. Then on Wednesday, our mobile billboard mounted on a truck began circulating around Capitol Hill with a plain message—"Oppose private accounts that take money out of Social Security." The billboard began its day parked outside the entrance to our national office for reporters to see when they came to our annual media briefing where we outlined our top priorities for the coming year. We made it clear that while we were pleased that the president had put Social Security reform high on his agenda, we believed that "taking money from Social Security taxes for private investment accounts would worsen the solvency outlook rather than improve it. This approach is risky, hugely expensive and unnecessary . . . And so we are strongly opposed to individual accounts taken out of Social Security. Opposing this approach—if it goes forward—is our top priority in 2005." At the same time, we expressed our desire to continue working with members of both political parties on a range of options to reach the goal of a Social Security system that is financially strong for current retirees and their children and grandchildren. And we drew the distinction between our opposition to private accounts created by taking money out of Social Security and our support for those created in addition to Social Security, but not at the program's expense.

At the same time that we were laying out the framework for the debate in Washington and with the national media, we began our outreach to other organizations and our own grassroots volunteer activists. We provided grants to fourteen organizations to conduct Social Security education and outreach: the Consortium for Citizens with Disabilities, Generations United, the Institute for the Puerto Rican/Hispanic Elderly, the Institute for Women's Policy Research, the Joint Center for Political and Economic Studies, the League of United Latin American Citizens, MANA (a national Latina organization), the National Academy of Social Insurance, the National Council of Women's Organizations, the National Partnership for Women & Families, the National Puerto Rican Coalition, the New York Public Interest Research Group, OWL: The Voice of Midlife and Older Women, and Rock the Vote. This last group was particularly important because Rock the Vote reaches young people just starting their careers, who needed to know the issues that would affect their futures.

During this same period, AARP members across the nation received a direct-mail call-to-action that was designed to spur large numbers of telephone calls and e-mail traffic to Senate and House offices on both sides of the aisle.

By the middle of January, the administration began to expand its public relations campaign to reinforce the message that Social Security was in "crisis" and to show that ordinary working people wanted the option of personal accounts. They also began a media ad campaign and brought out Vice President Dick Cheney and Treasury Secretary John Snow to make their case on Wall Street and with their supporters.

Congress was taking a "wait and see" approach, although there was a good bit of discussion. They wanted to see if the president could mobilize public opinion. They also wanted to see the specifics of his proposal, which were not expected until late February at the earliest. Many members of Congress were nervous about any suggestion of benefit cuts and of increases in the public debt, which would be the result of transitioning from the current system to private accounts. Some Republican senators wanted to go forward on a bipartisan basis, so they wanted the flexibility to make major changes in any bill the president would put forward. Much of the editorial comment from around the country (but certainly not all) was skeptical of the idea of diverting payroll taxes to fund private accounts.

Polls from various organizations showed that the public was still learning about the issue and forming opinions. Our own research showed that a majority of adults 30 and over wanted Social Security to be protected as a guaranteed benefit and not privatized. There was some difference among age-groups. The older segments were more opposed to privatization than younger ones. We believed that public attitudes would be the most important factor influencing the outcome within Congress.

As a result, we intensified our outreach to the grass roots. We continued newspaper advertising across the nation and made an extensive direct mail push to our activists. Social Security was the hot topic, and AARP was recognized as the leader in the debate. The media wrote and talked extensively about our position. We also spent a great deal of time talking regularly with television, radio, and print reporters. The media wrote and talked extensively about our position. And the impact was evident: On January 11 alone, we had 10,365 contacts with Congress as a result of our advertising, articles in our publications, and our Web site information. That brought the total congressional contacts since late December as a result of our campaign to over 106,000.

Following the president's State of the Union speech in February, the Social Security debate moved into a new stage. The president visited several states and held rallies in favor of private accounts. Meanwhile, members of Congress on both sides of the aisle held sessions with constituents back home to gauge their reactions to the ideas presented to date. The president's efforts to persuade the public on private accounts and to recruit additional support in Congress were not succeeding. Congressional leaders made a decision not to try to schedule an early vote on Social Security. Instead, they focused on holding hearings and educating the public. The president released specifications for the private accounts but not for solvency. He indicated that he would not oppose raising the wage base—the amount of salary on which Social Security payroll taxes are paid—as part of the solution. This seemed to be an acknowledgment that any bipartisan compromise in the Senate would need additional revenues. But Republican House leaders immediately criticized this idea as a tax increase they could not support.

With many House members not wanting to vote on such a controversial proposal, it began to look like the Senate would have to go first. This led Republican senator Lindsey Graham of South Carolina to put together a bipartisan centrist group to try to come up with a legislative solution. Apparently in order to give Senator Graham the maximum flexibility to explore a bipartisan deal, the president did not put forth a solvency proposal.

At the same time, the influential Federal Reserve chairman, Alan Greenspan, admonished Congress to "go slow." Although Greenspan favored private accounts, he also acknowledged the risk that transition costs pose to our economy and stated that private accounts, by themselves, do not address the solvency problem.

We continued our volunteer and staff meetings with Republicans and Democrats, and our media and outreach campaign aimed at public awareness was in full swing. We launched our next wave of advocacy advertising with the message: "If you have a problem with the sink, you don't tear down the whole house." The extensive TV ad campaign featuring a house being torn apart was a highly successful image. It acknowledged that changes were needed to strengthen the program, but there were wrong ways and right ways to go about it. The solution should not be worse than the problem.

Against this backdrop, our grassroots efforts continued to produce results. We generated more than 275,000 telephone calls and e-mails to members of Congress in the first quarter of 2005. We also trained volunteers to conduct forums and participate in other local events. We conducted dozens of community meetings as well as several nationally sponsored Social Security forums. Our focus was to impact public opinion back home, especially in districts and states where the elected representatives and senators were on the fence.

We also recognized that those who favored privatization were counting on the support of younger voters, a group that we at AARP traditionally had not reached. Our research showed that the 30–45 age-group would be a key constituency, because they were skeptical of the program's viability and therefore more open to private account ideas. This is where our partnership with Rock the Vote worked so well. We also tested our media messages with younger workers to be sure we were speaking their language.

Our strategy and work were paying off. Polling indicated that the public was becoming more negative to the idea of private accounts funded by the payroll tax. A front-page story in USA Today reported public support for private accounts slipping. The same poll found that AARP was the most trusted voice in the debate by far. Our media coverage had also been positive and extensive. And our board members and staff, who were conducting Social Security meetings around the country, reported positive responses to our position.

But the "carve out" fight was far from over. The administration had told congressional leaders that the next six weeks would be critical. And the leaders reportedly responded by telling the president that he must be the one to carry the ball. The administration then embarked on a "60 events in 60 days" campaign, featuring the president and cabinet officials, to build public support. The administration still had not put forward a proposal for how to make Social Security solvent for the future. Their message remained focused on the projected "unsustainability" of the current system and the need for change, along with the advantages of private accounts. Every place administration officials spoke, our volunteers were there to counter those messages with our own—that private accounts were a bad idea and would only make the problem worse. In addition, in states where the administration conducted events we ran print ads to thank those members of Congress who had resisted private accounts funded out of Social Security.

With the two-week congressional Easter recess approaching, we had generated over 350,000 contacts with members of Congress in direct response to our calls to action. And we were preparing to go out over the Easter recess with a new round of television and radio ads and print ads in *People* magazine and *Rolling Stone* targeted to younger workers (age 30–49) with the message that "over-reacting only makes things worse." We also appealed directly to African-American and Hispanic workers through targeted media. We instituted a Social Security page on our internal Web site that included daily updates and current activities. We sent this information out to our key volunteers in every state and placed articles about the debate in our Chapter News Update, which went out to our more than 2,500 local chapters.

This was an important time for Congress to gauge how the debate was playing in their states and districts. And it was also an important time for us to demonstrate that people strongly opposed the "carve out" idea. Based on several national polls as well as our own research, we believed that the public was growing more aware of the long-term fiscal challenges Social Security would face but was also increasingly rejecting the idea of private accounts carved out of Social Security payroll contributions. Congress was getting the same feeling. Negative reports from town meetings with their constituents fueled Republican nervousness on the issue and gave Democrats little reason to talk openly about compromise. Privately, Democratic members of Congress said they were even more resistant to bipartisan efforts unless the slate were wiped clean and private accounts were off the table.

As the leading opponents of creating private accounts out of Social Security, we were increasingly coming under attack from proponents of "carve out" accounts. House Majority Leader Tom DeLay called us "hypocritical and irresponsible." A fringe group, USA Next, the latest incarnation of the United Seniors Association, conducted a smear campaign against us. Several groups joined forces in a plan to flood our phone lines, Web site, e-mails, and state offices with contacts from disgruntled members threatening to quit if we did not change our policy and our campaign. Their stated goal was to enlist a million AARP members, and their tactics included direct mail, talk radio, e-mail, letters to the editor, and local word of mouth, including appearances at congressional and other town hall meetings. The barrage came to little consequence. We kept going.

CoMPASS, a business coalition, released a poll that claimed to show that our members supported private accounts. This poll received good media pickup, and President Bush referred to some of the poll findings during his news conference on March 16. Our analysis was that this poll was skewed by incomplete and loaded questions that referred to the positive aspects of private accounts without mentioning trade-offs and negatives.

While communicating aggressively in the public arena, we were also talking privately to all sides in the debate in order to clarify our position and better understand theirs.

As President Bush continued his controlled town hall meetings and entered the second month of his "60 events in 60 days" tour, the White House began talking about continuing the tour for another sixty days, which would have taken it up to the July Fourth congressional recess.

In the meantime, Senate Finance Committee chairman Charles Grassley, a Republican from Iowa, called for proposals on solvency and held the first hearing on Social Security (April 26), with testimony from the Cato Institute, the Heritage Foundation, and other groups supporting private accounts out of Social Security.

Despite the hearings, there were still no visible signs of any meaningful bipartisan discussion in the Senate. For our part, we continued our grassroots efforts and celebrated a milestone—more than half a million people had contacted their members of Congress to express their views on Social Security since January 1. We were now entering phase two of our campaign, which we anticipated would take us through Labor Day. While still speaking out against private accounts created out of Social Security, we began to put more emphasis on ways to achieve solvency in the system. Our objectives were to influence congressional action, to keep our members engaged and informed, and to move the debate more to solvency, benefit adequacy, and increased savings.

In the June issue of the *AARP Bulletin* (a monthly newspaper that reaches all our member households), AARP president Marie Smith and I published an open letter to our members on Social Security stating that "AARP is committed to working with both political parties to help ensure that Social Security remains strong for all Americans." And we laid out our six principles for Social Security reform:

- *A predictable and stable foundation that provides a risk-free retirement benefit that can't be outlived—for all who contribute.*
- *Disability and survivor benefits to protect workers and their families.*

- *Full participation—so the solution is fair to everyone.*
- *Adequate benefits for low-wage retirees—to assure at least a minimum standard in retirement.*
- *Benefits based on contributions for all who pay into Social Security.*
- *Annual adjustments that keep benefits up with the cost of living.*

This became the centerpiece of our phase two campaign. We used it as a discussion piece for volunteers to leave their members of Congress when they visited them at their home offices, and it was part of our "call-to-action" sent to more than 2 million activists to generate more contacts with members of Congress. We also used it to convey the same messages as we worked with our partner organizations, conducted community-level meetings, and spoke to corporate, civic, ethnic, policy-maker, and public audiences.

As summer approached there was no indication that public opinion was changing. Despite the administration's "60 events in 60 days" blitz, the concerted effort by various groups to attack AARP, and a pro–private accounts media barrage by supporters of the idea, private accounts still had not caught on. But neither was there much public appeal for an immediate fix to Social Security, even though the president had convinced the American public that the program has a long-term fiscal problem.

In what became a last-ditch effort to break the stalemate and create momentum for private accounts, a flurry of new legislative proposals was introduced prior to the July Fourth recess.

One proposed to use the Social Security cash surpluses generated between 2006 and 2017 to create private accounts. It did not address solvency and would have substantially increased the federal deficit and debt. Another legislative proposal called for achieving solvency by implementing various benefit reductions, but without any increases in revenues and without private accounts.

These and other bills were introduced with great fanfare, but as the details of the plans became known throughout the summer, the excitement waned. We analyzed the plans and informed our members, volunteers, and partners about their content and how they would work. None of the bills gathered enough support to warrant a vote. As other priorities moved onto the national agenda after the Labor Day recess, the Social Security debate faded unceremoniously into the background.

Though the obituary was never officially written, the idea of creating private accounts out of Social Security was dead. There was a robust national debate, and the public decided that it was not a good idea and would not strengthen Social Security for the future. Now the next and even more difficult step is achieving a bipartisan agreement on making the program solvent for generations to come. The partisan political climate and the bruising debate over private accounts indicate that it may take a while before Social Security is back on the national agenda.

> We have every opportunity and every encouragement
> before us. . . . We have it in our power to begin the world
> over again.
>
> —*Thomas Paine*, Common Sense

As these three case studies show, we do have the opportunity to make the world over again by advocating for a cause. Your cause may or may not be curbing tobacco use among kids, getting a prescription drug benefit in Medicare, or protecting Social Security, but as should be evident from all that I've discussed within these pages, opportunities for citizen advocacy abound. And many of them take place on a smaller, although important scale. Terry Baugh and Randi Thompson, two Porter Novelli alumnae and outstanding people, found their cause in advocating for children living in orphanages, foster families, group homes, and other facilities without parents of their own. That led them to start and grow Kidsave International. With a mission of ending the harmful institutionalization of children, Kidsave focuses on:

- *increasing awareness of the plight of children growing up without parents*
- *building model programs that move children without families into permanent, connected relationships with adults*
- *advocating with governments to create change in the way children without parents are treated*

Since 1999, Kidsave has been testing different methods for changing how the public and governments deal with children growing up in foster care and orphanages. Their goal is to develop a model program to help older orphaned children who have little chance for adoption. One such program is "Summer Miracles," which brings orphans from Russia and Kazakhstan to the United States for summer visits. Families host the children with the idea of finding them adoptive families while they are here. The program has been a huge success. Kidsave has found families for 94 percent of the children who were available for adoption.

These adoptive families have formed the basis of Kidsave's advocacy efforts to raise awareness of the problems of older orphans and change the way governments treat children without parents. For example, Kidsave sponsored a "Day on the Hill" event for children from Russia and Kazakhstan and their adoptive parents to tell members of Congress and their staffs about the needs of children left behind. They also hold gala dinners—with kids charmingly involved—to give families an opportunity to meet members of Congress and to present the "Power of Parents" awards.

The work of Kidsave and their citizen advocates is paying off. The U.S. Agency for International Development is now supporting Kidsave's Russia program. And Kidsave's Family Visit Model is being used in Los Angeles County, California; the Washington, D.C., metropolitan area; Smolensk and Yuzhno-Sakhalinsk, Russia; and Bogotá, Colombia. Terry and Randi are the engines, but Kidsave's growing success comes from volunteers, parents, and parents-to-be who love children and want to help them grow up healthy and happy. On the backs of Kidsave T-shirts is a well-known quote by Margaret Mead: "Never doubt that a small group of committed citizens can change the world; indeed, it's the only thing that ever does." Randi and Terry and the other members of their group are just such citizens.

The power of citizen advocates is also evident in New York State, where members of forty-five organizations have come together to form the Kincare Coalition to advocate for the state's more than 143,000 grandparents who are currently raising their grandchildren and the over 400,000 children who live in households headed by a grandparent or other relative. The Kincare Coalition's goal is to remove obstacles that make it difficult to meet basic needs and improve the lives of both the kids and those providing the care.

According to the 2000 Census, New York State ranks third in the country in terms of the number of grandparents raising their grandchildren. Yet these grandparents lack the legal authority to make decisions on behalf of the child or to obtain financial, medical, and educational services. The members of the Kincare Coalition came together to solve this problem.

By bringing the voice of these caregivers to members of the state legislature to help them understand the problems and what to do about them, the Kincare Coalition was instrumental in passing three laws: The Grandparents Caregivers' Rights Act helps grandparents receive custody or become foster parents of a grandchild. The Caregiver Consent law gives grandparents who do not have legal custody of a grandchild the ability to make important day-to-day decisions that affect the health and education of that grandchild. And a third law gives relatives an increased opportunity to become caregivers by requiring social services to conduct an expanded search for a child's relatives while making it easier for "kin caregivers" to become foster parents of a child.

Regardless of where our passion lies, we are all fortunate in this country. We have a unique system of government that affords us the opportunity to speak freely and to advocate change when we see something that we think needs changing. This freedom is built into our Constitution, and it is the soul of our democracy.

But our system also places an important responsibility on us as citizens. As Theodore Roosevelt said over a hundred years ago, "The first requisite of a good citizen in this Republic of ours is that he . . . show not only the capacity for sturdy self-help but also self-respecting regard for the rights of others." It is up to us to keep our eyes open, to recognize when society needs to change, and to work to make it happen. We have the power to make it better. And as you will discover in the next chapter, by following our passions and advocating for a cause we will not only make life better for others, but we will also leave our own lasting legacies for future generations.

eight

The Opportunity to Leave a Legacy

*The only worthy goal is to make a meaningful life
out of an ordinary one . . . make life your endgame.*
—*Peter Drucker*

Not long after the turn of the twentieth century, a young woman
paused at the entrance to Abraham Lincoln High School in East Los
Angeles. She was Ethel Percy Andrus, who was to be the founder of
AARP, and she was starting her career as a teacher that day. Seeing
the word "opportunity" engraved above the big iron gate, she took it as
a message for herself as much as for the students. No matter what lay
ahead, she was determined to approach her job, with fresh eyes and
an open mind, as an opportunity to learn and grow and give of herself
to others—and she did that all her life. She left a legacy that we at
AARP hold up as a model for ourselves, including our board, our volunteers, and our staff, as well as for all our millions of members.

Lincoln High wasn't an easy introduction to teaching, and a
novice might well have dropped out. But as a strong classroom teacher
Ethel Andrus seized the opportunity and made such a mark on the
school that she became its principal, the first female high-school
principal in America's history. She served there for nearly three decades, creating a new, vibrant community at the school, winning

many honors, and educating not only schoolchildren but also adults seeking new skills and a better life.

Dr. Andrus resigned abruptly and quite unexpectedly in 1944— shortly before the first baby boomers were born—to care for her ailing mother. They pleaded with Dr. Andrus to stay, but she said simply, "No, my mother needs me now." In time, she nursed her mother back to health. By then in her early sixties, Dr. Andrus might well have opted to retire at that point. But her mother told her to go out and do for others what "with great good fortune" she had done for her.

In truth, Ethel Andrus needed no such marching orders. She already believed deeply in what she called productive aging, which she defined as becoming more useful to those around her. As she often put it, "It is only in the giving of oneself to others that we truly live."

So she seized opportunity once again, this time to take on a problem she was sadly familiar with—the struggles of all too many retired teachers, who lived on meager pensions and without health insurance. Many of her own friends were in dire circumstances, including one who was living in what had been a chicken coop. In 1947, Dr. Andrus founded the National Retired Teachers Association (NRTA) to help them. The notion of health insurance for people over 60 was so outlandish in those days that she was turned away by literally dozens of companies before she found one willing to take on the risk. Then she promptly developed added benefits, including one that the country at large is only now catching up to: discount drugs for her retired members.

AARP evolved from NRTA in 1958 to address the same compelling needs of aging Americans all across the country. Many of these people—who had contributed so much to their communities throughout their lives—were living in poverty, ill health, and isolation. Dr. Andrus thought they deserved a better life and a brighter future. She knew that couldn't happen until they had pensions that would provide security after retirement. They also needed better health care and affordable insurance to help pay for it. And they needed opportunities to remain active, engaged, and productive members of society so they could continue to share the knowledge and experience gained throughout their lifetimes. She fought for all that for the rest of her life and saw much of her vision become reality before her death in 1967. It was Ethel Andrus who gave AARP the motto we still live by today: "To serve, not to be served." AARP is her legacy to millions of Americans, a monument to her vision of older people living with independence, dignity, and purpose.

It is a great privilege for me to oversee Ethel's legacy. We think of her as Ethel because she is still with us, part of the AARP family; when we reach a goal or overcome a problem, we tell one another, "Ethel would be proud." Our aim is to build on her legacy—and on everything that has been done before us. It is a goal that really makes me want to get up and get going, every morning.

This chapter demonstrates that we can all leave legacies. It's also something almost everyone wants to do: Our research shows that while people 50+ place a high value on caring for themselves and their families, they also have a strong desire to "leave the world better than I found it, give back to the world as much as I take, help those less fortunate than me, make a difference in the world, and be able to have an impact on the world around me." I know I feel that way, and I'll bet you do, too.

And for the boomers, the years after 50 offer an unparalleled chance to prepare a legacy. These are years of both tremendous change and self-discovery. Continued work, learning, spending time with grandchildren, traveling, and community service all can nourish our sense of well-being. And it is these years that give us more time to shape and polish the stamp that we mean to leave on the world.

LEGACIES LARGE, LEGACIES SMALL

> I wanted to change the world. But I have found that the only thing one can be sure of changing is oneself.
>
> —*Aldous Huxley*

There are many kinds of legacies and many ways to leave them. Some are made by people working to change society at large.

In the introduction of this book, I wrote about Dr. Ted Cooper, who created the most successful national public education program in U.S. history, the National High Blood Pressure Education Program.

Dr. Steve Schroeder is another person who made his impact on society at large. As I mentioned earlier, when he was newly installed as the president of the Robert Wood Johnson Foundation, he set out to persuade his board to make a major effort to reduce tobacco use in the United States. The debate was heated, and with the result still in doubt, the chairman of the board slipped Steve a note to drop the request. Steve tore up the note, the board eventually voted to follow his lead, and the foundation went on to make an enormous difference in tobacco control, both in the United States and internationally. It wouldn't have happened if Steve had taken the easy course.

There are lots of people who have used their money wisely in legacy creation. I have a master's degree because Walter Annenberg, the communications magnate, saw to it that every student accepted into the Annenberg School for Communication at the University of Pennsylvania and its counterpart at the University of Southern California was provided a full scholarship.

On a smaller scale, our family doctor in my childhood back in Bridgeville, Pennsylvania, Dr. Myron McGarvey, left much of his estate to the medical school at West Virginia University, even though his medical degree was from the University of Pittsburgh. Why? Because he decided that West Virginia needed the money more.

Others create a legacy by focusing on individuals. My son Peter is a fifth-grade teacher. He took a while to decide to go into education, with its low salaries and stressful work, and he had to pay for what was almost another whole undergraduate degree to become qualified. Now he's building an important legacy, twenty children at a time, year after year. Who knows what contributions those kids will make and what kind of impact their lives will have on others and our society? They will be Peter's legacy.

Two of my favorite teachers were Howard McCracken (algebra,

not my best subject) and Ray Donelli (junior high football and English). A few years ago I was given an award at the University of Pittsburgh and I invited them and their wives to the dinner, as a way of saying thank you. They made a difference in my life.

My mother-in-law, Laura Bickell, taught school in the little town of Victor and then in Missoula, Montana. She became the Director of Special Education for Missoula elementary schools and then went back to being a classroom teacher. She was considered a "master teacher" by the University of Montana School of Education, and they had a camera in her classroom so education majors could watch her in action. Over her career, she reached thousands of students and also influenced a new generation of teachers.

As you may have noticed—and as this chapter makes clear—I'm partial to teachers as legacy makers. Their job is a standing invitation to leave a mark on the world, and young people want nothing more than to be inspired. When the combination clicks, it's a joy to behold. Once I was invited to speak to a business-school class at Columbia University in New York. I was late and hurrying across campus trying to find the right building when I stopped a student to ask for directions. She wanted to know the name of the professor who had invited me. "Dr. Noel Capon," I said. "Oh, he's famous," she replied. I was intrigued enough to take the time to ask what he was famous for. "For being a great teacher," she explained. Now that's a legacy.

I recall Mara Flaherty's legacy with special fondness, perhaps because I had a hand in it. Back in my Porter Novelli days, one of our biggest and most important accounts was the National Cancer Institute (part of the National Institutes of Health). Mara Flaherty, one of our staff, was a cancer survivor who worked especially hard and effectively and made a major contribution to our work for the institute on cancer education and control. To the shock of our entire company, her cancer returned, and she eventually died of it. We decided to do something to honor Mara and came up with the idea of endowing an annual lecture at the Oncological Nurses Association. Last year I was speaking at a dinner of the Friends of the National

Institute of Nursing Research and a woman told me, "I just delivered this year's Mara Flaherty Lecture." Mara's legacy is alive and strong.

Mara was not the only colleague of mine who made a lasting impact. Last year Jerry Florence, a senior executive at AARP and a member of our executive team, dropped dead of a heart attack while shaving one morning. Jerry's death sent a wave of anguish through our organization. He had only been with us two years, but he had made a huge impact. I realized just how big when we held a "remembrance" for him at AARP two days after he died. I knew that Jerry was an impressive individual, but I was astounded to hear person after person stand up and talk about how much he had meant to them. Many young people spoke of him as a mentor. Later I heard still more about him taking kids to ball games, supporting charities, and helping others. We asked for ideas for permanently remembering Jerry and we implemented several of them, but nothing we can do will match the legacy of friendships, mentoring, and charity that Jerry left behind.

INDIVIDUAL LIVES, SINGULAR LEGACIES

> Do something worth remembering.
> —*Elvis Presley*

There's only one rule for preparing a legacy, and again it was Ethel Percy Andrus who defined it: "Do what you can, with what you have, where you are today." My father, Dominic Novelli, along with John Bowman and a few other men, exemplified the Andrus creed when they started an association for kids' sports in our small town near Pittsburgh, back in 1956. Today the Bridgeville Athletic Association is still operating, and thousands of young people, including my brother, Jerry, and me, have benefited.

In the final analysis, legacies are stories, stories that grow richer as we repeat and share them. I'd like to share a few more with you.

DON SCHOENDORFER'S LEGACY

A mechanical engineer with fifty patents to his credit, Don Schoendorfer had been haunted for decades by something he and his wife had witnessed on a trip to Morocco: a disabled woman, unable to walk, literally dragging herself by her fingertips across a street while urchins mocked and jeered at her. So he turned his attention to inventing a wheelchair inexpensive and sturdy enough to give the gift of mobility—and with it independence—to disabled poor people all over the world.

Don spent nine months tinkering in his garage in Orange County, California, getting up before dawn to spend three hours a day on his project before he went to work. His central inspiration came when he seized on the ubiquitous plastic lawn chair—light, virtually indestructible, and available for just $3 each—as the centerpiece of his wheelchair. With a welded frame, industrial casters, and mountain bike wheels from Toys "R" Us, the chair was all but done.

When a medical mission visited his church, he demonstrated the chair. The missionaries objected—"Do you know how much that would cost to ship?"—but he persisted until they relented, agreeing to take four of the chairs to India. He went along, presenting the first wheelchair to a father he met carrying his 11-year-old son, Emmanuel. The boy lit up, immediately wheeling and spinning, savoring his freedom. "Bless you for this chariot," the father said, and the missionaries were converted.

Don and a colleague, William Goodman, assembled the first 100 wheelchairs in Don's garage and set up a business plan for what would become the Free Wheelchair Mission. With initial contributions from two local foundations, they arranged to have the chairs made at two Chinese factories and distributed through evangelical missions around the world. Equipped with emergency brakes and air pump kits for the tires, the chairs could be made and shipped anywhere in the world, 550 to a shipping container, for just $41.17 apiece. (The price tag on a commercial wheelchair: $500 and up.)

In time, Don decided to devote all his energies to the project, while his wife went back to work to support the family. Donations trickled in, but the news media began to take notice, and the trickle swelled to $1.6 million in 2004. So far, 63,000 of Don's wheelchairs have been delivered to people in forty-five countries. He hopes to have 20 million chairs rolling by 2010, giving wheels to almost a fifth of the developing world's disabled people. His reward is the way their eyes light up at the sight of the chair. "It's the day they get their dignity back," he noted not long ago. Those shining eyes will be Don Schoendorfer's legacy, and he has indeed made the world a better place.

SISTER ISOLINA FERRÉ'S LEGACY

Tough as a spike, Sister Isolina Ferré would actually wade in and break up street fights in a section of Brooklyn that was plagued by gang wars. She went on to achieve the near impossible in 1969, uniting and rehabilitating a Puerto Rican community that had given itself up for lost. Where once there was nothing but despair, hope now shines in the faces of children and adults alike.

Sister Isolina was born into a prominent Puerto Rican family, and she was taught as a child to feel a deep concern for those less fortunate. Her mother welcomed orphans into their home, telling her own children that all were equal in the eyes of God. But Sister Isolina never accepted the injustice of poverty, and her desire to change lives led her at 21 to join the Missionary Servants of the Most Blessed Trinity. For two decades she worked among the poor in Puerto Rico and New York, giving both spiritual guidance and practical help in the form of medical care and social services.

She forged what would become her life's crusade in that rundown section of Brooklyn, where her gumption won her the respect she needed to curb juvenile violence and stop the community's decay. But her return in 1969 to La Playa, a neighborhood in Puerto

Rico's second-largest city, Ponce, would prove her greatest challenge.

It was a community in ruins, without a single doctor, nurse, dentist, or social agency. Thousands of people had been left to fend for themselves without a nickel to do it.

Sister Isolina went to work. Her first move was shrewd: She got the community to take a stake in her rescue effort by the simple tactic of asking people, "What shall we do?" They told her: Do something for the children and for the fathers and mothers. So she started the delinquency prevention program, which assigns local advocates to youngsters who turn up in court. These advocates help resolve problems with families, schools, police, and juvenile authorities. Better yet, they have gone on to reach youngsters before they get into trouble by offering alternatives to the street—programs that awaken creativity and develop job skills. It works. Delinquency in La Playa plunged after Sister Isolina's arrival.

In 1999, President Bill Clinton awarded Sister Isolina the Presidential Medal of Freedom, our nation's highest honor presented to civilians in service to humanity. She died on August 3, 2000, but her legacy lives on. Nearly forty years after her return to Puerto Rico, her work has grown into a chain of satellite centers in communities all over the island. Because of Sister Isolina's conviction that education is a lifelong blessing, her programs not only provide academic tutoring and courses in business and computer science for young people; they also teach adult literacy and vocational training for everyone. And since no community thrives without physical and mental health, her centers also advocate comprehensive health care, physical therapy, and counseling for children and families who need help.

Because of Sister Isolina's dedication, the people of La Playa have learned that self-help and united action create a community where dignity and competence thrive. We can help one another, she taught them, if we believe in and trust one another. Once downtrodden and desperate, they have been made to feel that they are important.

Sister Isolina has been called an angel. I won't dispute that, but I would add that she's an angel who has left a lasting legacy.

MABEL CLARE PROUDLEY'S LEGACY

Far from the island of Puerto Rico, a humble, selfless, and quietly charismatic woman, Mabel Clare Proudley, devoted more than a third of her life to the poor of Mexico. Until her death in 2002, at 87, she built houses and gave out food, clothing, money, and medicine. She paid children's school tuitions. But most of all, she dispensed love and hope to those too often deprived of both, and she inspired many others, blessed by fortune, to join her cause.

Mabel Proudley's own life was touched by tragedy. A gifted violinist and a protégée of the legendary Arthur Rubinstein, she was only 17 when she became the first woman ever to play in the Rome Symphony Orchestra. Her career was soaring, her future unlimited—until an accident permanently damaged her hand. She was still young, still gifted, still healthy—but Mabel Clare Proudley would never play the violin again.

Returning to the United States, she was floundering in a sea of uncertainty and resentment. Music had been her life. She knew nothing else. Now she had little left but rage at the injustice of it all.

But when grief and anger ebbed, Mabel decided that she could still help others to have healthy, happy, fulfilling lives. That's when she took up her second career as a teacher, working with children in her native Ohio. In 1950, she moved to Progreso, Texas, in the Rio Grande Valley, to work in a private school.

Then, in 1967, Hurricane Beulah roared through the area, leaving devastation. The misery of the Mexican people just across the river in Nuevo Progreso struck Mabel as an injustice even greater than her own, and she reached out to them. Joined by her sister, Elizabeth Proudley Davis, Mabel founded the Mexican Children's Refuge, a program that pays for school tuition and supplies. That was just a beginning; from there, Mabel and her sister expanded their efforts to provide free dental work, medical care, housing, and food.

The region is one of the poorest in North America, just across the river from the wealthiest nation on earth. The U.S. side is the winter home for many retirees from northern states—Winter Texans, they're called—among them Bob and Ester Scott, from Iowa. Like many others, the Scotts were moved and inspired by Mabel's actions. "When someone could just be sitting back and doing nothing," Ester marveled, "[Mabel was] working day in, day out, every day . . . working for the people in Mexico." Soon the Scotts, too, began building a legacy by volunteering to work on Mabel's projects.

Young people were also inspired. Teenagers from church groups who came to work with Mabel immediately identified with her simplicity and goodness. Kids can sense a fake, but there was nothing fake about Mabel. Her genuine concern for others touched both young and old.

Since Mabel's death and that of her sister in 2003, the work Mabel started has been carried on by volunteers, mainly Winter Texans. Mabel Clare Proudley, a woman with a heart that opened to help people who couldn't help themselves, left a legacy that will branch like a fruit tree as others join her cause and make it their own.

OLGA DAVIS MURRAY'S LEGACY

Olga Murray's opportunity to create a legacy was a long time coming—she was almost 60 and nearing retirement when she discovered a real need she could help solve. Until then, she had spent thirty years happily drafting opinions for justices of the California Supreme Court—a career that could have been seen as a legacy in itself. But all that was about to end, and then what? She was full of energy, but how could she channel it?

She thought she would like to work with disadvantaged children, but the right program seemed elusive. Then, when she was hiking in Nepal and exploring the Himalayan mountains, she found the work she was born for.

Olga Murray discovered her own Everest—the plight of Nepalese children, living amid beauty and poverty in tiny villages, far from the capital city of Katmandu. But the capital itself was full of rural youth who had come seeking work. When Olga began meeting these children, she says, "I was just blown away. No one could have been more disadvantaged. They were so poor. They were covered in rags. They didn't have enough to eat. But they had this amazing capacity for joy. They were so much happier than the average American child, and they all wanted to go to school. I said to myself, 'This is it. I'm going to do this for the rest of my life.'"

The way to help them dawned on her when she visited an orphanage for boys in Katmandu. It was a hovel in a noisy slum on the bank of a filthy river. All forty-five children slept in one room. The food was awful, the latrines indescribable, and there was no hot water. Yet the boys were bright, eager, and grateful not to be on the streets.

But when they turned 16 and finished high school, she was told, the streets would be waiting for them. Family connections are essential to get jobs in Nepal; they had none. Their only hope was to go on to college—many were good college material—but that would cost $300 a year, and they had no money.

Marveling at how little would go so far in an undeveloped country, Olga realized that she could do what she could, with what she had, where she was. She offered to provide scholarships for any of the boys who could pass the college entrance exams. That year, four boys passed—and thanks to the donors Olga has found to help the cause, every graduate since then who has qualified for college has been given a scholarship. By 2005, there were 160 students in college on Olga Murray's scholarships.

During Olga's first five years of helping Nepalese kids, she prevailed on a friendly foundation to process donations for her work so that donors could give tax-free. But when she found herself supporting some twenty college scholarships and ever more children in boarding schools, she decided she'd better launch her own foundation—the Nepalese Youth Opportunity Foundation (NYOF)—and its plate is full.

Olga says three-quarters of the funding comes from private donors she has cultivated over the years and the rest from other foundations. NYOF supports her scholarships, boarding schools, two homes for street children, a program to keep rural girls from being sold as indentured servants, and a nutritional center that feeds malnourished kids back to health while showing their mothers how to feed them properly. NYOF also covers the school expenses of 335 village children whose families can't afford even $50 a year for education. It pays special attention to 400 village girls, whose schooling is particularly neglected, and it helps train 100 teachers a year in rural districts. This year, thanks to Olga Murray's tireless work, more than 2,000 young Nepalese will attend classes ranging from preschool to postgraduate studies. Even in Nepal, all this doesn't come cheap. NYOF's budget is now more than $1 million a year.

All told, Olga Murray's "retirement" is making the world a better place—and making her happy, too. From her mother Olga learned never to say no to anyone in need. From her immigrant father, who taught himself English with *The New York Times* in one hand and an English-Hungarian dictionary in the other, she learned that education is the key to everything worthwhile. And applying those lessons to the children of Nepal, she says, has provided the best years of her life.

"I've had a good life, but these last years have been the best," she says. "I tell my friends to go out and do something for someone. That is what will make them feel good. The fact that you can't do everything doesn't mean you can't do anything."

A GENERATION'S LEGACY

He plants trees to benefit another generation.
—*Caecilius Statius*

Maturity and experience aren't essential for creating a legacy, and the 50+ generation has no monopoly on lending a helping hand. But I believe that having lived a few decades is a major asset when it comes to leaving this country better than we found it. And if they haven't done it already, it's time for boomers to ask themselves how they want to contribute. What will your legacy be?

Another way to put it is: "What did you do with the dash?" The dash is the one that will be on your tombstone, between your birth and death dates—for instance, "1956–2040." What did you do with your life? It's a question we must all ponder, and it takes on added urgency with each passing birthday. For me, it's summed up best by the poet Mary Oliver, who wrote: "When it's over, I don't want . . . to end up simply having visited this world."

Dr. Andrus said that when her alumni association at the University of Chicago wanted to honor a member for "pursuing the good life," they would give that member the title "Useful Citizen." The people whose stories you have read in this chapter have all been "Useful Citizens," and so have millions of unsung others. They all embrace the notion that while we live in an imperfect world, there is much we can do—individually and collectively—to make things better in our communities, our nation, and the world. They ask no reward other than knowing that they have done what they see as their duty. They represent the kind of people that Thomas Jefferson referred to as an "aristocracy of virtue and talent." By those they help or inspire they are simply called heroes.

And they are true heroes—no less than former presidents and senators and captains of industry. Heroes "do what you can, with what you have, where you are today." That's what can earn any of us the title of "Useful Citizen." It's what we can all do every day when we coach a youth soccer team, look in on a neighbor who lives alone, help out in a school, advocate for a cause, deliver meals-on-wheels, or volunteer in our church or synagogue. It's what Rosa Parks, an ordinary woman, did in 1955 when she kept her seat on a bus in Alabama with the simple sentence: "My feet are tired," thus triggering one of the great and ongoing transformations in our nation's history. Her story, her legacy, is still told and celebrated today.

Many heroes go unsung and unrecognized. For example, I don't know the names of the people who worked to get the Native American museum built on the Mall in Washington, D.C. But an executive of the Smithsonian once told me that these people made the museum possible and they worked at it because they had a theme they wanted to communicate: "We are still here." In other words, Native Americans aren't just a part of history but a living culture that wants its place in the United States. That's a story and theme I like to talk about. And even if those heroes remain unsung, the museum is their legacy.

SHARING OUR STORIES

> The universe is made of stories, not atoms.
> —*Muriel Rukeyser*

With a lifetime of knowledge and experience to impart, older people are naturally creators of stories. In fact, Dr. Gene Cohen, one of the nation's foremost authorities on creativity and aging, says mature people are inherently the "keepers of our culture." Transmitted to younger people, their wisdom can make dreams come true, create careers, encourage innovation, and provide the keys to a fulfilling life.

The world-famous violinist Jascha Heifetz felt his obligations as a keeper of the culture. After he left a celebrated international career on the concert stage to become a professor of music at the University of California at Los Angeles, he was asked why he would give up the glamour and rewards of performing to be a teacher. "Violin playing is a perishable art," he replied. "It must be passed on; otherwise it will be lost." He added, "I remember my old violin professor in Russia. He said that if I worked hard enough, someday I would be good enough to teach."

You don't have to be a world-famous violinist to be a keeper of the culture. Millions of people have lived through many of the seminal events in American history and have important memories, reflections, and insights to share. A couple of years ago, AARP, in partnership with the Leadership Conference on Civil Rights and the Library of Congress, set out to capture the extraordinary stories of a variety of people who had been involved in some way in the civil rights movement.

We called the project Voices of Civil Rights. These weren't the leaders who had been on television in the forefront of the civil rights and women's rights movements. They were the people who had been in the trenches or contributed in some other way to changing the nation's mind-set in those critical years. To collect these stories, we went out on a seventy-day, 12,000-mile bus tour across the United States to find the people who had lived them. All told, we collected more than 4,000 firsthand accounts of people involved in the civil rights movement.

I told my own small story, about the time in the 1960s when I went to check on Unilever products in grocery stores in Mississippi. I had my own epiphany about the workings of segregation when I learned from one store owner that he didn't stock our products (or those of our competitors Colgate or Procter & Gamble) because we all had black people in our television commercials.

We published many of these stories in the book *My Soul Looks Back in Wonder: Voices of the Civil Rights Experience,* written by Juan Williams, an Emmy-winning correspondent. Many were also included as part of the History Channel documentary *Save Our History: Voices of Civil Rights.* And all of the stories are archived at the Library of Congress.

One of my favorites in the book was told by Moon Landrieu, who was mayor of New Orleans from 1970 to 1978 and is the father of U.S. Senator Mary Landrieu. Moon Landrieu opposed segregation, both as mayor and before he was elected, and he had an extremely strong sense of legacy. As he put it, "I wanted to change the world, not just racially, but to make the world a better place. I had this flame burning inside me to make a difference in the world. I can't tell you where it came from. I just knew you could change the system, not in giant movements but like termites eating away at the pillars of homes in New Orleans."

Some of the stories by ordinary people have a flavor of "the worm turns," with the establishment getting a taste of its own medicine. José Angel Gutiérrez, for example, said his hero in high school was his principal—until he discovered that discrimination was the principal's way of life. Years later, Gutiérrez was elected school board chairman and suddenly he was his former principal's boss. When the school board announced that there was going to be bilingual and bicultural education, the principal said, "You mean I've got to learn Spanish?" "Yes," Gutiérrez told him, "but you've got three years to do it in."

When we started this project, I didn't realize just how extraordinary those stories would be. They are truly inspiring, because they demonstrate how everyday people, engaged and dedicated to a great cause, can change the world.

We can all learn from the stories of those who made this history. Some of them put their lives on the line to oppose segregation, get the right to vote, or get a fair chance at a good job. Their reflections are particularly important to the young, who may not realize what they owe to the courage and sacrifice of their forebears. Now the Library of Congress is continuing to collect more stories and build the archive.

There is an African adage that says: "When an old person dies, a library vanishes." But in handing off this archive to the Library of Congress we wanted to ensure that the library created by the many thousands of people who stood up for civil rights will never vanish. This collection of firsthand written accounts, photographs, and audio and video interviews will provide the foundation for a great national treasure—a broad mosaic of the quest for freedom and equality in the United States—truly a resource for generations to come and a lasting legacy. I really appreciated having a part in it.

The Library of Congress and AARP have also teamed up to create a similar lasting legacy in the Veterans History Project. Congress authorized this project—AARP is a major sponsor—to collect the stories and experiences of America's war veterans and the people back home who supported them. Thousands of volunteers, representing more than 100 organizations, collect the stories and experiences of veterans and their families, which are then archived in the Library of Congress to preserve our history and serve as a resource for scholars and future generations. I'm sure we all have family members who served in the military, in my case from World War II to the present time. I can recall my uncles coming home from World War II to restart their lives.

This is truly a remarkable collection of interviews and documentary materials, spanning much of the twentieth century. It contains compelling accounts of wartime service from men and women in both civilian and military roles, from admirals and munitions makers to GI Joe and Rosie the Riveter. Their stories are told in their own words through letters, diaries, and oral history interviews. Some amuse us, others sadden us, but all of them inspire us.

Most of the interviews were conducted by family members, friends, neighbors, students, and other volunteers. The interviews have taken place in private homes, retirement communities, VFW or American Legion halls, schools, and libraries. They touch on all aspects of America's war experiences at home and abroad, from the routine to the extraordinary.

Take the story of Donald Griffith, who served with the Marines in the Korean War. Captured by the Chinese, Donald spent three years as a prisoner of North Korea. His account of the ordeal reads like a laundry list of inhumanity, beginning with his captors' indifference to the wounds he suffered just before he was taken. He was thrown into a pigpen for a month and saw a fellow soldier lose his mind and eventually die. Donald watched in horror as another soldier's diseased feet literally came off with his boots, and he was temporarily blinded after being used in medical experiments by the Koreans.

Donald's experience taught him to be thankful for what he had. It was a message he wanted to pass on to others when he returned home. "One of the things I always try to instill in people is that we always just take too much for granted," he said. "We don't realize what we have." He would tell the people who worked for him, "Protect what you've got. You don't realize just how great a country we've got here, and things are so wonderful here compared to other countries and other people." He has been delivering that message for more than fifty years. "If we don't tell our story," Donald says, "then nobody will know."

Sharolyn Walcutt was among one of the first groups of nurses to serve in Vietnam. Arriving in 1965, she was stationed on the *Repose,* a Navy hospital ship anchored off the coast of Vietnam.

"Sometimes you'd see a perfectly healthy-looking eighteen-year-old who would be dead on arrival," she recalled. "And then, I was in triage one night and a man came in and he didn't have legs or arms, and he was talking. It was just mind-boggling."

But when Sharolyn attended the dedication of the Vietnam Women's Memorial in Washington, D.C., it was "one of the highlights of my life." People who had served on the *Repose* met at a designated spot, she said, "and I saw people I hadn't seen in twenty-five years. There was a patient looking for his nurse. He was an amputee, and he had come all the way across country to find her. We found his nurse, and I have never seen a happier person in my life. There he was without legs, and he just kept thanking us. It was very emotional."

Largely as a result of her experience in Vietnam, Sharolyn continues to build her legacy by working in a VA hospital in Ohio. "It's like I'm one of them," she says.

Like the Voices of Civil Rights, the Veterans History Project is a lasting legacy connecting our past with our future. And it has been created by ordinary people who wanted to make an impact and did something about it.

SHARING OUR STRENGTHS

Man is most uniquely human when he turns obstacles into opportunities.
—*Eric Hoffer*

When the strengths of a generation are passed along, all of society benefits. For example, SCORE, the Service Corps Of Retired Executives, provides hard-earned advice and training for entrepreneurs and small businesses. The Big Brothers Big Sisters program to recruit and train older adults as mentors is an excellent use of human resources that might otherwise be wasted. And the Experience Corps, a program that enlists people over 55 as tutors and mentors for children in urban schools, has also proved the benefits of connecting the generations. Not only do the students show progress in academic and social skills; the mentors also gain in health and well-being.

I recall sitting in a grade-school library in Philadelphia, in a little kid's chair, with a handful of AARP volunteers working on an Experience Corps reading program. One of the volunteers told me he had spent most of his life working on the Philadelphia utilities system. "I was in the sewers so much they called me Norton [the character on the old Jackie Gleason show]," he said. "And now there's nothing better than teaching first-, second-, and third-graders to read."

Older adults can also serve by helping children. Many work as individual advocates for abused and neglected children through the Court Appointed Special Advocate (CASA) program. Others engage in larger organized advocacy efforts. For example, AARP volunteers in Texas worked side by side with Children's Defense Fund volunteers to enroll hundreds of Hispanic children in the state Children's Health Insurance Program. AARP volunteers in Tennessee, New York, and several other states have also helped pass laws assisting children being raised by grandparents and other relatives.

And as described in chapter 7, AARP volunteers in advocacy are a powerful force for change. They come to rallies, lobby state and national legislators, and do much more. I recall standing in the legislative chamber in Albany and hearing a state representative say, "You know why that antipredatory bill passed? It was the sight of all those AARP volunteers in their red T-shirts surrounding us and watching up in the balcony."

Grandparents play an important role in the lives of their grandchildren. This is family legacy at its best. I love being with my grandkids, and my adult children speak fondly of their grandparents. Sadly, none of my grandparents left a written record of their immigration to the United States, so much of what I know about it comes from anecdotes. If you want to leave a legacy, it's important to write things down—especially a time line. I've been keeping a journal for many years, although I have a few gaps in it. AARP published a popular book, *For My Grandchild: A Grandmother's Gift of Memory*. It lets a grandmother tell her own story, and it has space for answering questions, adding notes, inserting photos, and so forth. I don't know why we haven't done one for grandfathers. We need to get busy.

A high turnover level among new teachers is threatening our education system, particularly in urban areas, where 50 percent of all the teachers drop out in their first three years. While this is a major problem, it is also another opportunity for Americans to leave a legacy. For example, the NRTA division of AARP has set up and tested a teacher-mentoring program in which older educators are paired with new teachers to give them the benefits of their experience and knowledge. The test results are being analyzed now, and in Chicago, one of the test sites, the portion of younger teachers who stay in the profession jumped from 50 to 91 percent. Now we intend to bring this program to a much larger scale. By helping new teachers these volunteers will also benefit the millions of children who are suffering from this high turnover rate.

In another NRTA program, With Our Youth, thousands of retired educators have volunteered more than 45 million service-hours to help more than 1.5 million young people, both in classes and in learning life skills, in 2,000 communities across the country. Like our driver education program, With Our Youth has been going for a long time. So has our Tax-Aide initiative, in which more than 32,000 volunteers help older people prepare their income taxes and make sure they receive their earned income tax credit. Last year, our volunteers served nearly 2 million people and helped more than 117,000 of them take advantage of the earned income tax credit. In all, that put more than $126 million back into their pockets.

To create a lasting legacy, all we have to do is open our hearts and minds to the needs of others. As this chapter shows, there is no shortage of opportunity—from the classroom to the courtroom, from the soup kitchen to the ball field, from the poverty-stricken residents of a distant country to the people in the house next door. And because the need for assistance, mentoring, and advocacy is huge, the ways in which everyone can contribute are limitless. All ages can join in, and the boomer generation, with its abundant spirit, energy, and optimism, is well suited to the challenge. I have no doubt the boomers will leave a legacy of lasting proportions, making this country a better place for all of us.

In the end, the legacy you leave is what your life has been about. The rest of the issues we have discussed—health care, transportation, housing, recreation, financial security, and so on—all are vitally important, but they are means to the end of living a meaningful life. The living is up to us.

We will all be remembered, and it is never too late to sharpen and highlight the features that will define your legacy. Growing older gives us time to reflect, to tell our stories and tend our families and friendships, to serve our communities and enhance whatever record we have made. What have you done with the dash? We can all improve on it. We can all make a meaningful life out of an ordinary one.

epilogue

Democracy is based upon the conviction that there are extraordinary possibilities in ordinary people.

—*Harry Emerson Fosdick*

All of the changes I've talked about in this book are possible, from transforming health care to reinventing retirement, from building livable communities to revolutionizing the workplace and the marketplace, and from advocating for a cause to leaving a lasting legacy. But none will be easy to achieve.

We can improve the quality of our own lives, and those of our families, by seizing the opportunities that spring from our increased longevity and our privileged place in the world. But we can also do much more. We can change society and make America a better place for all of our citizens, now and in the future.

But we need to pay more than lip service to the need for change. One of my favorite cartoonists is Sam Gross, who created many gems for *The New Yorker*. He did one with a pack of wolves howling at the moon, with one of them saying, "My question is: Are we making an impact?" And that's our question today. With all the potential we have, with all the wealth and inventiveness and wisdom, are we going to make an impact or just limp along while the world changes us?

The choice is up to us. In the book *Collapse,* author Jared Diamond argues that societies choose to succeed or choose to fail. It's not that people *deliberately* set out to pollute their environment beyond recovery, become irrelevant to their trading partners, be overtaken by other societies, or otherwise destroy their chances to succeed. But those and other devastating choices are made collectively, often by default, and the result is collapse. No one really expects the United States to collapse, but we don't want to just muddle through to avoid disaster; we want to be even better than we are today.

When I was a product manager in my early business days at Unilever, one of my colleague product managers was called to the chairman's office. You had to take a special elevator to get there. The company chairman said that he had been watching television the night before and had seen a commercial for the product my friend was managing. "Yes, sir," my friend said. "What did you think?" And the chairman said, "I think your commercial is somewhere between useless and downright harmful." When I heard this I asked my buddy what he did then. He said, "What could I do? At that point I argued for useless!"

Useless and downright harmful are not good choices, and "wait and see" and "muddle through" are not good strategies, whether you're managing a business, raising a family, pursuing a career, or working to make your community and country a better place. Business author Lou Vickery once wrote: "Nothing average ever stood as a monument to progress. When progress is looking for a partner, it doesn't turn to those who believe they are only average. It turns instead to those who are forever searching and striving to become the best they possibly can."

And that's who we are. As Americans, we strive to be even better than we are today. To make a genuine difference in all these things, we need to be activists, to become engaged in change. It's not too corny or overblown to say that we can all be activists for a better America. Every one of us can contribute. There's a story about the early days of the National Aeronautics and Space Administration, in the midsixties. A television network sent a crew in to interview NASA employees about their jobs. One of the people they talked to was a janitor, who was sweeping the floors. When the reporter asked him what he did, the janitor replied, "My job is to help put a man on the moon." Now there was someone who understood that everybody makes a difference.

There are lots of ways to make a difference. I talk to young people about entrepreneurship. By that I mean taking initiative, acting like your own boss, maybe taking the plunge and actually becoming your own boss. I tried it with Porter Novelli and liked it a lot. The Campaign for Tobacco-Free Kids was also a start-up. The J. W. Marriott company began as a husband-and-wife-operated root beer stand. But being an entrepreneur doesn't just mean setting up your own shop. We can be entrepreneurs in any setting. AARP's staff and volunteer ranks are full of entrepreneurs who are making huge differences in the lives of our members and their communities. I tell young people that they should try thinking of their group, their work team, their volunteer activities, or whatever they're part of as though it were their own company or organization and their own money. How would they do things if that were the case? In the same sense, we can all be entrepreneurs for change. After all, *it is our country.* Let's be bold and make things happen.

Of course, not everything is possible. As the old saying goes, you've got to know when to hold 'em and know when to fold 'em. There are a lot of programs, many in government, many in the private and nonprofit sectors, that don't work and probably should be altered or even scrapped. Part of being bold and making change is to admit this. But people who get things done don't always like to quit, to fold their cards and try another hand. The concept of "successful failures" comes to mind. The idea is to learn from something that didn't work in order to create something that does. An example is an AARP magazine that we produced a few years ago, called *My Generation.* Its purpose was to reach out specifically to boomers and to do it in their imagery and their lifestyles. After several years and a sizable investment, we decided we didn't have it right. But we did learn from the experience, and we incorporated our knowledge into our well-established flagship publication, *AARP The Magazine*. The "failure" of *My Generation* turned into a success as the readership and advertising sales of *AARP The Magazine* went up and our members responded with praise.

Creating change is messy. It takes what I call a kitchen-sink approach, where you throw everything but the kitchen sink at the problem and then sort out what's working as you go along. It's not a scientific process so much as an art. Look at obesity and lack of exercise, two problems I talked about earlier in this book that are highly resistant to change. It won't be enough to just tell people about the dangers. We need to make exercise and good eating habits the social norm, as well as work with individuals to assist them in changing their own behaviors. Families and individuals can work at this, of course, and many will succeed, but it will be a lot easier to sustain if the world around them—the social environment—supports their efforts.

Improving schools, fixing Social Security, making prescription drugs affordable, creating more livable communities, and providing better home- and community-based long-term care are all examples of changes we need to and can make. It will all take time, and we won't always get it right the first time. But we can get these changes done right eventually.

One of our biggest barriers to progress is the temptation to throw up our arms in despair. But despair is called a sin for good reason. We need to remember that progress often comes in small doses and not to get discouraged. Some years ago I was talking with the physician in charge of tobacco control for India. This was a time when the United States wasn't making much headway in stemming adult and youth smoking. The Indian doctor told me that their approach had to be a gradual one. "For instance," he said, "we have many people who smoke cigars with the lighted end in their mouth. When we get them to turn the cigar around, that's progress!" Likewise, it took a long time to develop effective strategies to reduce tobacco use among American kids. Many early campaigns were based on exhortation—"don't smoke; it's bad for you." Of course, kids already knew that and weren't motivated.

Social disapproval was also a strategy that had its run: "Smoking will make your breath and hair smell bad." It wasn't all that effective, either. Only in recent years did more effective strategies and tactics emerge, many of them pioneered by the states using money from their settlement with the tobacco companies. Getting youth involved from the very beginning of a program, so that it truly belonged to them, proved to be important. Using a variety of messages, channels, and activities that were designed by the young activists themselves was a key. And so was aiming youths' rebelliousness at the tobacco companies, rather than at their parents, teachers, and coaches. Progress came in fits and starts as we learned what worked and what didn't, but it came nonetheless. Incremental change does make a difference over time. Jenny Thornburgh, an activist who has devoted much of her time to making houses of worship accessible to disabled people, has a saying: "A ramp is not enough." But she'll take the ramp as a starter and push constantly for more improvements later.

One major obstacle to national progress is the current period of nasty, partisan politics in Washington. Historians tell us these periods occur in cycles, and we're definitely in a downturn now. Some of the same partisan gridlock is going on in our state governments, but it seems that the problem is much worse in Washington. I admire many of the senators and representatives I meet in Congress. They are smart, caring men and women who understand the issues and want to make the world a better place. But these days they're stuck in a quagmire of partisan bickering and striving for political advantage. This no-holds-barred partisanship is partly to blame for what I see around the country as disrespect for our national elected (and appointed) officials. This isn't good for democracy, and it's definitely bad for our country.

For a long time now, the quickest way to get a laugh out beyond the Beltway has been to crack a joke about Washington. I admit to having done it myself. For instance, it's easy to get an audience chortling by saying that you don't know about global warming, but the weather in D.C. has certainly been affected by all the hot air blowing down from Capitol Hill. Or you can quote Will Rogers: "There is good news from Washington today. The Congress is deadlocked and cannot act." And how many seasoned politicians do we see who pose as *outsiders,* promising to go to Washington to straighten out the mess? To add to the problem, we have the periodic political scandals that flare up when our elected officials get too chummy with lobbyists and skate on the thin ice of unethical behavior. This isn't new, but recent episodes are especially troubling and hamper the ability of our elected leaders to do the people's work.

We need to turn all this around. The combination of partisanship and cronyism on the part of our leadership and the resulting disrespect for government among our citizens is corrosive. When policy is debated only in terms of political spoils, the public loses. Instead of meaningful results, we get stalemate or worse. I think we can do something about this. And we must; it's the only way to face the huge challenges in front of us.

As individual citizens, we can call upon our elected representatives to reform the system, stop the pettiness, and work together for the good of the country. We need to *demand* that they come together on the big issues. Bipartisanship doesn't mean that both parties should or will agree on every issue. But they need to collaborate to reach viable solutions, as our elected leaders have done in the past. The two-party system has been a strength of our democracy. When it operates well, it ensures that different points of view are considered, issues are debated openly, and the will of the majority is carried out while the rights of the minority are protected.

There's an old adage that people distrust and dislike politicians in general, but they like their own congressman or congresswoman, whom they keep reelecting. I think it's time to *un-elect* some people, so that a clear message is delivered—*focus now on the people's work.* Of course, this requires information and thought on who should be reelected and who should be un-elected. That's our job as citizens and activists.

A point I've tried to make throughout this book is that these and other obstacles can be overcome by citizens demanding change. The most important thing we can do is weigh in on what we think is needed, helping to establish priorities and balancing short-term needs with long-term goals. This is not a new concept to boomers and their older brothers and sisters, who in their younger years mobilized to change America's public policies, attitudes, and culture. We now need to do it again, recruiting all generations to change our public policies, attitudes, and culture around the issues we face as society grows older.

By and large we know what needs to be done. The question is, do we have the will to do it? The United States is the wealthiest country in the world, but even we have competing demands for resources, at every level, from families to state government to Washington. That means we need strong leaders throughout society—including ourselves—who are willing to tackle the tough issues. We as citizens must demonstrate the strength of our convictions to require our leaders to lead or suffer the consequences. And we must be willing to look beyond our own self-interests to do what is good for the nation. After all, action is the ultimate measure of will.

I have always believed that true leadership must lead to change that translates into social betterment. There are loads of business and other books that talk about great organizational leaders at the top of the mountain, brilliantly creating the vision, seeing the future, leading the way forward. And of course there are many good examples of these visionaries in different places and settings. But true leaders are not only found on top of the pyramid. Everyone can be a leader, in setting examples, being active and an activist, and being a legacy maker. Part of this comes from the wisdom and experience of having lived.

There is a Brazilian proverb that says, "When we dream alone, it is only a dream. When we dream together, it is no longer a dream, but the beginning of reality." If we keep after the changes I've discussed within these chapters, we can grasp the tremendous opportunities that lie before us. We can create a new reality. We have the knowledge, the talent for innovation, and the technology to succeed. And by rediscovering the extraordinary possibilities that lie within all of us we can make America better not just for ourselves but for generations to come.